LITTLE PANIC

ALSO BY AMANDA STERN

The Long Haul

LITTLE PANIC

DISPATCHES FROM AN ANXIOUS LIFE

AMANDA STERN

GRAND CENTRAL
PUBLISHING

New York Boston

Grand Central Publishing
Hachette Book Group
1290 Avenue of the Americas, New York, NY 10104
grandcentralpublishing.com
twitter.com/grandcentralpub

First Edition: June 2018

Grand Central Publishing is a division of Hachette Book Group, Inc. The Grand Central Publishing name and logo is a trademark of Hachette Book Group, Inc.

The publisher is not responsible for websites (or their content) that are not owned by the publisher.

The Hachette Speakers Bureau provides a wide range of authors for speaking events. To find out more, go to www.hachettespeakersbureau.com or call (866) 376-6591.

Book design by Marie Mundaca

A full list of permissions is on page 392.

Library of Congress Control Number: 2017963706

ISBNs: 978-1-5387-1192-7 (hardcover); 978-1-5387-1191-0 (ebook)

Printed in the United States of America

LSC-C

10 9 8 7 6 5 4 3 2 1

For my parents, Eve and Eddie,
and for every little panicker and their loved
ones.

Contents

Author's Note on Sources

The images and IQ test questions that run throughout this book came from a variety of sources. The first is, believe it or not, my memory. When you take as many IQ tests as I have, they stick to your anxiety and never let go. Where I drew blanks, I turned to the actual tests and their guidebooks. They include: *WAIS Object Assembly* (The Psychological Corporation, 1955); *Measuring Intelligence: A Guide to the Administration of the New Revised Stanford-Binet Tests of Intelligence* by Lewis M. Terman and Maud A. Merrill (Houghton Mifflin, 1937), 102 (Form L / 4); *WAIS Manual, Weschler Adult Intelligence Scale* by David Wechsler (The Psychological Corporation, 1955); *WAIS Object Assembly H* (The Psychological Corporation, 1955). The images that appear are renditions inspired by Stanford-Binet and WAIS (Wechsler Adult Intelligence Scale) picture-completion and design cards.

Other books I read to refresh my memory and accurately portray the sequence of testing include: *Capturing the Essence: How Herman Hall Interpreted Standardized Test Scores* by James Shapiro (Joukowsky Family Foundation, 2004); *A Method of Measuring the Development of the Intelligence of Young Children* by Alfred Binet and Th. Simon (Chicago Medical Book Co., 1915); *Emotional Disorders of Children: A Case Book of Child Psychiatry* by Gerald H. J. Pearson, MD (Hayne Press, 2011); *Diagnostic Psychological Testing* by David Rapaport, Merton M. Gill, and Roy Schafer (International Universities Press, 1968); *Foundations of Psychological Testing: A Practical Approach* by Leslie A. Miller and Robert L. Lovler (SAGE, 2015). Since 1977 I have kept journals, and I also used those as reference.

I Am Not a Clock

TIME STICKS NUMBERS ON the world and marks spaces I can't see. My teacher says the hands do this, and clocks are how we know when to come and go, but I am not a clock, and I always know when I have to leave my mom.

I don't have a watch. My best friend, Melissa, does. When I learn to read time on a clock, I can get one, too.

"See? The small hand is on the two. The big hand is on the three," Melissa says. "And if you cover it, you can see it glow."

I nod. We are standing next to the bright light of the baby chick's cage, across the room from the fluffy red reading rug, and I'm hot. Does time glow when you hold your hand over its numbers, or only watches? I don't ask in case I'm supposed to already know the answer. I sneak a quick glance at our classmates, who are playing a clock game I don't understand. Our teacher, Allegra, asked Melissa to help me, but I know I'm being left behind.

Melissa's fingers are gummed with orange juice from recess. I duck my eyes down to the trapped neon, green under our cupped hands. The raised black plastic surrounds the clock glass like a medieval fortress, but the numbers are just horses standing in a circle—they mean nothing to me. I like the watch's buckled bigness and I want one around my wrist for the comfort, the extra weight when my body turns into a leaf and floats away. Maybe Melissa will let me try hers on.

When I look back, Melissa's face is bigger than before. She's pushed

in close to me, warming the air with her nearness, making energy out
of the nothing between us. The sudden change reminds me of the truth
about time only I seem to know: It can't be trusted. To me, time feels
good or bad, but to everyone else, time isn't a feeling, it's something outside their bodies they can see; it doesn't hurt them. If time is visible to
others, why won't anyone catch it and make it stop, so I never have to
leave my mom? Maybe the meaning of time is taking people away from
each other.

"So...what time is it?" Melissa's nose is an urgent inch away. Her
eyebrows are impatient. I feel the dread before school every day; I feel
the dread leading up to weekend visits with my father. I know something
is wrong with me. I feel the dread all the time.

Our classmates are running clockwise on the reading rug, calling out
minutes and hours from the center of the room. Their clapped vibrations catch in the middle of my body; their carefree jumps pass from the
floor into my feet and knees.

Allegra claps twice, and everyone freezes. In the corner of my eye,
I watch Naomi whispering to Kyra, eyes locked on me. Melissa asks
again, but I still don't know the answer. Once I understand what they
do, we can join the game, but until then, I'm keeping Melissa stuck. My
lungs feel tight. What if she's worried I'll never let her go?

"You can play with them if you want," I tell Melissa. "You don't have
to stay with me." I don't mean it. The instant I say it, I am homesick
for her.

"I can't," Melissa says, frustrated. "Not until you know the time." She
lifts her wrist to my face and lumps out my view. "How 'bout now? What
time is it now?" She's not even looking at me. Outside of my mother,
my sister, and my brother, Melissa is my favorite person. Her hair is always a little tangled, and her dresses are always the wrong size, so she
looks messy, like me. We have lots in common. When I don't understand something, she waits for me. When I accidentally suck my fingers
at school, she knocks them out of my mouth or signals from across the
room—a tug on her hair; but now something sounds gone. She's not

being motherly, and her voice rings the emergency feeling in my body telling me to hurry up, hurry up. This makes the world speed up and everything goes double.

"Is it a.m. or p.m.?" Melissa thinks she's helping, but she's not.

I look at the board where a chalk sun rises over a.m., and the moon sinks down to p.m.

"It's a.m.," I say. There is too much going on around me. I am in nineteen different places at once.

"No, it's p.m."

"But the sun is out," I say, pointing.

"At twelve things turn p.m.," she explains.

"Then what turns everything a.m.?"

"Twelve," she says. "There are two twelves. One turns everything p.m., and the other turns everything a.m."

I look back at the clock. Melissa steps in and out of her clogs.

"Where's the other twelve?" I ask.

"The one twelve is two twelves," she says. "All the numbers happen twice."

"When?" How can one number mean two things? This makes no sense to me.

Melissa pushes her lips together, frustrated. "When the clock says."

Does everything mean two things? When Allegra writes things on the calendar, like "Class Picnic" or "Field Trip," they become true. Before she wrote them, they didn't exist. Before I was born, I didn't exist either, and after I die I won't exist again. What else of the world can't I see?

I look back at the watch on Melissa's dark-haired wrist. Two hands stand perfectly still while a third skips past in a race by itself. How is 2 p.m. different from 1 p.m.? They both feel exactly the same, and they both happen over and over, day in and day out. Maybe they even happen at the same time. Time changes, hands move, but the same things don't always happen at the same time. If someone fell down every Tuesday at 2 p.m. in front of me, then I'd always know, Oh, today is Tuesday, and it's 2 p.m.!

If I never understand, will I become a stay-behind kid who stops growing older? No one says it's possible to just *not-learn* something, which means it doesn't happen to regular people, only people like me. None of my friends have to watch their mom all the time to make sure she doesn't die or disappear.

My mom tells me over and over that nothing bad will happen to me, or to her, or to my big sister, Kara, or to my brother, Eddie, or to anyone when I leave home. She says, "Trust me." I do, but I also know with my body that bad things happen. If I turn away for just one second, the world might swallow my mom, or me, and I will never find her again. I worry that I'm the only person who knows about this, and I am in charge of this knowing, which is not a job I want.

Melissa starts playing with her necklace. A bright yellow *M*. "It's really not that hard. I promise," she says. A spicy-cool peppermint rises sad from my belly and closes hot and tight in my throat. I want to cry. This means she agrees with Allegra, who acts like there is only one type of world, one way to feel and be and think, and even one way of knowing. I am beginning to worry all people think this way.

"Can't you just tell me?" I ask.

"I'm not allowed," she says. "You're supposed to learn it by yourself."

If my mom were here, she'd tell me. At home she always tells me the time so I don't have to do it myself. Is Melissa changing her mind about me? Is she ashamed to be my friend?

"The game's almost over," she says.

"I know," I say. "I'm sorry." I can't hear my voice.

"It's okay," she tells me and then leans down. "It's twenty after two," she hot-whispers.

"But...I don't even see a twenty," I say.

Melissa sucks in an inside-out breath and sighs. "The four is twenty. And the three is fifteen, and the two is ten and like that."

Why isn't the two just two and the four just four? If everything really does mean two things, why can't I ever understand the second thing?

The sound in the classroom has quieted. My classmates have stopped running; they're staring. Everyone is waiting for me to get it: Melissa, my family, my teacher, the class, the street, the Village, the entire city; everyone in the world is waiting, but I will never get it. Something is wrong with me, and no one is helping me fix it.

My body feels drained, like I've just finished ten back-to-back relay races, and my head is crowded with cloudy chatter whose words don't make sense. I want to go home, where I'm safe, and get back into bed with my mom. Everyone is ahead of me; I'm always trying to catch up, but I never do. I'm always the littlest and the last to understand. I picture their brains with long legs racing down the block, but my brain has little-kid legs, too short to keep up. Melissa understands things on the first try, but not me. The space between us is growing; I can feel her pulling away, and I'm afraid she'll stop being my friend. A burning glows in my throat when people leave. The only way to keep my family close, to keep my friends, is to try to make my brain keep up.

"You get it now?" Melissa asks, eager for me to say yes.

The edges of the room smudge with black fog, and a slow suction pulls me away from her, from all of them. Soon my classmates will be far ahead of me. I'll watch them move without me to the grade above, and the grade after that, and they'll go to college and get married and have babies and families and jobs and houses, and I'll be right here, still trying to tell time, still trying to understand the secret second thing, stuck and alone and six forever. Maybe like the number twelve, there are two worlds. They're in one together, while I'm in mine alone.

Everyone wants me to learn how to read time, but no one understands that I don't want more ways that say good-bye.

INTELLIGENCE TEST: NUMBER CONCEPTS

This is a clock that is missing some numbers. You have to figure out which numbers are missing. Can you see which number is missing? No, eleven is right there, see it? What number should be here? Yes, good, twelve. Now, can you point to the minute hand? Are you sure that's the minute hand? Right, good, yes... Can you put the hands at nine fifteen? No, no... Three is fifteen, remember? If it's nine fifteen, can you tell me what time it was a half hour ago? Do you want to say your words out loud, or would you rather keep nodding? Nodding, okay. Look at this clock. You have to draw the numbers and the hands. Can you draw noon? Can you show me where twelve is? Can you put your pencil on twelve? Good. Now draw a little line. Now where do you draw the minute hand?...Are you okay? Dizzy? Do you want some water? Do you need a snack? What will help with your dizziness? You want to go visit your mom? Okay. Okay, let's stop for now. Let's take a little break.

Not the Right Kind of Human

I'VE BEEN TESTED FOR ambidexterity, amblyopia, astigmatism, auditory processing disorder, focal dystonia, and essential blepharospasm (eye twitching). I've been evaluated in language, learning, speech, and motor skills; tested for visual and hearing disabilities; rated on intelligence, cognition, aptitude, personality, development, and functioning. I've undergone Wepman's Auditory Discrimination Test and Auditory Memory Battery, the Beery-Buktenica Developmental Test of Visual-Motor Integration, the Beery Tests of Oral Comprehension, the Draw-a-Person Test, the Denckla rapid automatized naming test, the Peabody Picture Vocabulary Test, the Detroit Test of Learning Aptitude, the Illinois Test of Psycholinguistic Abilities, the Spache Diagnostic Reading Scales tests, the McCarthy Scales of Children's Abilities test, the Kaufman Assessment Battery for Children test, Frostig's Developmental Test of Visual Perception, the Gray Oral Reading Tests, Raven's Progressive Matrices test, the Bender Visual-Motor Gestalt Test, and neuropsychological batteries including the Wide Range Achievement Test, the Wechsler Intelligence Scale for Children, the Wechsler Adult Intelligence Scale, and the Stanford-Binet Intelligence Scales test, four times each.

I've pointed to pictures of shapes, cartoons, numbers, and letters, hoping my final answer matched what belonged in the empty grid. I've told them what was wrong with that picture, what was silly about it. I've drawn pictures and written stories. I've recited number sequences backward and forward. I've reconstructed cube patterns in the allotted time. After a while, all the patterns began to look the same.

My brain has been divided into fourths, eighths, and twelfths. I've been measured and sent to labs, measured and weighed against calculations, measured and assigned diagnostic codes, measured and measured and tested and compared to the standards by which measuring was held. I've spelled words I'd never heard, guessed their definitions. I've suffixed, prefixed, compounded, conjugated, diagrammed, defined, duplicated, reiterated, guessed, multiplied, divided, added, subtracted, elided, recited, confided, lied, cursed, and cried. I've repeated numbers, words, and rhymes. I've seen doctors, learning specialists, and tutors; I've stood on scales, languished in waiting rooms and on examination tables; I've raced against stopwatches; I've hung upright in trays affixed to the backs of doctors' doors. I've sat at Formica desks and in play areas, and been surrounded by white coats, pantsuits, pearl necklaces, bifocals, year-old issues of *Highlights*, *Cricket*, *WOW*, and *Dynamite*; I've climbed poles, marked on boards, put together oversized puzzles, threw suction darts, sat at low worktables to draw with colored chalk; I've met more new receptionists in more clinics than I can recall.

I've filled in the blanks: Mary had a _____ lamb. Boys run; babies _____. I've been timed, watched, and notated.

I was confused by the tests. I couldn't understand why adults believed that state capitals, equations, or analogies could determine why I was always afraid. I waited for someone to tell me the answers to what was inside me, but the focus was on what I didn't know, and never on what I did. The tests didn't care about my experience of the world; no one asked me questions they didn't already have answers to. There was a way I was supposed to be, and I didn't match. I was off the charts I should have been on, below the percentiles I was expected to reach, and outside the limited check boxes inside which I didn't easily fit. There were norms, categories and particular systems too narrow to include me. There was a single standard used to evaluate everyone, and that meant there was a single standard type of person, defined by a basic human trait that I did not possess: intelligence. I did not match the person I knew I was supposed to be. I feared I was not the right kind of human.

I knew where to go, what time to be there, and the name of each doctor, but I could not tell you why I took those tests, I could not tell you how I scored, or what they were supposed to teach me, my mother, or my doctors. Until I was twenty-five years old, I could not tell you what was wrong with me.

Dr. Rivka Golod

Language and Learning Evaluation
Developmental History

Pregnancy, birth, and developmental history were all normal. Amanda has no allergies and no unusual cognitive problems were noted in early childhood. Strengths of Amanda's include her ability to play piano by ear, her good memory, and acting skills. Amanda's mother and father separated when she was two years old. Mrs. Stuart is remarried and Amanda currently lives with her biological siblings and three stepbrothers and sister.

Maybe I Am Not a Person

ON MACDOUGAL STREET BETWEEN Bleecker and Houston, a row of multicolored houses, dyed like Easter eggs, backs up to a matching row on Sullivan Street. In the middle is a secret garden, reachable only through the homes. Its cobblestone and grass stretch the length of the entire block. Almost thirty kids live here, including my best friend, Melissa, and we think it's the greatest place on earth. Bob Dylan used to live here, too, but he's long gone, and besides, I don't even know who that is. Still, people ring our doorbell and ask for him all the time. I say, "He moved away. Now good-bye to you, home invader!"

On the street side we have an extra-wide stoop, which we share with our next-door neighbor. At night, the local bums, Ciggy and Sasquatch, turn the stairs into beds. Unlike the steps of normal stoops, ours lead up to the street, not down, sinking our house below the sidewalk. During the day, tourists duck down and peer through our kitchen window; we see their maps and wide, curious faces. Ten seconds later our doorbell rings.

"Is this a restaurant?" They crane their necks to look around me.

"Nope." I can tell they're trying to see into our secret garden, but I won't let them.

"What happens here?"

What happens here is a question that asks what we're hiding. As though being a family isn't good enough. I don't like disappointing people, so I say, "I'm not allowed to tell," or "You don't want to know." This way, they won't feel I failed them. They might be embarrassed by their question, but that's fine by me since that's how I feel most of the time. (Sometimes it's nice to have a break.) Even when I want to lie and say this is the headquarters of the Members-Only Evel Knievel Fan Club or the Truant Officer School for Juvenile Delinquents, I don't because then they'd want an explanation I don't have. People always expect right answers to their wrong questions. All that happens here is us, and we're not questions and can't be answered.

"Who is it?" my mom, still in her nightgown, yells from her bedroom upstairs. I can tell from her voice she's talking on the phone.

"Beats me," I say, shutting the door on the tourists, shoving my two sucking-fingers into my mouth and hurrying back to her.

*   *   *

The secret garden is where I'm not erased. Some people think I'm funny; the adults call me a character. Outside of Melissa, my favorite garden friends are Marcel and Margaux, and although adults are always smacking my hands out of my mouth whenever I bite my fingernails, I like everyone. Some people fight, but mainly we tromp in and out of one another's houses, sharing toys, food, and moms. When I'm not cursing, or teaching other people how to curse, I speak with a fake Russian accent or pretend I'm an old-timey spy. Once I cut Marcel's hair with pinking shears.

We climb trees, read books on the branches, and rope-swing our way down. We tap-dance on the sandbox cover, circle the entire garden on the low balance beam of bricks without touching the ground, play freeze tag, and have chestnut and bottle-rocket wars. We build igloos, and we ice-skate when snow freezes over in wintertime. In the fall, I peel apart the helicopter wings and stick them on the end of my nose. We set up ramps and ride our Big Wheels like they're scooters and jump daredevil-style from one to the other. On the jungle gym swing, we lay the seesaw across the canvas seat and stand a kid on each end while someone turns us round and round until the ropes are twirled, as tight as they can go. When you unspin, the colored houses, the trees and the fences, the sandbox and the cobblestone all swirl together, mixing up a fast new world in a brand-new color. You can feel the air of that new world whoosh your face, and the tight sensations in your belly are from excitement nerves, not worry ones. I am always happy when my body remembers to feel things other than scared.

There are garden rules and garden meetings and garden gossip and garden life. We're like a small town with traditions and holiday celebrations. On Halloween we have a haunted house and our own parade with prizes; on Easter we hunt for eggs in the bushes; on Digging Day we plant grass and repaint the green benches and black gates. In winter we have weekly Christmas-caroling rehearsals in different living rooms. My mom throws her own Christmas party every year, even though we're Jewish.

On the garden side, houses are sun-bleached and worn, the color of faded vegetables. Ivy covers only a couple of house faces, and a lucky few have their own balcony. I take pictures of everything to keep life permanent.

Everyone shares the big garden, but the little garden is your own. Ours has a sour cherry tree. There's a cobblestone area for tables and chairs, and a small rectangle of grass where you can plant flowers if you like that sort of thing. Sometimes I set out a blanket in our little garden and bring snacks and a book and pretend the blanket is a raft and the grass is the ocean. I crank the crooked pole round and round and watch the awning open, imagining it's a sail. The dark green cover makes me feel safe. I shut my eyes and feel the raft bob over gentle waves and smell the salt water. In the middle of the ocean, I'm protected from the whole scary world. When I open my eyes, my house is still there. It never leaves me.

When it rains the maple leaves grow heavy and brush against the house like a bedtime back rub, taking care of us. It is a home sound, one that happens only here. In the mornings, we hear birds before humans. Light catches and holds in wide stripes on the wood-planked floors.

Kara, Eddie, and I lie sleepily on a couch near the garden doors, listening to the country sounds in the middle of the city, letting the spill of the sun warm our faces. When I was a baby, we lived uptown with our dad and mom. Kara and Eddie remember that, but I don't. I only remember living here. I want to only ever live here, in my same house, always.

The garden has legends, like Dead Man Smith, who lives under the Lesters' house and comes out only at night. But even with Dead Man Smith, it's not dangerous here. If time worked the way it does in the garden, I wouldn't have any problems telling it. When the high-pitched clamoring of small lungs first shrieks a hole in the weekday quiet, it's 3 p.m. The quick flick of the bell from Minnie Lester's wrist chiming Arthur and John to dinner is 6 p.m. When you wake up to voices and running, it's either the weekend or the summer. When I'm in the garden, I can always feel my mother. If I need her, I know where to find her. The brownstones protect us. Like uptown doormen, they guard us from murderers and intruders, keeping us safe inside our secret world. We're reminded of the outside only when the subway rolls its vibration under us.

The world is scary on the street side of life. Even my mom thinks so. When people don't look right at her, she stiffens her body and rushes us past, her mouth set tight, her eyes propped wide and straight, holding back her blinks. When we walk through Washington Square Park, she clutches her purse to her chest, and she walks so fast I have to run behind her to keep up. My dad tells us stories about people who go missing and three days later they find them dead. The news tells you what happens. The radio too. People disappear without a trace and are found strangled in Boston. If you go on the subway, people push you onto the tracks and escape as the train splurts out your bloody guts. My mom is afraid of the subway, but Kara and Eddie still take it to school, even though they are only eleven and nine. When you're too famous, people come to your door and shoot you in the face. Who wants to grow up when there are so many ways to get killed?

I ask my mom all the time if these things will happen to us, but she says no, absolutely not. Things like that just don't happen to children, she says. That makes me feel better, but I still worry about what will happen to me when I grow up. My mom's a grown-up, and she's afraid of the world, too. I can tell.

From my bedroom window, through my rainbow decal I watch the days unfold into evenings on MacDougal Street. Legs bent under me, I study the street side of things: the smoking adults, the kids practicing tricks on their skateboards. The church bell chimes, and wood cracks against a baseball in the Houston Street playground across the street, signaling the end of the day.

Across the street is Caffé Dante, where the artists go; and next door to that is Joe's Restaurant, where Vito serves vodka to the grown-ups and Tony slides plates of fried zucchini piled high like green volcanoes. In the morning when we're walking to school, and in the afternoon when we're returning, Vito stands outside and makes sure the St. Anthony's kids don't beat us up. Whenever I pass him I yell out, "No black eyes yet!" so he knows he's doing a good job.

At Al's Candy Store kids run in and out, while teenage hoodlums shop for drug equipment at the head shop next door. Al sells Tootsie Rolls for a penny, and I load up on those, as well as Swedish Fish, with the prize money I receive for finding my mom's lost things. She loses earrings, glasses, rings, to-do lists, books, and even the glass she was just drinking from (which is always right in front of her). She doesn't look for anything before she starts yelling out that something's missing, but if she did, I wouldn't have so much reward money right now. No one else in the house is as good at finding things as I am. When I'm searching, no area goes unexamined, except for at night, when I will not go down to the basement. Not even with Jimmy, my mom's boyfriend, whom I like because he lets me climb all over him even when he's reading the newspaper. His kids, Holly, Daniel, and David, told me Norman Bates lives in our basement. Norman is a psycho who killed his mom, and I am not going to let him kill mine. He doesn't live there during the day, though.

Sometimes in the evenings, we walk up Sixth Avenue to Brentano's.

None of us ever wear shoes, including my mom. We walk around the Village barefoot, and sometimes people look at us weird or yell, "Someone's gonna get hurt!" On special occasions, we go to Canton restaurant on Division Street where the owner, Eileen, orders things for us that aren't on the menu: lettuce wraps, sautéed Chinese broccoli, and salt-and-pepper shrimp. We are allowed to have whatever we want, including sugar, and Eddie and I always order orange soda. Afterward, we walk down the block to the Chinese arcade and pose like strongmen in the photo booth and feed dimes to the dancing chicken. Sometimes we go to Guss' Pickles on Delancey Street, where they let us stick our dirty fingers into the cloudy barrels and pull out a sour that's too heavy for just one hand. When we want a snack we go to Balducci's, where we stand at the openmouthed crates and pop raw vegetables into our mouths, one fast sugar snap pea after another. On the way home, Eddie and Kara walk together, trading secrets they don't share with me. They do it because I'm the youngest. When I'm left out, I feel erased. We pass Jimmy Alcatraz, who sits outside the mafia store with the red curtain.

"Hi, Jimmy Alcatraz!" We wave.

Jimmy Alcatraz is the mafia; he keeps our neighborhood protected. Even though he knows our names, he and all the other Italians call the garden people the Americans.

A few buildings over, in the late afternoon, old Italian women in their nightgowns call down to kids below and lower metal pails filled with grubby loose change and warm fistfuls of crumpled dollar bills. "See how many Loosies these'll get me!"

Melissa and I inflate with pride at their husky shouts, as though they've been waiting just for us. When we return, out of breath, and drop the change and goods back into the pail, Ciggy appears out of nowhere and lunges his arm in, but he's never fast enough.

"Get your filthy mitts outta my pail, Ciggy!"

Off he goes, scouring the curb for stubs the Italian women throw out their windows. Unlike Ciggy, the other neighborhood homeless man, Sasquatch, never asks for anything. Ciggy's gray hair is unraveling and his nose is a fistful of warts. Sasquatch is a redheaded ogre, but they are our bums, and when they disappear for days at a time, we notice and worry, and when they die, we'll miss them.

Every moment in my neighborhood is fun and sad at the same time. Sadness is my regular temperature and joy is a lucky surprise, one I feel mainly in the garden. I wish I could feel something else, something better. Even now, sitting on my own bed, safe at home, the soothing sensation of my house rectangled around me, I feel the spot in me where homesickness fills. Even when Melissa is here, I am always sad for something, but I never know for what. Ordinary things, like the dimming sun, lowering lights, the fresh spray of stars, or the first smell inside a new season's breeze, fill me with grief, a pressing dread, although I can never figure out what I'm mourning. Even when there is nothing to feel afraid of, I feel a fear, like something very terrible is about to happen. My chest and stomach fill with butterflies, a heat presses up under my skin, and my body vibrates like someone's drawing a chaotic black-and-white scribble and won't stop. I feel like this almost all the time. I wish the sky, the timer that sets the world, that sets the days and hours and weeks, that sets you and everyone I know, didn't *unset* me. Every day, when the sun starts to lower and the colors thicken the sky, my chest clogs. When the pink smears its sadness across the sun's cheek, that same pink sadness streaks in me.

The church bells chime. One, then two, all the way to the chime of now. The clouds smell like smoke, firewood burning. The bells chime and the sun dies. It dies every day, and the chimes tell the whole world why.

I want to feel safe, but I don't know how. One day I'll have to live on the street side of life. On the garden side we look after one another, making sure that all the children are here, that no one is missing or lost. We have each other's backs. I wish our secret garden were a real little town with its own bank and post office and school. Then maybe our father could live here and I wouldn't have to leave my mother in order to visit him, in order to do anything. If only this were the entire world. If only the garden could hold us all.

June 1981

Dr. Rivka Golod

<u>Language and Learning Evaluation</u>
<u>Presenting Problem</u>

Amanda was referred for a language and learning evaluation because of her low scores on the E.R.B. Intelligence Test done on February 24, 1981. Amanda performed particularly poorly on the subtest of verbal reasoning and there was concern about "language processing problems." Amanda is also reportedly "terrified of tests" in general. Other behavioral difficulties include a notable problem separating from her mother and a general fearfulness. Teachers report that Amanda has difficulty understanding concepts and struggles to extract meaning from abstractions—parents state that Amanda had difficulty learning to tell time. There is no question that Amanda is a learning disabled child.

How to Say What's Wrong

A GRAY-HAIRED LADY stands on the corner of MacDougal and Houston where the playground fence meets in the shape of a stick figure's nose. Unlike Sasquatch and Ciggy, whose hair has grown tangled into something that isn't hair, the gray-haired lady's bob is always the same length; even her bangs never get long. Do homeless people get haircuts? She stands on that corner every day, all week, every week, all month, every month, waiting. I know she's different from Ciggy and Sasquatch; I know she has a story hanging over her. But no one else seems to see it.

"I don't think she's waiting for anyone," Kara says, pressing her fingers into her chest and coughing out a wheeze. She leans over me at the window, cradles the inhaler between her lips, pushes down the top, and breathes in the medicine it releases. I'm dying to try it.

"Why not?"

"Because she's a crazy lady. She's just doing what crazy ladies do; they stand on corners."

"She's drunk," Eddie announces, shoving contraband Oreos into his mouth and wiping the crumbs off his Ace-bandaged knee onto my bed. At school he jumped down a flight of stairs, and his teacher had to carry him home because he couldn't walk. Eddie and I fight a lot because he's mean to me, and right now he's breaking the law by being in my room. I want to citizen arrest him, but I don't know how.

I know the lady on the corner is waiting for her mother. The part I don't understand is why her mother isn't showing up. Did she get hit by a car or move to Europe without telling her? Maybe the lady's been standing there for forty years, since she was a girl, because her mother told her to wait right there while she ran a quick errand, but she never came back. Maybe the lady on the corner doesn't know she's turned into a grown-up. Whatever she was supposed to become, whomever she was supposed to make a life with, it never happened. It's been so long, now she can never leave.

There's no one to tell her how to be a grown-up now. No one explains anything to me, so maybe no one explained anything to her either. How do people find jobs? Or get a house? What happens at a bank? Where do you find a husband, and how do you make sure they don't kill you? When I ask my mom she says I don't need to worry about that kind of stuff for a long time, but if I'm already worried, can't she just tell me so I'll know how not to be homeless? My mom says I will never be homeless. When I ask how she knows, she says, "I just do."

"Can I live with you when I grow up?" I ask.

"Yes, of course," she says. I calm down. She is lying on her bed, as usual, cheek propped in her hand and two pairs of glasses on her head. Her bed is her safe place, like she is my safe place.

"Here in this house?"

"Of course in this house; where else will I be?" She is distracted, trying to find a phone number in the white pages.

"I'm never going to college," I tell her. "I want to be with you always."

"You'll feel differently when you get older," she says, her voice distant.

But I know I won't. "What if we spend all our money and we lose the house?" I ask her.

"That's not going to happen," she says. She sits up, presses her finger into the page, and dials the number. "Goddamn it," she says. Busy signal. When my mom's tone changes to mad, it happens fast, and it scares me, even if it's not my fault.

"How do you know?" I ask.

"Because one day this house will be yours, so you have nothing to worry about." She tosses the phonebook down, still annoyed.

"What about Kara and Eddie?" I ask.

"Theirs too."

"It will?" I ask.

"Yes," she says, propping up pillows behind her and reaching for a book.

"So I can live here always? Even when I'm a grown-up? You promise?"

"Promise. No matter what, you will always have this house."

I exhale. I want to dance. This house is my best friend. Knowing I will never lose it protects me inside a coat of shiny armor. Uncertainty throws me away from the world, but as soon as I know something for sure, I'm dropped back to earth, living and breathing with everyone else.

"You promise?" I ask one last time.

"I promise," she says, turning to the thick middle of her novel where she left off. "Why don't you go make a project?" she says.

When I'm at home, I feel guarded. I can be myself and put on shows to make my mom laugh. I dress up and do impressions of my teachers and even of her. I'll put two pairs of her glasses on my face, and yell out in my mom's high-pitched voice, "I can't find my glasses! Where are my glasses?" And my mom, doubled over with laughter, will say, "You're so mean to me!" but she doesn't really believe that.

Whenever Kara and Eddie and I get bored and want her to play with us, she always says to make a project and show her when we're done. This is why I've written, directed, and acted in fifteen plays. I'm also building a robot out of a shopping cart and tinfoil, which is why we keep running out. No matter what, every time we're deep in the middle of writing a play, or making a puppet show, she'll yell out for one of us to bring her this medicine or that medicine. We always have a good hard laugh when she asks me to bring her Titralac. I can't believe someone put the word "tit" in their medicine.

When one of us has a headache or feels sick, my mom opens her overstuffed medicine cabinet. I'm relieved she has something for everything, but if there are that many medicines for different things, then there must be hundreds of different sicknesses that I could die from.

Whenever I am afraid, worry sounds itself as sixty maybe seventy radio channels playing at the same time inside my head. Refrains loop around and around my brain like fast jabber, and I cannot get any of it to stop. I know there is something wrong with me, but no one knows how to fix me. Not anyone outside my body, and definitely not me. Eddie says a body is blood and bones and skin, and when everything falls off you're a skeleton, but I am air pressure and tingly dots, energy and everything. I am air and nothing.

If I try to explain to adults how I'm feeling, they say I'm being over-dramatic. Adults always say that kids have it easy, that they wish they could go back to childhood. The kids around me are carefree and happy, but I'm not, and life doesn't feel easy for me, ever, which means I'm being a kid in the wrong way.

You can't see the wrong on my outside, but I wish you could because then my mom would get me fixed. My mom can fix anything; she knows every doctor in New York City. Kara and Eddie always have something wrong with them; they're so lucky. Kara is allergic to everything, and her asthma means she gets to miss school all the time. Sometimes she even gets to go to the hospital. Eddie doesn't have things wrong with the way his body works, but he's accident-prone. A couple of years ago, he got hit in the back of the head with a metal swing and got stitches, but then a guy put bird feed in his hair and a pigeon swooped down and plucked the stitches out of his scalp. Once he broke his arm playing on the escalator at a department store when he wasn't supposed to. He lied to my mom and said he walked into a wall. She believed him because she believes everything, but the doctor wasn't fooled. When I started sobbing because I thought broken meant dead, the doctor crossed his arms and looked at us funny, like someone wasn't telling the truth.

Grown-ups can see how to fix Kara and Eddie. I feel my wrong things all the time, but no one else seems to see them. Eddie's cast is covered in drawings and signatures and I stare at it all the time and imagine my arm inside. He gets to wear it for six weeks and I'm so jealous. Sometimes I wear his sling and it fills me with a deep comfort, like I'm being swaddled next to my mom. Eddie is a daredevil. I'm the most daredevil of the girls in the garden, but no matter how hard I try, I never seem to break anything.

Maybe the lady on the corner was a tomboy, too, flying her scooter off ramps in a garden. Probably not, though—she keeps her hair so neat, even now that she's homeless. She probably hates being dirty. My mom probably wishes I could keep my hair like that. My mom likes things that are beautiful. My mom is very beautiful; everyone says so. She is skinny and glamorous; in the daytime, she wears oversized sunglasses, batik halter tops, and wraparound skirts. Her hair is dark brown and wavy, and it falls down her back like a movie star's. She has a lot of friends who are always talking about how she's "fabulous" and "too generous." She's all those things, but she's also daydreamy. She doesn't notice things everyone else seems to notice, and sometimes when you're talking to her, her eyes go glassy, like she's somewhere else, but I never know where, and I miss her, even though she hasn't actually gone anywhere.

She doesn't wear shoes, but she loves nice clothes and jewelry and is always put-together and perfect, like our house. This is one way we are not the same. I am not pretty, and the way I like things is worn-in and torn-up. I am the opposite of the things my mom likes. Instead of a regular bar of soap in the bathroom, there are little pink perfumed soaps shaped like seashells that we're not supposed to get dirty. I like being messy, and I keep my hair short like a boy and wear boy's clothes because I don't want to be a girl in the way that girls are. I want to be a girl in the way I am, which is more like a boy. I care about climbing trees and cursing, not dolls or being a bride. I don't want boys looking at me with sexy eyes. Grown-ups are always telling me that playing sports and cursing isn't ladylike or feminine, but I am a kid. Kids can be girls and act like boys and the other way around, but that upsets grown-ups, and I don't know why.

My mom gets upset when we spill something on the fancy lace tablecloth she makes us eat dinner on, and when I curse she gets mad and says I'm being "fresh." If I keep biting my fingernails, she says, no one will want to marry me, and if I keep my hair short, no boy will ever ask me to dance. She wishes I wore dresses. She thinks good things happen when you're pretty, but I know that's not true. When she makes me wear a dress, grown-ups say I look pretty, but I am not pretty, I'm cute. I don't want to be pretty. *They* want me to be pretty. I don't think it's fair that there's only one way to be a girl. When you're pretty boys want to sex on you. At night, on the street side of my house, the Jersey kids come and press their tight jeans against each other, swapping spit between their bad-accent mouths and long hair. I don't want to be pretty because I do not want sex, especially after that time Frederick and his mother came over. It was a special occasion, but I can't remember what we were celebrating.

The best part of Truth or Dare is Dare, but Frederick is older and I'm seven, so he was the boss of me, and I had to do what he said. Truth or Dare isn't a top secret game, so he shouldn't have covered the escape way of the hidden cubby in Eddie's loft bed. After he asked me the first Truth question I wish I hadn't said, "What is that?" because then he showed me what it was. When he asked the next question, I didn't say "What is that?" but he tricked me by asking, "Do you know what that is?" When I shook my head, he showed me what it was. I should not have asked, and I should not have shaken my head. I wish I hadn't been wearing a dress. I didn't want to play anymore, but he wouldn't stop. It wasn't fun at all. Finally, he said I could put my clothes back on. He let me out only after I promised I'd never tell—if I did tell, he'd have someone take my mom away.

That's what happens when you're pretty. Funny is safer than pretty.

When I worry about bad things happening to me, like getting kidnapped, my mom always tells me bad things like that don't happen to kids. But I know they do. And she does, too—some nights, when I make her sing me songs or read to me, it's always about babies dropping out of cradles and children turning into ash and falling down. Madeline rushes to the hospital in the middle of the night with a bursting appendix; a boy finds a rotten peanut, eats it, and dies; a pig loses her life; and people are always disappearing. My mom sings that I am her sunshine, and asks me to please not take myself away. How could she think I would ever do that? I want to stay with her always. Sometimes I wish my mother sang me different songs and read me different books, but if I tell her to stop or change, she'll think I mean forever, and I'll accidentally send her away.

My worry that something terrible is going to happen when my mom and I are separated is a thick, blurry sadness that covers everything, like cracked plastic sleeves in an old photo album. It sits on top of my *Family Circus* books, Etch A Sketch, Magic 8 Ball, posters of Philippe Petit, John Travolta, and the Fonz. Even the rainbow decal on my window looks sad. Sometimes I feel like I'm watching a movie about myself. I am always in the future somehow, separated from my body, and it's from there I feel sad for the moment I'm living. Soon this moment will be gone; it will turn into another moment that will go, and I think I must be the only person who feels life as though it's already over. This is the weight I feel every time the sun goes down. No matter how hard I try to stop the feeling, I can't. Even if I run from it, it meets me wherever I land.

At night when I'm in bed, I try to hear the house sounds that comfort me: the low mumblings of my siblings, the tamped-down warble of the radio, the needle's skipped return over scratches inside a song, the ceramic clatter of plates being rinsed, and the first turbulent bumps of the dishwasher before it coasts into its varoom lulling hum. My mother's voice talking on the phone curls its way to my room, and I pull it toward me, past the other sounds, and try to swallow it inside me. When I can't hear her at all, I look out my window to make sure she's not running down MacDougal Street to join another family. Or to just live alone, which is one of the worst things I can think of happening when I grow up.

I don't know where the lady on the corner sleeps, or if she even has a house. My mom can't tell me where the lady gets medicine when she gets sick, but when I ask if she can live here with us, my mom says no. When you have a safe house that loves you and a person needs help, that's the right thing to do. When I am older and this house is mine, I will let her live here with us. Isn't she afraid out there at night by herself? Night is scary, even in here. When she sees all the house lights turn out, does dread drop its stones in her stomach like mine? Lights-out means my mom is going to sleep, too. Turning out all the lights tells the bad people of the world that we're asleep and now is the best time for them to break in and kill us—except I'm *not* asleep, and I am going to have to watch it happening. If I'm the only one still awake, then I'm in charge of protecting everyone, and no one is in charge of me. If I do manage to fall asleep before the lights go out but wake up in the dark, I worry I'm too late, and I can't hurry fast enough to my mom's room, where I climb onto her couch once I'm sure we're all alive.

Our mom is a night owl. She stays up until 3 or 4 a.m., and then in the morning her alarm sirens the rest of us awake. She sleeps right through it, which makes me worry she's died in her sleep, and my breath flips on its side, horizontal and too wide to go through my lungs. The only way to wake her is to put ice down her back. She doesn't take us to school, though, so during the week we don't ice her. If we don't wake her, she sleeps until noon.

When we were very little, before we lived here, we lived in a hotel, but not with our dad. Kara was six, Eddie was four, and I was two. One day Kara came home from school and found my mom fainted on the bed. I don't know what baby-me was doing, maybe just crawling around. The ambulance took my mom away to a hospital, and we had to go live with my dad until she came home. I don't remember that, and I don't know how long we were apart, but it makes me cry to think of my mom being taken away from us. My body feels like it is always worried it's going to happen again, any second.

Now Kara makes banana smoothies for her in the morning because the hospital says she has low potassium. Other days she can't get up because she has a headache and needs Kara to make her a fruit smoothie and bring it to her in bed. She wakes up with a lot of headaches. I get a lot of headaches, too; so do Kara and Eddie. Also earaches, and my nose bleeds all the time, but mainly on the weekends I have to spend at my dad's house. Sometimes, when Eddie and Kara leave for school before me and she's still asleep, I sit on the end of her bed and stay with her. When she opens her eyes, I ask her if I can stay home and she says yes. When she wakes up at noon, she doesn't remember why I'm not at school, but by then it's too late to take me, so we go shopping or to the toy store. I know she is safer if I'm with her.

I know my mom doesn't want us to leave her either. Since she was little, she's hated being alone. She was an only child and her parents never played with her. Her parents competed with each other for her affection, and her mom was so strict about how she looked, she sewed her winter coat pockets up so it looked more streamlined. My mom's hands were cold her entire childhood.

"Do you wish you had brothers or sisters?" I ask her sometimes. The answer is always the same.

"Why do you think I had so many children?" I never understand what that means. Are we her siblings?

I worry about my mom, and myself, all the time. Even in the moments when I've found a way to stop worrying, just for a minute or two, something abrupt always stabs the calm. Usually it's my own mom, who screams out emergencies, like "OH GOD!" or "JESUS CHRIST!" and I jump into action and zoom down the stairs, terrified I will find her bleeding and dead.

"What happened?"

"Oh, I dropped my pen," she'll say. Or Kara spilled something, or Eddie tipped a chair back. When she reacts this way, with her worried hospital panic, it's hard to calm down again. Her responses mean the world *is* just as scary as I thought, and I'm right to stay alert. That's why I can't sleep at my friends' houses, or even let friends sleep over here. Because even when I'm home, a sleepover is a distraction that might make me miss an important cry for help.

I worry so much that at school sometimes my teacher's words turn into thick fingers rubbing inside my ears so I can't hear. The only voice

I hear is my own, and it tells me that while I'm trying to listen to the lesson, my mom is answering the door to a stranger who's shoving a sock into her mouth, tying her up in the basement, and burning down our house.

It's not just that she drops things or loses glasses and rings, it's also that she believes everything everyone tells her—like that Eddie broke his arm walking into a wall—which means one day, she might get hurt. She's always asking people what to do, or what to think or say, and whenever I ask her anything she says either "It just is," or "It just won't," or "I can't explain it," which means she doesn't know. I worry she'll forget I love her, which is why when she says she loves me, I say, "I love you more." Now she's started saying, "No, I love *you* more," and I'm worried she thinks I don't love her enough, which is worse than her not loving me enough. I need to be home; I need to make sure she can see me, can feel my love. Otherwise, she might forget. She forgets important things. She forgot the sleepover code.

Margaux is always asking me to sleep over. I don't want to be scared, because it makes life harder. So a few months ago I decided that the next time Margaux asked, I'd say yes and push myself to try. But still I worried.

"What if I say yes to a sleepover but then decide later that I need to come home?" I asked my mom.

"We can have a code," she said. "If you want to sleep at Margaux's house, when you call, you ask, 'Mom, can I sleep at Margaux's house?' Otherwise, you should ask, 'Mom, Margaux wants to know if I can sleep over.' When you say their name first, I'll know that means you don't want to. Got it?"

I smiled. My mother is not only very beautiful, she's also a brilliant genius. "I get it."

A few days later, when I was at Margaux's and it was almost dinnertime, she asked if I wanted to sleep over. Although I'd felt ready a few days ago, it wasn't true anymore, but now I had a code to get out of things like this.

"Let me call and ask," I said.

Margaux stood next to me as I dialed home.

"Hello?"

"Hi, Mom. Margaux wants to know if I can sleep over," I said. I hoped I didn't sound so obvious that Margaux would figure out our code.

"Okay, that's fine," she said.

I held the phone, paralyzed. "No, Mom. I said Margaux wants to know if I can sleep over!"

"Manda, I just said it's fine."

"What's she saying?" Margaux asked. I didn't like how close her ear was to the receiver.

I looked around the kitchen. It made me sick to imagine all the lights of this house turning out for the night. I turned my back to Margaux, covered the receiver with my hand, and spoke directly into the pinpricks.

"But Mom . . . ," I tried again.

"Manda, I have something in the oven. I said yes; yes, you can sleep over at Margaux's!"

"Code, Mom! Code!" I whispered hard into the phone.

"Oh! I completely forgot! No, you may not sleep at Margaux's!"

I hung up and looked at Margaux with the saddest face I could manage. "She says I can't."

"Why?" Margaux asked.

But the only thing I could think to say was, "I can't explain it."

A few hours later, when I was safely back in my own house, it sank in. If my mom couldn't remember a code she invented, and I had to remember it for her, then it really wasn't safe for me to leave her. What else was she forgetting?

Rules always change on me when they aren't supposed to because I'm right about the world—the things that people say won't happen do happen. Nothing stays the same. It feels like every time I try to get past my worries, my tries get erased. So now it's back to how it was.

On the street she's not careful either. Just the other day, at the corner, she started to cross without looking at the red light. I yanked her back, and my lungs burned like in breaststroke. Now I know for sure she can't be left alone. She doesn't even know how to properly cross the street without me.

"You can cross if no cars are coming," she said. Now, how on earth do I keep someone like that safe?

My mom always talks about "the right thing to do." She never makes mistakes and doesn't like when other people make mistakes either, which is why I am always trying my hardest. But crossing the street when the light is red is not the right thing to do, and I don't know why she doesn't know that.

Sometimes I wish my mom would trade places with the lady on the corner. That way I'd know where she was all the time, and that she was standing still. John, one of my babysitters, takes me to school and picks me up. He takes me to activities and doctors' appointments. When I'm with my babysitter I don't know where my mom is, but if she stood on the corner, I'd always know. At night, I would bring her back home for dinner and then bed.

My siblings don't mind separating, not the way I do. Our mother spits on her finger to wipe our faces, and we always smell like her saliva. "I don't want to smell your mouth on me!" one of them complains, stomping to the sink to scrub her away. When she eats some of Kara's apple: "Now every bite will taste like lipstick!" Or when she takes a sip of Eddie's water: "I can taste your bad breath!" But if she wants, I'll let her lick my entire face.

Why don't they want to be that close, and why do they cheerfully look forward to visiting our father every other weekend when it means leaving our mother? Why don't they want to smell her stale, airless breath in the middle of the night, to spend every last second with her?

Sometimes I feel like the world and I are the same. Like I am part of its feelings and it's breathing me. All the days that lie ahead of me are filled with each of these exact hours, and I worry this sadness will always wait for me, no matter how old I get or where I live. Every time the sun goes, it tells me about all the days I've lost, and the one I'm losing now, even though I'm not finished living it.

The sky can see and feel everything, and I feel everything, too, even things I know aren't mine. I know when my mom is upset. I know when my mom is sad. Sometimes, when I hear her cry, I barrel toward her bedroom where she's lying on her bed, and I hold her hand and ask her if she misses her mom, which makes her cry harder, but always she says yes, and always I understand.

People make mean comments about the lady on the corner. They want her to stand somewhere else. They don't understand, but I do. She spooks me, too, but not for the same reason. She scares me because I know that her waiting means it never goes away. The worrying, the waiting for something terrible to happen, the dread. Sometimes it gets worse as you grow up, so bad you find yourself at age forty-five standing on the corner still worried about your mom. Your hair's gone gray, your skin's loosened, you've got no job, no kids or family of your own, because all this time you've paid attention to only one thing: your mom. This is what forever looks like.

INTELLIGENCE TEST: PICTURE COMPLETION

"I am going to show you a picture that has something wrong with it. Here is the first card. Can you tell me what is wrong with this picture?"

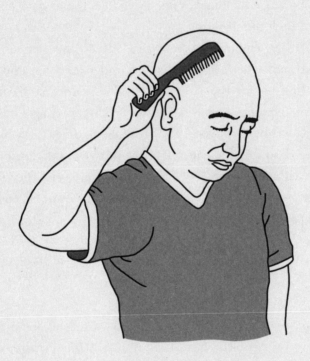

"The man is using a comb, but he has no hair."

"Here's another picture. Can you tell me what's funny about this picture? What's silly about it?"

I look at the picture. There is too much to take in. It's not like the first picture, which was simple; this one is busy. Look at the picture. She's timing you. The sand is running out. Focus. Girl. Tree. Grass. Okay, now I can see the picture. This is a trick question because there are lots of things wrong. For instance, it's windy and the girl isn't wearing a warm enough jacket. Two, the girl is too young to be out without a grown-up. Three, the girl should have worn darker socks to match her outfit. She doesn't look neat and put-together. Four, the wind is going in the opposite direction from the way her hair is blowing; and five, the shadow on the ground looks wrong.

Dr. Rivka shifts.

"Just one funny thing?" I ask.

"Just one."

"Could it be the trees?" I ask. "That they're blowing a different way from her hair? Maybe that's it?"

I look at the girl in the picture again and then over to the doctor.

"Is that a question, or your answer?"

"It's a question," I say, hoping she'll just say I'm right so I can say the answer and know I'm right.

"I need just an answer," she says.

I do not want to be wrong. What if she yells at me? I feel myself separate from my body so that it can answer her without me, in case I'm wrong.

"It's the trees?" I say. "That they're blowing a different way from her hair?"

"What about this picture, Amanda? Can you tell me what's foolish about it, what's silly?"

She's not saying whether I'm right or wrong. Was it her jacket, or that she was outside without a grown-up? I stare at the card. I stare at the dog. I stare at the man. I will never know anything.

The man has footprints and the dog doesn't, but maybe the dog is walking on a sidewalk and not in the snow. It's hard to tell. Looking closer, it seems the man isn't wearing shoes, and walking through the snow barefoot is funny, and wrong, as well as foolish and silly. But there's the matter of the dog not being on a leash. Also, the dog isn't wearing a collar. The man has his hands in fists, so he must be cold, which means he forgot his gloves. Not to mention the world is missing.

The sand timer is draining. What if the card is supposed to be in color and my answer is about the footprints? What if the man isn't dressed warmly and my answer is that the card is black and white? What if the dog is supposed to be a cat, the man a woman, the dog a child, the man a dog? What if I can't see the exact same things she sees?

"Don't overthink it, Amanda. Just say the first thing that comes to your mind."

"Is it that the dog has no footprints but the man does?" I ask.

I wait for her to say, "Very good," or "Right on!" or even "Good job, kiddo!" but she just puts another card in front of me.

"Amanda, there is something missing from the pictures I am going to show you. You have to tell me what is missing. Here is the first picture. Can you tell me what is missing?"

I sigh. "Is it the dad's glasses? The nose part? Is that right?"

"What about this picture?"
I will never know whether or not I'm ever right.
"What's missing? Amanda?"

"The baby."
"Anything else?"
"The mom."

The System of the World

I AM NOT MARRIED. I have never been married. I am single and childless and thirty-nine years old. It's 2009 and I'm still looking for someone I won't lose. For now, though, my life is just me. Me and no one. Me and no one at a dinner party. Me and no one at a wedding. Me and no one at a funeral. People ask why I'm not married, tell me I should get married, or say how lucky I am that I never married. All strange things to say to a person with no one to marry, not only because it's predicated on the idea that I'm deficient as I am, but because it suggests marriage is a product, an item on eBay I neglected to bid on. I'm not against marriage; marriage would be nice. At the very least, it would give me a reason to list someone other than my mother as my emergency contact. A family, I think, is what I'm after.

My siblings, friends, and acquaintances seem to have effortlessly found their right someones. But for me, finding love, and the family that follows, feels like the NYC housing lottery. Every time I go to fill out an application, I've missed the deadline by a day.

I've had plenty of horrible boyfriends and have twice escaped marrying those bad choices. Yet, despite not making the mistake of marrying the wrong person, single people are still looked down upon, even by the unhappily wed.

*　　　*　　　*

People who were once single right alongside me have now coupled off away from me, as though they've suddenly realized I'm contagious. Now they're on the other side of the divide: inadvertently making single people feel ashamed, egging me on to entertain them with dating stories, the bad ones especially, because it's been *so long*. Thing is, they mean well, which is why I don't tell them how much it hurts. The longest relationship I've ever had is with my therapist.

I want a child. I want a family. I want to be like everyone else. I thought I'd have that with Peter the Literary Agent; at one point I even thought it about Caleb the Clown, whom I followed to Europe when he was cast in the Cirque du Soleil. All I've ever wanted is to feel like I belong to this world. I want to raise a child who feels like she belongs here, too, a child who doesn't worry I'll die or disappear, who trusts I know how to take care of her because she sees I know how to take care of myself, who knows I can teach her to manage her fears, push her to face and conquer reality, and to rely not on me, but on herself. The longer I remain without a family, the more I feel I don't belong anywhere, and I've grown so tired of that feeling.

People tell me, "If you really want a family, you'll get a family," and that "it happens when you're ready, when you least expect it, when you love yourself." I disagree with that point of view, but the world has a fixed timeline, and I'm incompatible with its system; just like the growth charts of my childhood, there's no space left for me to be plotted.

While I've been close to marriage, anxiety makes losing harder than loving, and I've lost more than I've been able to love. I haven't let go when I should have; I've pushed when I should have pulled, and I waited when I knew to run, and I've always known, right from the start, whether or not a particular guy is the one. But once I'm connected, separation feels too harrowing, even if all my love has turned sour. Somewhere early on I learned that attachment meant love, and now I can't find my way out.

I want something I don't even remember having—a family I can trust to stay. I am trying to return to a place I can't recall and I'm being driven by memories I don't have—by unconscious urges so ancient they crumble at my touch. All my efforts to make a family fail. I'm inadequate, and I'm afraid. My anxiety is so deeply embedded, I'm scared I'll never be free.

I worry anxiety has been keeping me from the pieces of my life lying in wait underneath me. Have I been allowing the happiness that should have been mine to move on to someone else? What if all this time I've accidentally been donating the life I've been too afraid to live to someone less frightened?

June 1981

Dr. Rivka Golod

General Observation and Behavior

Amanda is small for her age and of slight build. I found Amanda to be a gentle, sweet, and winsome child. She seemed quite anxious about the testing, and while overwhelmed by the content of the questions, taking some very literally, she was eager to please and cooperative. Rapport with me was easily established and I felt I was able to ease her anxiety. By the second visit Amanda appeared more relaxed and easy about the evaluation.

Nevertheless, it was soon evident that Amanda equates performance with acceptability. This, I think, is a critical factor feeding into her anxiety around tests and, possibly, resistance around risking herself when challenged intellectually and academically. That is, my impression was that Amanda may be so fearful of failing and so anxious about not being liked and accepted that she'd rather choose the safe alternative and not learn so that less will be expected of her.

Countdown to Karen Silkwood

MY PARENTS LIVE ON either side of Manhattan, uptown and downtown. By cab my dad is twenty minutes away, but that's time, and time doesn't work for me. I like being downtown always; I like when it's just the four of us: my mom, Kara, Eddie, and me. But Kara and Eddie don't mind leaving downtown. They remember when we lived together with my dad as a family, but I don't. I don't even know how old I was when they divorced because my parents tell me different ages—and when I ask why they divorced, my mom says it's none of my business, which means I'm the reason.

Even though I know he's my dad, he always feels new to me.

I try to get my mom to let me stay home, and I can tell she doesn't want me to leave, but no matter what organ hurts, or how hard I cry and beg and plead, I still have to go. When I was in preschool, my teachers told my parents I was too young to be leaving my mom. They said I was saying and doing things that meant leaving was not good for me, but my dad got really mad and insulted and said too bad, and that was that. My mom says, "What was I supposed to do?" When I was five, my dad married Sallie and I thought we wouldn't have to visit him anymore, but my mom said that's not how marriage works. I guess I'm glad, in case Mom ever marries Jimmy.

I want someone to either make my feelings go away, to make me feel okay about going uptown like Kara and Eddie do, or let me stay with my mom. Instead, everyone just repeats the same things over and over, like

"You'll be back before you know it," and "It'll be over in the blink of an eye." But what about before it's over? What about the part that means "during," the part that means "being away"? That's what scares me most, but everyone skips over during. Everyone ignores the things I can't, and I don't know why.

When people try to explain that uptown is not far, or that a weekend isn't long, it makes me feel worse, more afraid that my worries are right, and that the world I live in is different from the world everyone else lives in. That means *I'm* different, something I don't want other people to figure out about me. Something is wrong inside me; I've always known that, but I don't want anyone to ever see that I'm not the same as they are. If they find out, I'll feel humiliated and want to leave the world. Still, I don't know if I can pretend for my entire life. What if someone unsafe sees through me? I think my dad already knows—he is always telling me I was hatched, not born. I don't miss my dad when I'm not with him.

We are not supposed to be our downtown selves uptown, so I don't feel like myself when I'm there, which means I'm separated not only from my mom, home, garden, and the Village, but from the me of me. My uptown self can't keep track of all the rules, and I am always afraid to make a mistake. I don't like making mistakes because then my dad gets mad. My mom and dad are alike in that way. Also, nothing is good enough. If we get a silver medal, he wants to know why we didn't get gold. He makes us compete, and I hate competing. Uptown, I feel confused all the time, like a baton someone suddenly dropped.

Everything uptown is different. Uptown we have to comb and part our hair and take a bath every night and wear fancy clothes so that we look "halfway decent." The three of us hate this. Uptown we "Mr." and "Mrs." everyone, while downtown adults have first names. I don't know what I'm supposed to call uptown people if I accidentally see one downtown. When we go out to eat, I have to wear cardigans with slippery buttons and dresses with doilies for collars. Our clothes are ironed and tucked in, and the feeling of my halfway decent clothes scratching rough against my skin makes me want to cry and pull out my hair. Uptown we have strict manners. Uptown we have a new baby brother named Nicky.

At my grandmother Puggy's house, which is also uptown, you have to stand behind your dinner chair and wait until she sits before you can. Even if you're starving your face off, well too bad for you; you can't start eating until Puggy takes the first bite. Then, once you start eating, you can't stop. You have to finish everything on your plate, or it's rude. Elbows off the table. Feet on the floor. Sit up straight. Look people in the eye. Downtown we ask to be excused, but uptown we have to wait. Don't scrape your fork on your plate, even by accident. Don't talk over anyone, but speak clearly when someone asks you a question. Downtown we race down the stairs barefoot and take the first seat we see and serve ourselves. When my mom's boyfriend, Jimmy, comes over for dinner with Daniel, David, and Holly, the boys punch one another in the head, yell at Jimmy, are mean to my mom, and knock things over at the table. Usually there's crying and yelling and even though they don't live there, Jimmy's kids stomp away and slam doors. At my dad's we retire to a formal living room after dinner where the piano is and everyone but the kids talks. Uptown we are rich. Downtown we are "comfortable."

When the sun is out, it's not scary, and I can have fun. On sunny days we play touch football in Central Park. When we go to the country, where my dad has another house, we wash his car to music and tie-dye shirts in buckets. I run wide stripes of zigzags into the big field of grass, chasing after his dog, and I ride my bike with no hands down the hill. But when the sun begins to set I'm always knocked back to the beginning, afraid again from scratch. I try to make it through, but I never can, and I call my mom crying and she tells my dad to bring me home— sometimes all the way back from the country. The second she does, the vibrating terror falls right off my body knowing I don't have to be away from my mom any longer. But too soon I wake up into Monday and countdowns-to-uptown start all over again.

Before I go to my dad's, my mom draws "I LOVE YOU" upside down on my belly, but no matter how many hundreds of times I lift my shirt to stare at the indelible black heart, she is still too far away. If we're not at home taking care of our mom, then no one is taking care of our mom. Who will make her the special smoothie for her potassium, or the blended fruit drink when she has a migraine, or give her all those arm and back rubs? Who will get her a glass of water or her glasses or a cold cloth for her forehead? Who will put ice down her back when she doesn't wake up in the morning? When I'm at my dad's, I can't hear her shouting and make sure she's okay. I don't trust the world to keep my mom alive, and I don't trust my mom to keep herself alive either.

"What if you die when I'm at Dad's house? What will happen?" I ask.

"That's not going to happen," she says firmly.

That's when I feel dragged toward the black quicksand waiting at the bottom of my worries that wants to drown me dead. How can I stop worrying if no one will talk me through the what-ifs? I need to know what to do. I need to know who I'll live with, and if I can stay in our house. What if she forgets she has kids and moves to Europe? What if I get hurt when I'm at my dad's? He might not know that something is worse than it actually is, which means he won't take me to a doctor and I might die. When I go to my dad's house I can't see my mom and I can't see the house. I worry that without my eyes on them, my mom will leave and take the house with her, and when we return, all that will be left is the black empty space where our house, and all our memories, once sat.

Kara and my mom always tell me nothing bad is going to happen when I leave home, that every time I go and come back the world is exactly the same, but it's the next time I'm worried about. Everywhere I go and everything I do, I always feel the leaving. I feel it in hi-ing and good-bying, in sunset and sunrise. They call it homesickness, this feeling of mine, but that word never feels strong enough because even when I'm home, I ache in that leaving way. When I hear my mother say "home-sickness," it reminds me of countdowns, which I hate most of all.

Countdowns are how my body tells time. Everyone else lives in a clock-and-calendar world, but my clocks and calendars are countdowns that start light and safe like ocean bubbles, and end dark and dangerous like animal extinction. Countdowns come in stages that change color and sensation as they move from deep to shallow. They tell me in advance when I'm going uptown to visit my father; when my mother is going out to dinner with Jimmy, to a movie, or on a two-week vacation and leaving us with a babysitter. If my mom and Jimmy go away while I'm uptown at my father's, or we go away from New York with my dad, that's a double countdown, which is the worst possible countdown a person can have. Countdowns happen for everything. Before a weekend with my dad, they look like this:

MONDAY: When I wake up and remember that it's Monday, five entire days until I have to go to my dad's, the doom lifts and my relief grows. On Monday, Friday is far enough away. I'm in Deep Countdown, which is pale yellow and pulses in the distance. Deep Countdown is tricky because it fools me into thinking I have enough time to be cured before the worst of the countdowns come. Maybe I've outgrown it since last time. This is what Deep Countdown wants me to think.

During the day, the world is one glob of noise and action. The day's sun makes me feel like we're all connected, but daylight makes a promise that night doesn't keep. Nighttime is when we're all inside together. The darker it gets, the closer it is to bedtime, and bedtime is when I have to leave my mom by herself in the world. Dinner moves me one space ahead, cleanup is two, bath is three, and on it goes until it's time for sleep, where I may never wake up.

TUESDAY: I wake up and feel relieved that I didn't die. Another minute to feel the world, which tells me I'm still in Deep Countdown. The pulse is there, but now the dull tugging is a bit closer. Unlike yesterday, if today someone says the word "Friday" or "weekend," if I hear a number that matches the date I'm leaving, or I smell something like grilled cheese, which I eat only at my dad's, I feel a wave of Middle Countdown. I try to steer clear of all the things that set off Middle Countdown, but it's hard because the radio likes to announce what's coming up on Friday or the weekend. The world is always freeze-tagging me.

WEDNESDAY: I wake up into Middle Countdown, which doesn't have color. Middle Countdown is a vibration. Once I'm in Middle Countdown, I feel mad at myself that I didn't appreciate the safe feelings of Monday and Tuesday enough, that I didn't prepare myself. Middle Countdown doesn't wash over me from behind; I walk right into it. It's a tunnel I enter; sometimes the tunnel lasts only a flight of stairs. Other times the tunnel is the length of recess, or the entire day, crawling toward Shallow Countdown, which is the most dangerous. After school everyone is already talking about Friday like they can't wait.

That's when the sky lowers. A heavy day cups us close, catching the future, dragging it closer. Melissa never says "Friday" or "weekend" to me, and she protects me when other people do. I don't even have to tell her; she just knows.

THURSDAY: When I wake up into Shallow Countdown, my limbs feel heavy and hard to lift. I can smell last night on my pillow, but I am not in last night anymore. Shallow Countdown can't be ignored. You don't accidentally walk into it or get zapped by its sudden flash. Shallow Countdown paints over the stars and city lights. Shallow Countdown is feeling the things you're not supposed to feel, like the settings that hold your teeth in place. Shallow Countdown is forgetting the names for familiar things like bed, dog, and window. Shallow Countdown is knowing you're about to die. Every bite of school lunch is flavored with it. A new word, the last song in the school play, the smell of cooked mozzarella on after-school pizza, the squeaking effort of sneakers on a gym floor, my mother's closed eyes when she laughs, my siblings' huddled whispers, the sun warming the cobbles on Wooster Street, the sound of skin sticking to a summer banister, the air on my face as I run down the street. The flavor won't come out. When the sun starts to set, my dread grows. Night pulls people apart. The shorter days mean Shallow Countdown starts sooner, and the darkening sky is like the subway doors closing: even if you stick your hand in the way, they still close.

FRIDAY: The worst day of the week. I wake up and know what today is about. My skin feels tight around my bones. Balloon air takes up all the room inside me, making it hard to swallow, skimming just the top of each breath. There is no gap between times of fear—fear is all there is. I feel the cracks and shadow places between the bones of the world, which is stripped of rules I can depend on. I feel things I know I shouldn't, like the spinning of the earth.

On those Fridays before my dad arrives I cry, cling to my mother, press myself into the banister. I hide in my closet, but never for long because it's too far away from my mother. My temples tense with sharp headaches; my stomach hardens into a stale-fisted chestnut. I want to scream and throw tantrums, but I stay very still, afraid of any sudden movement. How come no one except me understands that my heart must be near my mom's heart in order for us both to survive? When I'm gone my mom might forget I exist, wander across the world, and never send her new address. It's when I'm gone that she might cross on red, get hit by a car, and die; lean too far out a window and crush her brains on the sidewalk; get mauled by a dog, tetanus-ed from a rusty nail, or stabbed by an escaped mental patient from Bellevue. She might accidentally burn down the house or open the door to a killer who just robbed a bank. Anything can happen when I'm not there.

And then, countdowns change into the actual events, weekends I almost never make it through. I press myself against Kara in the cab ride uptown, and she puts her arm around me. Out the window patches of color fall behind and tumble downtown. Things turn gray at Eighteenth and Park Avenue South, and the buildings change from homes into businesses. To distract myself I try counting the passing buildings, but my eyes are too slow. By the time I feel caught up, we're already at the Pan Am Building and it's too late; we're inside the tunnel and slowing down for the turn, so slow that there's nowhere I can look to avoid the graffiti: "KAREN SILKWOOD WAS MURDERED." That sign is my enemy. If my mom is murdered, will my dad know how to care for me, or will he make fun of me all the time, like always? Last summer, we lived uptown at Jimmy's house, and the Son of Sam killed people and the city had a blackout. What if the Son of Sam comes back? What if an uptown waitress puts acid in my milk and I die like Karen Silkwood? The world moves too fast, and I'm too slow dodging out of the way. I keep getting crushed by life's revolving doors. No one tries to save me because it's all invisible to them. No one else sees how hard the world keeps pressing against me. Well, maybe Kara, but she's only eleven. I hold Kara's hand and she rubs her thumb back and forth across my skin, which means she loves me.

Two Fridays ago, on a Dad weekend, Kara's friend Marci Klein was kidnapped. Everyone tried to keep it from me because they knew I'd be scared, but I heard about it anyway. My mom talked about it on the phone, and teachers whispered about it at school, and my friends told me what happened. What happened was Marci was on the bus going to school, when her babysitter stopped the bus and said there was an emergency and Marci had to come with her. The emergency was that Marci's mom was in the hospital, so of course Marci went with her, but the babysitter lied. Her mom wasn't sick. Instead, Marci's babysitter took her to a place of ransom and hid her until her dad dropped off a bag of big money inside the Pan Am Building where Karen Silkwood was murdered.

Ten hours passed before her parents got her back. I was glad she was found, but it's the in-between part I can't stop thinking about, the part when Marci realized they weren't going to the hospital, and she didn't know what was going to happen. When she didn't know if she'd ever see her mom again. During is the scariest part. I know if someone came to my school and said my mom was in the hospital, I'd go with them, too. Why would a person use moms in such a terrible way? Would my babysitter do that to me? When someone is kidnapped, they are stolen from their regular world without any warning. My mom said that kind of thing is very rare, but I feel kidnapped when my dad comes and takes us away from our mom, and that happens all the time. Downtown is safe because Jimmy Alcatraz, Vito, and the rest of the mafia are protecting the neighborhood; but uptown, no one's watching.

It makes me feel a little better knowing that Marci knew the person who took her, but I still don't understand why grown-ups enjoy scaring little kids. My dad scares me all the time. When I ask, "Can I go home?" he says, "Didn't anyone tell you? You're never going home." This makes me feel like I have no skin. One time, when I was four, he took us to Arizona. A few days in, he woke us up shouting that it was time to leave, and I jumped out of bed, delirious with happiness before he yelled, "April Fools'!" He's the kind of dad who would play hide-and-seek with your birthday present and then put it in the basement where Norman Bates lives. It's only after I cry, and feel myself turning into dust the world will blow away, that he tells me he's just kidding. When we get a paper cut or a scratch, he says instead of a Band-Aid, we should get our limbs amputated.

My dad's feelings get hurt when I want to leave, I can tell. I like my dad, but I am scared of him. I think he is funny and silly and handsome, but he doesn't live with me, so I don't know the rules of him, and he doesn't know the rules of me. I've seen my mother naked. I've seen my mother in her nightgown in the morning. I've smelled my mother's bad middle-of-the-night breath when I sleep in bed with her; I've sat in the bathroom when she's taken a bath, peed, brushed her teeth, and put on makeup; but my dad is a mystery to me. He is always spiffy and polished. He is formal like a museum where you get yelled at if you lean too close to a painting, and he teases me. But then, when I want to go home early, he makes jokes that are funnier than all the other jokes. He'll tickle me or put on a record I really like, trying to convince me to stay. He'll tell me about the fun thing we're doing tomorrow, or the plans he has for us tonight, but he could tell me that I'll grow eight inches in my sleep, wake up with blond, stick-straight hair, and still I'd want to go home. I am not worried my dad will die, so it's okay to leave him, but he doesn't agree.

The next time I have to leave downtown, it always feels like the first time. No matter how many times I follow a schedule, I never know what's coming next. When my teacher announces nap every day, worry wraps around me. I wake up into surprised relief; I can't believe my classroom looks the same, that my teacher and classmates haven't disappeared, that Melissa is reading on the cot next to me. I feel such relief that nap is over, that I made it through, and that I never have to do it again, except I will, every day, again and again and again.

If things pass quickly for everyone, why don't they pass quickly for me? Time is always what people talk about when I am afraid, but minutes and hours are the same length when I'm gone because they all mean "away." Away is what time is made of; away is counted in fear-seconds, not number-seconds. Everything I sense when I'm afraid sticks to the thing that scares me. When I hear the sizzle sounds of pork chops, smell potatoes roasting from my dad's kitchen, time sticks to the smell, which sticks to my homesickness and makes dinnertime mean sadness. Out in the world, I can always smell my feelings.

Even though I know I'm going "uptown" and "to my father's house," and that we might "see a movie" or "go out to dinner," those words don't tell me what will happen once I'm there. How do I pick from the menu without making my dad mad because I ordered something expensive? What if I can't finish everything on my plate? Going "uptown" doesn't tell my brain not to grow slippery if my dad plays the math game at dinner, which is not a game but a trick that tells everyone I'm dumb. He sounds like an auctioneer when he asks, "What is ten plus eight minus three times one divided by seven plus twelve times fifty minus six plus forty times three and three-quarters?" What I want to know is, who will take care of me? Why does everyone always want school answers from me, when it's feeling-answers I need? When I go to my dad's house all the regular words my brain knows fall out, and I never understand what's being asked. Sometimes I hear things backward or inside out. If my dad says, "Don't do that," I hear "Go do that," and then he yells at me when I do.

Because I'm scared of him, and because he teases me, I can't ask him all the things I need to know. When we are downtown, Kara and Eddie leave me out of things, and Eddie and I usually fight, but uptown things are different. We defend each other; we're a team. My dad has two entire floors and lots of rooms, but we don't have our own bedroom there. We sleep in the maid's room, which is very small and behind the kitchen. It's as far away from Dad and Sallie's room as you can get; their room is near baby Nicky's, which is the biggest room in the house, and another room that is empty and waiting for another baby if they have one. In the maid's room, if we screamed, we'd be dead by the time they heard us. We don't have our own toys there or get to leave anything behind, and we keep our clothes in our suitcases because Sallie's winter clothes take up the closet. Eddie brings his security pillow, Kara has her medicine, I have my two sucking-fingers, and we have one another.

Before this house, and before Sallie, my dad lived in another apartment where we also shared a room, but it was our own, and had a triple bunk bed. That's when he had a lot of different girlfriends. I can't remember all their names. One good thing about the maid's room, though, is that there's a telephone in the kitchen, which I secretly use to call my mom and tell her to come get me. This is something my dad does not like about me.

Taking our picture is one of the activities we do with our dad when we go uptown. He's a really good photographer, which is why it's okay that he takes thousands of pictures. The ones he likes best go up on the wall. In some we're laughing, running in a field, curled up and sleepy, or sunburned on a hotel chair. The ones with the three of us together are always the same: Kara, and Eddie with his pillow, standing loose next to each other; and then me, pressed into Kara's side, as close to her as possible. The bump on my middle sucking-finger has grown really big. In every picture, I have to check if it's visible. If anyone else sees it, they'll know I suck my fingers like a baby, and I'll be humiliated for the rest of my life.

My dad loves practical jokes. He's not gullible like my mom. His favorite musician is Tom Lehrer, who sings funny songs about math and Jews, and his favorite prankster is Hugh Troy. My dad and Hugh Troy went to the same college. I don't know if they knew each other. Once, Hugh Troy walked into the Waldorf Astoria with a friend, both carrying ladders and dressed like city workers. People moved out of their way as they climbed carefully to the top of their ladders and removed all the lightbulbs from the ceiling. When they were done, they folded their ladders and made their way out of the darkened hotel lobby, taking the lightbulbs with them. This story is supposed to be funny, but I always worry a little for the people stuck in the dark hotel with no way out.

When we're on the street, or in a store, and a little kid calls out, "Mommy!" my dad yells back, "Yes?" This either scares them or makes them laugh, depending on the kid, but even if they cry and run away, my dad thinks it's hilarious and keeps doing it. In the summers, after telling us that yes, we can go swimming, he'll wait until we've jumped up and off the diving board and are in the air before yelling out—"Just don't get wet!"

The first time he says this, I panic, paddling the air before slamming down into the cold chlorine. When I'm underwater, I know I did the wrong thing by getting wet, even though he said I could go swimming, and I worry that once my head pops out into the air, he'll yell at me, and I'll get spanked. In the car, he tells us we should hold our breath when we pass a cemetery if we don't want bad luck. So we suck in all the air and hold it while our dad drives past, slowing down halfway through. We gesture, wave, and flap at him to hurry, pointing to our puffed-out cheeks, and he pretends he doesn't understand.

"What? What's the matter? You want me to slow down?" He slows down more.

We shake our heads no, pushing our hands to indicate hurry, pointing forward.

"Yes, I should slow down?" he asks, lifting his foot off the pedal even more, and we jump up and down in our seats until we exhale and say, "Dad, no, we wanted you to speed up." Then he says, "Oh, why didn't you just say so?" and hits the gas and flies past the cemetery. Bad luck forever.

I know how to make my dad laugh. I know how to make my mom laugh, too, just not the same way. My dad loves when I curse. He thinks it's really funny, and sometimes he records me cursing. I know more curse words than anyone my age. Maybe more than people of any age. More than my grandmother Puggy, who didn't even know the word "asshole" until I taught her. She'd never even heard it before, and I was proud that out of all her grandchildren, I was the one to teach her something, and I'm the youngest.

But even though we sometimes laugh together, I don't feel safe at my dad's house, because he makes fun of my worries. I know it's a joke when my dad says that I was hatched, but it's funny only to him. Also, I don't understand this joke because chickens are hatched and I am not a chicken. Maybe because my hair is soft and woolly like a chickadee's, my dad thinks I look cracked out of an egg. Or because I don't look like Kara and Eddie as much as they look like each other. The three of us match because we're all small and skinny, but Kara and Eddie have bright red hair—his straight, hers frizzy—and skin so white they look like brand-new lampshades. My hair is sandy blond and feels like quilt batting. My skin is olive-green in winter and honey-tan in summer, and when you put my arm next to Eddie's or Kara's, we look like different races. I don't act like them either. Eddie is wild, and Kara is very grown-up and polite.

Dad took a picture of me hugging Nana, his sheepdog, which makes him laugh and say we're siblings. I don't think I look like a dog. Being hatched means I am not related to Kara and Eddie. It means my mother isn't my mother, and I'm not human, which is sometimes how I feel, and now I worry my feeling of not being like everyone else isn't as secret as I thought. The joke is saying something about me, but I'm not sure what. Maybe it's not just my inside that's wrong but my outside, and I never knew. Maybe it's not that I have fuzzy hair, or that I'm little, but that I'm fuzzy and little in the wrong way. Maybe I'm not a person. I worry my dad can see something about me I don't want anyone to see.

He doesn't want me to be different either, which is why he tells me to eat more brussels sprouts. He says brussels sprouts make your boobs grow. Even though I like doing boy things, and I am too young for boobs,

I want to make sure I get my puberty. That's why I take extra helpings of brussels sprouts.

When we are not home, Kara is my home. She knows it, too. She might leave me out of things downtown, but at Dad's house, she takes care of me. I follow Kara and do what she does so I can try to get things right. She is my protection. I make sure I can smell her hair because her hair smells like home.

Uptown, a weekend lasts an entire month.

"I'd like to show you some pictures."

"Okay. I like pictures."

"Good. I'd like you to tell me what they're about, all right?"

"All right."

"Here is the first picture. Can you tell me the story of what's happening in this picture?"

"Yes, I can tell you. The dad is carrying the daughter back to her mom. The daughter is dead. She died from having to leave her mom and visit her dad. She didn't want to go. She knew she would die if they made her leave, but they made her even when she tried to explain, even when she screamed and cried. They didn't listen to her; they never listen to her, and so, when she got to her dad's house she died, and he didn't know what to do, so he brought her back to the mom who is the only person who knows how to fix her. Once the mom gets the daughter alive again, the parents apologize for not listening to her, for making her leave, which is what killed her. They promise they'll never send her away again."

The Underside of Perfect

CHOOSING THE RIGHT SOMEONE to make a family with feels like trying to answer a timed test question everyone else but me can hear. Long after the sand's run out and everyone's gone, I'm still shouting guesses. But, just like the homeless lady on the corner, no one has ever told me how to make a family. How do you get close to someone when you're always worried about the end when you have to continue on without them? And what happens when you actually want to be free, but your anxiety can't let you go? All I want is to know that *this* is the one, this is the relationship that will work out, but that's the information no one has.

When I turned thirty-four, the universe cracked itself open and handed me what I thought was the answer.

Since I was a kid writing plays for my mom and the garden kids, I'd wanted to be a writer. In my late twenties, I wrote a novel and got a literary agent. In my early thirties, I got a book deal. My life was going surprisingly well. But the thought of entering the literary world, where I had no footing or friends, was daunting, so I decided to create a community where I might belong. Two months before my book came out, I started a literary event, the Happy Ending Music and Reading Series, in which I challenged authors to take risks onstage and musicians to a sing-along. Every week, in a small red velvet bar in Chinatown, I invited different authors, artists, and musicians to converge and together we'd put on a show for the crowd. It wasn't until the third year that I realized what I'd truly done—re-created the secret garden on the street side of life.

Peter was a literary agent and we'd been flirting on and off for years. After my novel came out, we found ourselves single at the same time. At first, Peter had come to Happy Ending events only when a client read, but soon he was showing up every week.

There were many arguments against dating him, including how often he flirted with me even when he wasn't single. But he was unlike anyone else I'd dated. For starters, he wore a suit. He was old-school and masculine, and I felt protected. He walked curbside to protect me from splattering mud; rented us cars and fancy hotel rooms; took me on trips, to spas, to concerts; bought me expensive presents and dinners. He spent money like it self-replicated in his pockets. Two weeks in he told me he loved me. Two months and he moved in, called me his home, his everything, told me we were getting married, that I was perfect, made lists of our future wedding guests, noting possible venues, and named our babies. I worked hard to overlook the sexism of his romantic gestures, the speed and fury with which his affections were being thrown at me. He didn't just sweep me off my feet, he swept me off-balance, right past the awful uncertainty of a slow and steady beginning and into a happiness that made me feel crazy. He spun me hard, and I suffered real moments of terror that he would be taken from me as quickly as he was given. No one had ever courted me that way, and I was ashamed of how much I liked it.

"Why do they say relationships take work?" he asked. "This is so easy."

I felt slightly possessed by my love, and I was so glad I didn't listen to my fucking gut. Stupid idiot. This guy was everything. I'd never had anyone be that attentive to me. Is this what real love feels like, off-kilter and semi-insane, or is this something beyond even that? Had we stumbled upon a love dimension no one had ever before experienced?

I'm the one, I'm the one, I'm the one. I loved hearing it. He said he'd been waiting his whole life for me. He wouldn't stop telling me I was perfect, so I started adding "for you," and he said, "No, you're perfect." Full stop. Period. This made me uneasy; I'm fond of myself, but I also know I'm the underside of perfect.

"I'm very emotional," I said.

"I love that about you," he told me.

"I can be very sensitive," I added.

"My kinda girl!"

"I have a lot of anxiety. I'm in therapy. I've been in therapy a very long time," I explained, not wanting to fall too far from his pedestal should he ever witness a panic attack.

"That means you have depth," he said. "You're the one. We're getting married and you know it," he said, winning the conversation.

I called everyone I knew and told them I'd found the One.

"What's the rush?" my therapist asked.

"When you know, you know," I told her.

"Tell me what it is you know," she asked.

"I can't explain it," I said.

Peter and I talked about everything, foot to foot on the couch. I lobbed him soft test questions.

"If your partner wanted you to go to couples counseling, would you do it?"

"Of course. I've already done it," he said. "It works. I'm a big believer."

This was my guy. He was forty years old, never married, never even lived with anyone. Everyone told me that was a red flag, but I broke the mold; he told me that himself. "I've been waiting forty years for you," he said. "I never thought I'd find you, but here you are."

We nested, and ordered in every night and watched movies. We barely left, got fat, and suddenly it was winter, nearly Christmas, when he said, "Let's dress up and go shopping on Fifth Avenue." He took me to Tiffany, Cartier, and Harry Winston, asking me to show him what I liked. Were we ring shopping?

"What about that one?" he asked, pointing to a diamond engagement ring. Holy shit. He was going to propose to me on Christmas. He didn't know my style, so I took him downtown and chose a more bohemian-looking ring from a store called Fragments.

Everything was in fast-forward, skipping over the discomfort of getting to know someone else and deciding, at a more natural pace, whether you even liked them—thank God. Even if my therapist said Peter seemed to talk out both sides of his mouth and my gut was jazz-handing for my attention, I ignored both, seduced by his promises of certainty and security.

I've only ever experienced the world with my body, but growing up I was told my experience wasn't true, that the world was safe and nothing bad would happen, that my feelings were a learning disability. I was conditioned to trust people older than me, especially those in authority, to believe what people said at the expense of my intuition, actions be damned.

At Christmas, there was no ring. Instead he gave me a laptop, which made me uncomfortable because it was so expensive. As I studied my new computer, I sensed an old, familiar feeling. A tightening below my rib cage warned me I was entering Deep Countdown, something I hadn't felt in a long time. My body had more to tell me, but I didn't want to hear what it had to say. I wanted to make a joke. I wanted to say, this laptop isn't my ring size. Instead, I thanked him, and I installed everything I could get my hands on, overstuffing my computer with information, making it eat its emotions in megabytes.

It was springtime and we'd barely left the house, but I felt ready to advance from nesting. I wanted to go outside. I made plans for us to see my friends, ignoring my vibrating worry when he seemed put out. We met my friends at a bar and he was rude and silent the entire night. I fought off the prickling heat until at home he said, "Well, that was three hours of my life I'll never get back." I wrote my friends apology emails. What happened to the charming guy from a month ago?

On my thirty-fifth birthday Peter lifted a black velvet box from a Fragments bag and placed it on the bed. Oh my God, I'm getting married. I'm going to have a family. We'll make friends with other couples, and their babies, and join playgroups and throw pirate-themed birthday parties. Here I am, getting what I thought I'd have to trick someone into giving me. This is actually happening and I thought it never would. I'm not defective. He sat down next to me on the bed.

"Holy shit," I said, and looked at him.

"Open it," he said, smiling.

As I pulled the lid off the box, he said, quickly, "It's not what you think it is."

Inside was a silver necklace shaped like a crescent moon. Not what you think it is.

"Do you like it?" he asked me.

"Yes," I said, confused. Something is wrong with this picture. Can you tell me what's funny about it? Can you tell me what's missing? Heat had concentrated itself in my face. He said one thing but did another.

"Should I read into this?" he asked when I exchanged the necklace for something else.

"Should *I* read into it?" I asked.

"I'm not ready yet," he said.

"But... you were ready months ago," I said.

"That was the beginning."

"So?"

"In the beginning people say things they don't mean," he told me.

Was it possible I fell in love with someone I didn't even like? We never went out unless it was with people who could advance his career. His clichés and aphorisms made him sound dated. He was forty years old, but he still talked about high school. I worried I'd heard everything he had to say. Middle Countdown washed over me.

He drove me to and from my reading series, which I had to host even when it was hard to get out of bed. When I wanted to go alone, he insisted on bringing me. I was not allowed to say no. Like being uptown, there was always something I was doing wrong. I have bad allergies, and one day he stormed down the hall of our apartment, stared at me, enraged, and asked, "Do you need a tissue? You're *sniffling*."

"Oh, sorry," I said.

"Don't be sorry," he said. "Just blow your nose."

We went to a movie, and when we got there, we discovered it had started a half an hour earlier. He was infuriated.

"What's the big deal? You got the time wrong. We'll see the next one."

He spun on me. "I love how you just automatically blame me. I'm not the one who got it wrong; the newspaper printed the wrong time. Do you think so little of me that I can't even get the time right?"

"I . . . I'm not blaming you."

"Well, you're blaming someone, and it sure isn't the paper," he said, storming home.

When I eventually admitted to him that I felt like I was walking on eggshells, he exploded at me.

I said, "I think we should go to couples counseling."

"No fucking way."

I felt kicked off reality. "Why not?" I asked.

"I don't believe in it," he said. "It doesn't work."

I woke up every night at 3 a.m. and couldn't breathe. I was in Shallow Countdown. I had to get out of this relationship, but I didn't know how. I only know how to avoid what I'm afraid of by staying. Leaving is death. I couldn't get out of bed.

Or stop crying.

Or staring at the wall.

I felt trapped by him and by my anxiety, both of which I was too frightened to fight back against. I tried again: "If I told you that going to couples counseling was the most important thing to me in the world, would you do it then?"

"No," he said.

I wanted to die, but I was too tired. Suddenly I couldn't stop sleeping. It's all I did. And it was glorious. When I wasn't awake, nothing was wrong, and all my answers were correct.

It would take me another six months to break up with Peter. To fill the empty space, I found a roommate, a South African psychologist named Calvin, who I thought was gay when we first met. (By the time I understood he wasn't, it was clear we weren't each other's type.) Calvin, it turned out, had also recently broken up with someone. We commiserated together in the kitchen at night drinking wine and smoking cigarettes. Despite his advice, wisdom, and his vast library of psychology books, even my in-house therapist couldn't help me get over Peter. It took me four more years to trust I'd never fall for someone like him again.

June 1981

Dr. Rivka Golod

<u>Summary of Test Results</u>

No problems were noted in the areas of somatosensory or visual perception. Her grapho-motor coordination is good. Her productions on the Bender Design and Drawings of a Person were excellent. The content of her drawings were childlike for the full-bodied drawings. However, she also drew a picture of just a male face, which was more sophisticated in its emotional expression. It was somewhat of a caricature image of an angry man's face.

My Real Family

EVEN THOUGH IT'S AROUND the corner from our house, my new school feels too far for me. I know I said I wanted to switch, but now I'm not so sure. The four of us walk across Bleecker, toward Sixth Avenue, to the Little Red School House, which is waiting to swallow me into its unknown world. A streamer of squeals, racing feet, whistles, and laughing passes me: the noise I know as other people's normal. Groups of kids collect on the steps, parents hug. Red hair, brown hair, black hair, a blond girl tips forward, gliding off her unicycle. Overalls, Pumas, and Afro picks. Everywhere, a striped shirt. I feel like I am inside someone else's body. I want to go home. Eddie and Kara wish me luck, tell me they love me, and then sprint ahead and leave Mom and me behind. Kara calls back that she'll come find me later and I try to nod, but I can't feel my skull.

Through the red doors, past the front desk woman, who waves and smiles at everyone. This school smells different from my other school. Not spaghetti sauce and finger paint, but sawdust and Elmer's glue. When I told my mom I wanted to be with Kara and Eddie at their school for third grade, I didn't think about leaving Melissa behind because I knew I'd see her in the garden. But then she moved out of the garden and now I worry I made a mistake because I don't know anyone, I don't know when I'll see Melissa next, and my skin is jumpy. Inside, excited kids high-five and hug. Two girls huddle; how do they already have secret whisper-things? A girl passes. Her upper lip has a steep purple widow's peak. Maybe it's stained grape from a recent pouch of Pop Rocks, or she's a private vampire and secretly drinks blood. Kids younger than me yell good-bye to their parents. Someone pushes his mom toward the door, wanting her to leave. At the end of the hall on the first floor is Marie's office. She's like the mom of the school. If you're homesick or scared, if you don't feel well and need Tylenol, that's where you go. I try to memorize where it is.

My mom goes up the steps, pulling me behind her. When I glance back, kids are jammed behind me and my breath gets trapped. If I let go of my mom's hand and try to run home, I'll get trampled and die.

My teacher, Faith, has none of the warmth her name promises. Her body is low and plump. Her voice booms from somewhere down near her belly button. Her gray curls are short like mine. The long hair sticking out from her chin mole looks like a rotten flower stem. With my finger, I press against the sharp headache stabbing at the back of my eyeballs, which accidentally tips out tears. My mom spells out letters on my back. She writes, "You Are A-OK." She is writing things that are opposite to how I feel, and if I look at her, or tell her to stop, I'll start sobbing. I can't bear it when my mom sees the world through a different window than I do, because that means our hearts are separating.

Faith claps her hands and bosses us into a circle of chairs. My mom squeezes my hand and tries to let go, but I clutch until Faith pulls me to a chair facing away from my mom. I keep turning around to make sure she's still there. A blond girl who's as little and skinny as I am slides into the seat next to me. I like her navy Adidas tracksuit and her dimples when she smiles at me. But smiling back is too hard.

"Don't worry. Everything will be all right," the girl says. Her voice is thick and musty, like she's talking underwater. "I already did third grade last year. This is my second time with Faith. It's really fun." Something about her voice sounds foreign, like the words and her lips don't match. I try again to smile, to be polite, but I'm confused by her, and my own talk muscles are too shy to say anything. She tucks her blond hair behind one ear and then the other, revealing two tan-colored cartridges hugging her ears.

"I'm deaf," she explains. "But I can read lips."

I've never seen hearing aids until right now and I'm instantly envious; I wish my outside body told the story of my inside body. If I had hearing aids, everyone would know something was wrong with me, and they'd treat me extra carefully, explain things patiently. If I broke my arm or leg, I'd probably get to sleep in my mom's room without asking. If I were deaf, I probably wouldn't have to go to my dad's house, ever. I give her a huge smile.

"My name is Imogen. I'm the oldest kid in the class."

Everything about her is different: her name, her ears. And she's safe because she's older than me, like Kara.

"I'll be your friend," she says.

When she says "friend," the empty space between me and everyone fills with the same soothing yellow comfort I feel at home. Imogen knows what to do and where to go; now that we're friends, I can follow behind her like on a bridge.

I turn, nod at my mom, whose eyes ask, Are you sure? I blink. I am never sure. But I think it might be all right for her to leave, although I already miss her and will feel in five minutes the mistake of letting her go. She stands quietly and leaves the classroom, while I grip the sides of the chair so that no one can see if I float away.

Imogen's my partner in line to gym, and we run into Kara, who hugs me in front of my whole class. I breathe in deep, taking a strong smell of her to carry me through the rest of the day. Our coach, Omar James, is waiting for us on the basketball court. He has long matted ropes for hair that are secured into a ponytail with a rubber band. Just like Imogen, he has something different: Instead of a hand, he has a hook. I need something on my outside, too, a sign that something is wrong with me, like Eddie's casts and slings but permanent. If I had that, no one would expect the same things from me as from other kids. All I've ever wanted was for someone to see my inside and get it fixed, but how could they, when there is nothing on my outside to show them what's wrong?

I can't wait to tell Melissa about Imogen's hearing aids and Omar James's hand. When I was little we were in a car accident with my dad, and glass went into my head so they shaved all my hair off and wrapped white bandages around my skull, but I don't remember it. Or that time I was a baby and my mom tripped and spilled a pot of boiling water on me. Why did all the good things happen when I was too young to remember? We must have had so many bandages then.

After my first day of third grade, I hurry home and wrap one of Eddie's old Ace bandages around my wrist. It's not bad, but it still doesn't look like a real cast, with the white fluff sticking out like a long sleeve. I start again, rolling toilet paper around my palm this time and then wrapping the Ace bandage over it. This will help tell everyone about my insides.

Before dinner, I unwind everything and hide it in my closet, excited to have something besides my sucking-fingers to make me feel secure. Over fried chicken and peas, I watch Kara fiddle with her palate expander. It's like a music box in her mouth and turning the key makes her cry. Everyone feels bad for her, including me. But I also feel envy.

My mom's boyfriend, Jimmy, and his kids are always around now, and our quiet house turns loud and chaotic. At the dinner table the boys get into physical fights and yell at Jimmy, who sticks his tongue into the side of his cheek, picks at his whiskers, and ignores everyone. They tell him he's bad at his business, that he's too fat and needs to lose weight. He's supposed to be on a diet, but I've seen him late at night from the window scurrying across the street to the gun club for steak and fried clams.

Holly, Daniel, and David used to be our neighbors uptown before their mom died, which is the worst thing that can happen to a person. I feel sad for them, but having them around makes my brain hurt. Daniel and Kara are the same age, and Eddie and Holly are the same age, but David and I don't have an age twin. Nobody plays with me because I'm the youngest. Holly doesn't like me and I am convinced she is always trying to kill me. She was only six when her mom died, and afterward she changed. Now she's mad all the time and I know she wants to hurt me. The other day she came up behind me in the garden and covered my mouth and nose with her hand so I couldn't breathe.

"Now you'll know what it feels like to die," she said through her two buckteeth. I thought I'd never see my mom again. The free-falling, burning, wild flapping in my chest made me bite her hand until she dropped it. When my mom and Jimmy were out to dinner, and I was standing on the banister trying to reach a book, Holly shook the bookcase so hard I was sure it would fall on me. Instead, it was just me who fell.

Soon Jimmy and his kids will sleep here all the time because he and my mom are getting married. The original family I had with Mom, Kara, and Eddie won't exist anymore. Now I don't always get to sit next to my mom at dinner, and I can't sleep in her bed because there's no room for me. There are so many of them that I can't hear my mom from another floor like I used to. But at least when Jimmy stays over I feel relieved from my job of having to protect everyone while we sleep. I love Jimmy, even though he's really old and always says "What?" because he never hears anything anyone says. My mom says he's a different generation, but he and I are alike because we both care about safety. We are interested in alarm systems and double-locking the front door. Jimmy always finds things in the house to fix, even when they're not broken.

After dinner, I practice limping. I drag my right foot and let it drop like a dead rabbit down the steps in heavy, delayed thuds behind me. This will probably get me orthopedic shoes, or even a wheelchair. Worst-case scenario crutches, but I don't want a cane because then people will think I'm old. I limp past my mother. She's on the phone, filing her nails, and she doesn't notice, so I limp past again. Still nothing. I bolt upstairs and try limping past my siblings, who are tossed all over the place reading and doing homework. No one looks up at me, so I start to head back downstairs to my mom.

"Wrong foot," Kara says.

I turn around, confused.

"You were fake-limping with the right foot a minute ago, and now you're fake-limping with the left. You better get your facts straight if you're gonna fool anyone."

"You're such an idiot," Eddie says, and he and Kara laugh.

I put my fingers in my mouth and scramble to my mom's room, throw myself on her bed, and try not to cry. I am not trying to fool anyone, and I'm not an idiot. I'm trying to tell the actual truth; I'm just doing it through acting. I want something wrong on my outside, but I don't want doctors to think I'm sick because when you are sick you might die, and I don't want to give anyone any ideas. Holly, Daniel, and David's mom was sick. She had a brain tumor and died a few years ago when they were at sleepaway camp, which is just one reason I'm never going to camp. Being afraid my mom will die if I leave is one thing, but living all the time with people whose mom actually died when they left is another. I hope it's not contagious.

If I die, will people forget me? Will they just go on living life the way they were?

When I complain to Mom about all the times I think Holly tries to kill me, she says I have to be nice because she's had a hard life. She says I'd be angry, too, if she died. She's wrong about that, though. If she died, so would I. My mom is putting Holly's bedroom right next to mine so the girls are all on one floor, which I don't appreciate at all. When Holly found out she said, "Better sleep with one eye open." I hope she doesn't murder me in my sleep.

*   *   *

The first week of my new school I make my mom sit in my classroom every single morning and let her leave only when I feel a certainty in my belly. The certainty is Imogen and friendship, and knowing that soon I will find a way to make my inside wrong visible on the outside.

Faith gives us an assignment to make a family tree. We have to begin with our birth certificates, but no one can find mine. My classmates' trees are filling out; birth certificates sparkle from one end of the wall to the other like big, white teeth. Day one and I am already behind. Imogen's family is small and she's halfway through. On day three, I'm in knots and Imogen's tree is all finished. Kara and Eddie suggest that the reason no one can find my birth certificate is because I'm adopted. They think this is funny, but it feels too plausible for me to laugh, and it feels just as awful as when Dad says I was hatched. I *feel* adopted. And now no one can show me proof that I'm not.

At school, Imogen tries to help. She stares at me from every angle. Maybe I look like my mother, she's not sure. She's never met my father, so she can't say, but I definitely don't look like Kara or Eddie. "I don't know, you might be adopted."

At dinner, Holly says, "We had a substitute teacher today, he was really weird."

"Maybe he's Amanda's real father," Daniel says.

Eddie spits out his water and slaps the table, hysterical. Kara starts giggling and all the blood rushes to her face, tears stream down her cheeks, and her shoulders shake. Even my mom is laughing. Jimmy too. Holly's smile gathers steam as she realizes her comment made this happen at my expense. She glares at me. See? her eyes say. You may be the new youngest, but I'm more powerful. At night Holly stands in my doorway and whispers that the homeless woman on the corner is my real mother, and either Sasquatch or Ciggy is my real father, maybe even both of them. My siblings pick the worst adults to torment me with, and the game spreads outside into the garden. Any new adult who appears is "Amanda's real father."

At first I'm just fighting mad, but then a tingling begins to zap through my entire body. If I was adopted, then this isn't my real family, and my mom isn't my mom, and Kara isn't my Kara, and my real mom is somewhere else and I've been without her all this time. I don't like the feeling of not having a family. Of not belonging. I don't like being in the in-between of whether or not this is true; it makes me feel like I'm lost in black space and the person I really belong to doesn't know where I am and no one can even see me. Like I've been kidnapped and locked in a dark basement somewhere and no one knows to look for me. If I am adopted, then this isn't my house. I don't want to live in any other house, or with any other family. What if my other family changes their mind and wants me back? Will I be able to bring my mom with me?

"You were not adopted," my mother keeps telling me, but she says it through her own laughter, her irritation, her discomfort at my discomfort. "If you don't believe me, call your father. He'll tell you."

I turn the rotary dial carefully, pulling each number back and letting it go entirely before dragging the next one. Everything about this conversation has to go right, including the dialing. On the fourth ring my dad answers.

"Hi, Dad," I say. "It's Amanda."

"Amanda who?" he says.

"Your daughter!" I say, not sure if he's joking.

"I don't have a daughter," he says. My stomach falls. "Oh wait, yes, I remember now. What is it, daughter?"

"Was I adopted?"

"I don't know," he says. "Ask your mother." Then he hangs up. I walk on shaky legs back to my mom. "I called Dad."

"See? I told you," she says.

"He said he didn't know if I was adopted and I should ask you," I say and start to cry. I feel like an orphan.

"Oh, he's such an asshole," my mom says. "Do you want me to call him?"

"No," I say. I go up to my room, throw myself down on my bed, and wail. When I'm done, I wrap the Ace bandage around my wrist and secure it tightly.

My mom is talking to her friend Lydia, another garden mom, on the phone. I can hear her Southern accent through the pinpricks. "Tho what," I say quietly. "Theriously, I'm not mething around with you." My voice sounds good with a lisp. My mom won't stop talking on the phone and I want her to see my fake limp and take me to a doctor. Now I can't remember which foot I used. I squinch my eyes at her, closing one eye then the other, so she bounces side to side like feet in Double Dutch. I squint and make her go double. Then I start closing them really hard, which feels good. I do it over and over again until I hear my mom.

"What's wrong with your eyes?" my mom asks, alarmed.

I sit straight up. "I don't know," I say. "I might be going blind."

"Lydia, I have to call you back. Something is wrong with Manda." She hangs up and comes closer to me, concerned. "Does it hurt? Do you want to take something?"

"No, it doesn't hurt," I say, squeezing them closed again.

"It looks like an eye twitch."

"Yes!" I say. "That's what I have. An eye twitch!"

"You sure you don't want to take anything? Should we put ice on it? Or a heat compress? I'll call the pediatrician first thing in the morning. Dr. Fine will tell us what to do." My mom makes herself a note.

I'm ecstatic. I'm not sure glasses are the right type of sign, though. This is why I also drag my foot. Maybe they'll give me crutches, or a cast. Anything people can plainly see, even while they're on the telephone. Something serious-looking, so everyone knows I'm fragile.

June 1981

Dr. Rivka Golod

<u>Summary of Test Results</u>

   Her spatial and temporal orientation appear adequate at this point although she kept leaving out one month of the year (Oct or Sept) when reciting the months, or confusing the order of September and October. I wonder if this could be related to the extreme anxiety she's exhibited around school, as these are the months when the school year begins.

   My observations of Amanda during these tests is that it is fraught with anxiety for her. My impression of her attitude was that she was convinced she could not think on a high level and was somehow comfortable with simple concrete answers. This suggests not simply a fear of being wrong, but a fear of effort. As though guessing and being wrong is so frightening, she'd rather stay safe and not try. It seems to me she's developed an unrealistic expectation that the solution will be provided for her if she can't find it herself.

Not-Melissa

WHEN WE GO VISIT Baba, my grandfather, I bring my question with me. Even though Baba is a quiet person, I know he'll tell me the truth, because he is gentle and not a liar. Also, he's bedridden and probably bored. This could be a good mystery for him to solve. When my mom leaves for the bathroom, I lean over and whisper in his ear.

"Baba, was I adopted?"

He pats my face with his stiff, veiny hand, but he doesn't answer. His fingers are long and delicate, but the skin is chapped and sore-looking. He smells like talcum powder and old man. Maybe he thought I was just kissing him. Maybe he's not allowed to tell me the truth. Maybe I actually *was* hatched, and I've confused him by asking about adoption. I'm about to ask him again, but my mom comes back, and I pull away. I pat him again to show her I am extra careful with my Baba. He is very fragile. My mom says he's a hypochondriac, that he's been that way his whole life. That means he always thinks something's wrong with him when there's not, or that he'll never stop bleeding if he gets a cut; I can never remember which. I do not want my grandpa to die. He is not only my grandpa, but my mom's dad. She doesn't have a mom anymore, because my mom's mom died the same day my dad's dad died, which must have been the worst day in the history of the world. I don't like to think about that day, but sometimes it accidentally happens, and I have to sit down. How did my parents survive after losing so much in just twenty-four hours? Now, if Baba dies, she'll be an orphan. I do not want that to happen to her.

Baba doesn't like that we live in the Village, and when my mom moved there from uptown without my dad, he said he'd never come and see us, but he did. One time when his nurse took him to the bathroom too late, he left a big wet stain on the couch cushion. I was terrified by it. I never sat in that spot on the couch again. What if inside that very pee was the sickness that he's always in bed for now, and he can't get better because the sickness never made it to the doctor's office? Now it's inside our couch, and I might catch it.

I love Baba, but ever since he peed on our couch, it's all I can think about when I'm near him. What are you supposed to say to a sick person? If I say something like "I hope you feel better," I might ruin his life with the news that he's sick. I love Baba, but I don't like going uptown to visit him, and I want it to stop. My mom says that soon he'll go to a nursing home all the way uptown. Hopefully I won't have to go there to visit him. A nursing home is filled with sick old people who are contagious.

One terrible day, a thought skids across my brain before I can stop it, and the thought hits the air before I can figure out how to take it back. I don't really wish Baba would die, I just wish we could stop going uptown to his house. I don't like leaving our house on MacDougal Street, and I don't like how close Baba's apartment is to my dad's. I worry that my mom will forget it's not a Dad weekend and accidentally leave me there. I quickly tell whatever power makes things happen that I do not want my grandfather to die, of course I don't, and that I am truly not a terrible person, but it's not enough. Now I know that if my grandfather does die, it will be my fault. But when days pass and Baba doesn't die, I am grateful that whoever is in charge of keeping people alive heard me.

Tillie from the garden is turning seven and having a birthday party at her house. Melissa will be there and I'm excited to see her. Now that we're at different schools, I haven't seen her in months. When I arrive, I hear "Y.M.C.A." playing on the turntable and small fits of laughter punching up from the basement. A table off to the side is set up with gift bags. My favorite! Outside I catch a glimpse of an enormous colorful ball hanging from a tree—a piñata! My other favorite! I race downstairs and see all the kids clustered on one side of the room playing Pin the Tail on the Donkey. There's Tillie, her brother Cosmo, Marcel and Margaux, some friends from her grade, but no Melissa. A boy is lounging on the oversized beanbag chair reading Marvel's greatest superhero battles. Marcel turns around and waves me over, and I kick my sneakers off, sink my feet into the plush, thick rug, and go stand next to him. Someone is jumping down the stairs, and I turn to see who it is, but it's no one I know. I notice a girl playing by herself on the other side of the room, and she's wearing the same long-sleeved blue dress with flowers that Melissa has. The girl looks up at me, and smiles, and I smile back, confused. Her cheeks are puffy and swollen, like two baked potatoes, and a red bandanna is wrapped around her head. I can't see any hair. The girl is wearing Melissa's yellow *M* necklace, and Melissa's yellow clogs are on the floor by her feet. Why does Not-Melissa have all of Melissa's stuff? Not-Melissa waves me over, and I go, a little nervous, and stand over her.

"Hi!" she says, using Melissa's voice.

"Hi," I say and sit down. Her lips look chapped and raw and she's got a sweat mustache.

"How's your new school?" she asks.

"It's pretty good," I say. "How's yours?"

She shrugs. "I don't really know."

I'm so confused.

"Wanna play?" Melissa asks.

"Sure," I say. I stare at her, even though I know I shouldn't. Where did all her hair go? Did she get stung by a bee and go all puffy? I don't know how to ask what's wrong. It's easier just to pretend nothing's the matter.

"You be blue," she says. "I'll be yellow."

We're too old to be playing Candy Land, but we don't care. It's always been our favorite game.

"You don't want to play Pin the Tail on the Donkey?" I ask.

"No. I don't feel like standing," she says. Her eyes travel down her legs to her feet, which look raw and burned.

I feel afraid of this new Melissa I've never met. She changed without telling me. I know something is wrong with her, but I don't know what, and if she doesn't know, I don't want to be the one to tell her.

The whole time during Candy Land, outside as we hit the piñata, sing "Happy Birthday," and cut the cake, I can't stop worrying and wondering what happened to Melissa. When the party is over, I rush home with my party bag to tell my mom, Eddie, and Kara about Melissa. That's when my mom's face changes and she puts on her trying-not-to-scare-us voice.

"Melissa isn't feeling very well lately," my mom says.

"Why not?" I ask. How did she know this already?

"She just isn't, but she's seeing a doctor about it and she's getting the exact treatment she needs."

"But why is she wearing a bandanna?" I ask. "What happened to her hair?"

"The medicine that makes her better is very strong. Sometimes it can make your hair fall out, but her doctors know what they are doing, and it's the exact right medicine she needs, so you don't need to worry."

"Is she very sick?" I ask, knowing the answer will be no because bad things don't happen to kids.

"It's nothing for you to worry about," my mom says.

That's not quite a no. "Is she going to die?" I ask.

"She's not going to die," my mom says.

Now that's a no. "Then why was no one playing with her at the party?"

"They weren't?"

"Maybe they didn't recognize her."

"Maybe they were afraid of her," Kara says.

"Why would they be afraid?" I ask.

Kara shrugs.

"There's nothing to be afraid of," my mom says. "What she has isn't contagious."

"What does she have?" Eddie asks.

"She's been getting a lot of bad headaches," my mom says.

I get bad headaches, too, but the medicine I take doesn't make my hair fall out.

"Can I get a bandanna?" I ask.

"Of course."

It turns out I hadn't seen Melissa for so long because she was sick, but now that I know, we can see each other again. In Melissa's apartment, where I go when she feels well enough, we make gingerbread houses and eat ginger candies one after another, surprised every time the edible rice paper melts on our tongues. We play Candy Land and read WOW magazine. Melissa has a coin bank in the shape of a pig, and when our change reaches the top, we're going to figure out how to get it out.

The piggy bank is almost all the way full. I watch as she slides in another quarter. Dark hair used to cover her arms. Now it's gone, and where it was is empty skin. Inside the pillow forts we build, we're the closest we can be without touching, and I notice her eyelids are two shiny ridges; her eyelashes are gone. Without them, she looks like the plastic dolls we played with as babies. Her lids don't stick when she closes them, though, so I don't have to push them open with my thumb. We make up stories about who we're going to marry, and I wonder if her hair will ever grow back, but I don't ask because what if the answer is no?

My mom keeps telling me I can't catch what Melissa has. It's not like a cold or the rash caused by poison ivy. The type of sick she has is only hers, like a mosquito bite. Plus, she has very good doctors and doctors know what they're doing. We are always trying to figure out special codes for how to save each other if we get kidnapped. We decide that we'll say each other's full names, and that way the other person will know we're in trouble. I like having a plan because I really don't want to get kidnapped like Marci Klein. Especially not by the Son of Sam. Melissa doesn't either.

She doesn't come over as often to play, but when she does, I remind everyone in the garden to be gentle with her now. Even though third grade is almost over, it's only now I feel guilty that I'm not with her at school, because who helps her when I'm not there? Who will know that her mouth is sore and she needs something to suck on? Who will know that she's too tired and needs to sit down?

Even during the summer I'll be too far away. This year, my mom is making me go to the camp Kara and Eddie go to. When my mom asked if I wanted to go to sleepaway camp with them, it was snowing outside and the idea was too far away to feel. Camp is something Kara and Eddie have in common; it's what makes them closer to each other than they are to me, and because I don't like being left out, I said yes. But I meant yes to not being left out, not yes to being away. Now it's not an idea anymore. It's close enough to feel, and it's grabbed me by the throat. I know I can't do it. I can't stop thinking about Holly's mom, who died when she was away. A big countdown set off in me and hasn't let go. Two months is too long—something bad will happen if I leave, I know it will. People might die or disappear. What if the house disappears? I want to tell Melissa how scared I am, and I want her to soothe me the way she used to do, but I'm worried she can't anymore. So I just shift the bandanna on my head and hope that my hands and feet don't stay this cold forever.

"Why are criminals locked up?"

"If they're not locked up, they'll kill us."

"Why should women and children be saved first in a shipwreck?"

"So they don't drown."

"But why should they be saved first?"

"Because moms and daughters should never be separated."

"What would you do if you broke something at a friend's house?"

"Is it a sleepover?"

"It's not a sleepover."

"Because I don't sleep over. I don't want to sleep over."

"You're not sleeping over. You're just visiting."

"During the daytime?"

"Yes."

"Okay. If it's the daytime and I'm not sleeping over, that's okay. I broke something? Was it an accident?"

"Yes."

"Then I'd tell the mom of the friend and say I was sorry."

"What would you do if you found yourself alone in a strange city?"

"Where is my mom?"

"She is here, in New York. But you are in a strange city, all by yourself, without your mom."

"How did I get there?"

"That's not the question. The question is, what would you do?"

"I disappeared from my house?"

"I guess so, yes."

"My mom said that can't happen. She said that doesn't happen to kids."

"All right; well, let's say, just this once, it did. What would you do?"

"But she said people don't just disappear."

"Let's just say that it happened to you. One day you were home and the next, you woke up in a strange city. What would you do?"

I have asked my mom a million times what I should do if something like this happened and she says the same thing every time. "That won't happen," I say.

"Amanda, I need you to try to answer the question. What would you do if you found yourself alone in a strange city?"

I have disappeared from the room. I am in a strange city right now. "I would cry."

"Okay, let's move on, and we'll return to that question later."

Someone Kicked the Earth

IT'S MEMORIAL DAY WEEKEND, and everyone's away except us. Outside feels like a hot, wet sweater. There's no one to play with and nothing to do. Imogen is in Hoboken, Melissa is upstate, my mom is upstairs on her bed reading, and Jimmy is at the hardware store buying parts to build a phone intercom system for the house. One day soon he's going to install a video camera so we can see who's at the door before we answer it. Jimmy and I really think alike. He says I can be his assistant. All my siblings have their doors closed. I'm supposed to be doing my eye exercises, but I'm too mad about it to bother. Who knew something would actually be wrong with my eyes? I have two wrong things with them, but neither one meant glasses or getting out of anything. What it meant was eye exercises.

My tutor, Anton, gave me homework, but it's boring and I'm not happy because my mom is making me do more school even after school is over. Besides, no one even told me what I'm being tutored for. Deep Countdown wants to capture me and make me think about sleepaway camp, but I keep trying to dodge out of the way. I pick up *Beezus and Ramona* and start reading it for the twelve hundred and twelfth time when the doorbell rings.

I throw the book down and skip to get it. Maybe it's mail! Maybe it's a package! Maybe it's someone looking for Bob Dylan! Through the side window I see a light blue button-down shirt and a shiny gold medal. Up top there's a police cap. Even though police are from the street side of

life, they're safe because safe is their job. I open the door and the policeman holds up a large photo of a little boy and asks if I've seen him.

The boy is a couple of years younger than me and very cute. His name
is Etan Patz and he lives a few blocks away, in SoHo. We have the same
sandy-colored hair, except his is straight and mine is fuzzy. His bangs are
a little crooked, like he cut them himself, and he has an after-nap look
on him. I like him instantly. But as soon as I realize I like him, I know
something terrible happened. Maybe if I look closer at the photo, I'll remember seeing him and be able to help the policeman find him, but I
shake my head no. I haven't. When a person gets turned into a photo,
it's a very bad sign.

"Do you mind if I come in and have a look around?" he asks, stepping
into my house without waiting for my answer. I am suddenly relieved
and elated. I don't know how he knew this was the exact right place to
find missing things, but I'm glad he's here because I know he'll find the
boy. Etan is probably just having a snack in our kitchen, or playing in the
garden, or hiding in the closet, which is where I go when I threaten to
run away but never do. When I leave home, coming back to my house
solves all my problems, so it makes sense to me that strangers would
know, just by looking at my house, that it was magical and saved people
who didn't like being away.

I follow behind him, up the stairs, and up the next set of stairs, waiting for him to start looking for Etan. But a slow inky heaviness builds
inside me as he passes every room without looking in. He doesn't open
any closets or cupboards and doesn't even get on the ground to look under the beds. My mom comes out of her bedroom, and the policeman
shows her the picture and asks if she's seen him, but she hasn't either.

"How do you get to the roof?" he asks her.

"Manda, show him how to get to the roof."

He follows me to the top floor and I point to the door that leads to the
ladder that leads to the manhole cover that lets the sky inside, and up
he goes. I stay where I am, confused because he's doing this all wrong.
Maybe on the way down he'll get on his hands and knees and look under

the beds? I begin to worry about the boy all over again, before I remember Jimmy Alcatraz is right down the street. Of course the boy is safe; we have the mafia on our side. Soon the cop returns and heads down the stairs, passing by all the rooms again. Does he not know how to do his own job? Downstairs he makes his way to the basement where Norman Bates lives, but it's not nighttime, so the policeman's not scared. Then he leaves, without even checking the kitchen. Without even looking in the garden.

After the cop goes, I hightail it upstairs to my mom, who's back on her bed, reading. I peek out my window, hoping maybe the boy is playing in the Houston Street playground, but the park is empty. The only person there is the lady on the corner. Maybe she saw Etan Patz! Maybe Ciggy or Sasquatch saw him, or the Italian ladies who hang their boobs out the windows. I wonder if the policeman asked them. I look in my closet. Nothing. On my way down to the garden, I stop and look into every room, but he's not here. Maybe he already went back to his mom? I'm confused and disappointed that the cop didn't know how or where to look for the boy. We're supposed to trust cops, but this one did everything wrong. Maybe they just sent a bad one to our house. I walk right into a feeling of doom, but I remind myself of all the times I worried bad things would happen and they didn't.

Later, when I'm in our little garden, I can hear Antsy Stevens talking with her husband Walter. Cops came to their house, too, and also only went to the roof.

"He just disappeared," Antsy Stevens says. "Into thin air."

"Who are these monsters who keep kidnapping little kids?" Walter asks.

A vine of chills wraps around me. My mom says that people don't just disappear into thin air. She promises she won't evaporate when I'm not with her, that terrible things don't happen to little kids. With Marci Klein it was different, because the person who took her was her babysitter. Strangers don't take kids. It's just not possible, but I overheard Antsy say it, and Walter, too, and they're grown-ups. I run to my mom's room and climb next to her in bed.

"Someone took him," I say. "A monster kidnapped him."

"I think he just ran away," she says, rolling her nap breath over in my direction.

"Antsy and Walter said he was kidnapped."

"They don't know what they're talking about."

"Why did the cop go to the roof?"

"I guess he thought he'd have a better view."

"Why didn't he look in the closets?"

"I don't know, sweetheart, but you don't need to worry. Nothing bad happened to him. He's probably already home. You'll see. Tonight on the news, they'll tell everyone there was nothing to worry about."

That night on the news, they show the same photo of the little boy. The anchor tells everyone the boy is six, and yesterday morning he walked to his school bus stop alone for the very first time, but he never got on the bus, and he didn't make it to school, and now it's been more than twenty-four hours. When I hear how long it's been, that he disappeared yesterday, and not today as I had thought, I get light-headed and my brain drops into my stomach with a tangled, dreaded flump. My body knows he didn't run away. My mom is wrong; he's probably in a cold, damp dungeon right now, crying for his mom and unable to get warm. Why couldn't anyone find him? Why didn't the people who protect us protect him? Maybe the Guardian Angels will find him. They patrol the subway, which is very dangerous, and do karate and arrest people. Maybe they'll do a better job than the cops. Every time I spot their red berets, I know I am safe.

"I'm sure he's just at a friend's house, and they just don't realize everyone is looking for him," my mom says. "I'm sure they'll find him."

I want to believe this, but I know she's wrong. I don't understand why we both heard the news say one thing and she's still saying another. Not knowing who to believe makes his disappearance scarier. On the street, police loudspeakers are yelling, "Have you seen this little boy?" They describe what he looks like, what he was wearing, the bag he was carrying. She says the police know what they're doing. She promises, but I saw, with my very own face, the cop doing only wrong things and not being a good looker at all. On the street there's a jangle of leashes, a stampede of paws scouring the sidewalk as bloodhounds try to sniff their way to the boy. That night a spotlight swipes past my bedroom window. Since the cop left, my house has smelled different to me, like cold clouds in winter.

How will Etan survive being away from his mother for so long? Someone has to save him. What if all the adults believe what my mom does, that he's fine? Then no one will be looking for him. Maybe only kids know how to find other missing kids. Maybe I'm amazing at it. When I think about his mother, I feel myself spin, because I know what must be in Etan's head right now. I feel what he and his mother must be feeling, knowing that it's a trillion times worse because it's *actually* happening, instead of just my worries.

Maybe I can help her. I will help them find him. I will look and look and look until he appears. Then my mouth suddenly fills with the metallic taste of Shallow Countdown: My mom is sending me away to camp, for two entire months. Now that Etan is missing, I know I can't leave. If I leave, they'll never find him, and if I'm sent away, they may never find me.

When I wake up the next morning on my mom's safe couch, my first thought is that they found him overnight. But in the kitchen, my mom is on the phone talking about him. He didn't come home. It's officially Day Three. On the street side, kids have been biking around, calling his name, but he never answers. I imagine him underneath the street, down below the grates on the sidewalk, huddled up and hungry, crying and scared of the dark. I look for him in all the right places, but even I don't find him. He's not in our house. My dread expands, rushes down my street and the surrounding blocks, crashing over rooftops and breaking onto the sidewalks like a twenty-foot wave. What if my whole neighborhood is unsafe?

On the kitchen table, the newspaper says they're doing a rooftop-by-rooftop, backyard-by-backyard search, but they didn't search our backyard. The article says he disappeared between 8:00 a.m. and 8:10 a.m. How can such a big thing happen in such a small period of time? It's the between time I'm most afraid of, and it was in the between time that he went missing.

Bad things don't happen to kids my age, but they do because Etan vanished; he's disappeared. I'm seeing it with my own eyes. Where do you go when you vanish? What even is "thin air," and how does it decide who to take? If you're missing, do you still exist? Is "gone missing" the same as death, or worse? I don't know why someone would take that little boy. Doesn't anyone know what being scared feels like? And if they do, why do they want other people to feel that same horrible way?

Now when the church bells stop chiming they leave a trace in the air, a gloomy after-clang, the sound of olden times when townspeople watched the day's execution.

The spotlights continue to pass by my window, pinning my eyes open each time I am supposed to sleep. The helicopter goes in circles. People are crowded outside the gun club across the street from my house. What if Etan is there? I slide my blanket off the bed, tuck my pillow under one arm, push my fingers into my mouth, and make my way to my mom's room.

"Can I sleep in here?" I ask my mom. "I have a headache."

"Do you want to take something?" she asks.

I shake my head.

"You should take something."

After I take some Tylenol, I climb onto her couch, and when I'm finally tilting toward sleep, Melissa's puffy face appears in my head and I open my eyes wide but close them again, turning onto my side, not wanting to follow the breadcrumbs my brain is dropping for me.

At school all we can talk about is Etan, and we're worried, except for some jerk kids who pretend they're not scared. Imogen and I are going to look for him after school on our bikes. Josh M. is absent, and soon everyone is worried that maybe he's been kidnapped. Maybe the kidnapper is taking all the kids, coming for us one at a time until no kids are left. When is he coming to get me? I imagine cars following kids as they walk home, and then the kidnappers grabbing them and throwing them into the trunk. I make sure to walk as far away from the actual street as possible. If the world doesn't do bad things to kids, did the world change its mind? Did someone overhear me worrying about people disappearing and get their own ideas? If the world isn't a safe place to live in, where will we go?

Before, we had no rules downtown, and now there are too many. A specialist comes to our school to talk about "Stranger Danger." We have to peel off our shiny gold name decals; tear our identities from jackets, shirts, and backpacks; unstitch each embroidered letter of our names. Everything of Imogen's has her name on it. If a stranger knows your name, they can trick you. They can pretend they know you because they know your name. How would someone even think about that? Imogen's been undoing her name tags for days. If we think someone is following us, we shouldn't stop at our house, but keep going and walk into the first open store to ask for help. Otherwise, the stranger will know where we live and come back and kill us. Do not talk to strangers, do not accept candy, which could have poison or razor blades in it. I picture myself with a mouth full of blood, a Jolly Rancher drowning on my tongue. Some adults are monsters, but kids aren't monsters. I look at all my classmates suspicious now. Who among us will grow up to be that bad?

Etan is six and I just turned nine, but he is braver than me because I don't want to go anywhere without my mom, and he wanted his mom to stay behind while he walked alone to the school bus. Tuesday, my school takes the day off to hang missing posters all around the Village. I keep thinking about what we were doing on Friday morning while Etan was getting disappeared, and I feel ashamed of myself that I was doing regular things while someone was in trouble. If I had known, I would have done something. It's too painful to miss home, and if I can stop that feeling from happening inside others, I will. But on Friday, I did what I always do and got dressed, ate cereal, tried to get out of going to school, ate lunch, had library, then spelling bee, and came home. By the time I got home it was 3 p.m., and Etan had already been missing for seven hours, and no one knew a thing about it, not yet. Not even his parents. Why didn't the school call his mom? Why didn't the bus driver? In those hours when he was in trouble, and maybe even being tortured, we were running and laughing and eating candy and being carefree. We were happy when we should have been scared. Why didn't I feel the tugs inside me when someone was in such bad trouble? This is what happens when you're not paying attention. Melissa and I call and remind each other of our secret kidnapping code, feeling lucky we came up with one, but sad for Etan that he didn't think of it.

People claim to have seen him all over the Village. The guys at Prince Street Lumber say he'd been there with a friend. People saw him on the subway and in a candy store. It's been five days, then suddenly seven, and I don't have an appetite. If he was on the subway, then why didn't the Guardian Angels protect him? Are they not looking in the right places either?

Everyone around me keeps living regular life, which feels unbearable to me. Someone kicked the earth and shook everything out of place. More and more cops are out on the street, but they just stand there.

Did Etan's mom tell him what to do if anyone kidnapped him? I can't stop imagining his terror, that absolute, end-of-life feeling.

"What should I do if someone tries to kidnap me?" I ask my mom.

"No one is going to kidnap you," she says.

"But what if? Just pretend. I need to know what to do. If someone drove slowly after me, opened their car door, and pulled me inside, what would I do?"

"Never talk to strangers," she says.

"I know that. I know all the things not to do, but just say something happens; what I need to know is what to do!" I am getting so frustrated.

"Do not raise your voice at me!" my mom snaps.

I fly away. "Sorry." I start to cry and run to my bedroom. Later, she comes up to check on me.

"I promise you," she says, rubbing my back while I lie facedown on my pillow. "No one is going to take you. Nothing bad is going to happen to you, or me, or anyone you love. You don't need to worry about it. Do you feel better now?" she asks.

I nod. But I don't feel better. I feel worse. More afraid than before. Only my mom knows how to protect me, but she won't tell me how to do it, and I won't know what to do when she's not there.

The Guardian Angels promised to make the streets safer, but they didn't, so how am I supposed to believe them anymore? They didn't guard Etan Patz. Why aren't the grown-ups finding him? They found Marci Klein. They found her before the day was even over. Maybe her cops should be in charge here. As soon as we find him, we can go back to the world where kids don't vanish. I have to bring him back home.

When the cops come to our house again, they take Eddie in the police car to interview him because he saw Etan in Washington Square Park, walking with an older man. Eddie always gets everything I want: broken arms and casts; and now he's going to be the one to find Etan. I watch him in the car, making sure the cops don't take my brother away like someone took Etan. But he comes back right away. He didn't see the right boy, and I feel guilty for being relieved.

The Lester boys have friends over, and we start a game of freeze tag. As I tag one of Arthur's friends, I instantly recognize his choppy, self-cut bangs, his after-nap look. I freeze him, looking back to make sure he can't move, and sprint through my house and down the street to the cop at the end of the block to tell him I found Etan Patz. He doesn't believe me, but I drag him back. I will save all the kids from all the kidnappers. I will save the world.

Triumphant, I point to the boy with the crescent smile.

"That one?" he asks. "Near the rope?"

"Yes," I answer, annoyed at his hesitation. "That's Etan Patz."

"That's not him."

I don't know why he is saying this to me, so I insist. Close to tears, I tell him again he's the one.

"No, Etan Patz is white."

"White?"

"Not Chinese," he says softly.

His words make no sense. White, Chinese, what does it matter—that little boy is Etan Patz. I stare at the Chinese boy. He smiles back at me. I blink up at the cop. "Even now? It's still not him?"

"Even now," he says, and then he puts his hands on his hips and walks away from me forever.

I know the boy isn't Etan. I knew he wasn't Etan even when I tagged him, but maybe he would become Etan because that's what I really wanted. Because what if we never find out what happened to him? The not knowing will be the worst part. His mother and father don't know. His sister and brother don't know. No one knows where Etan is, and nothing is safe anymore.

The street side of life brought a bad omen that changed the entire world: I've been right all along and the adults have been wrong. If adults can't save us kids, then they can't save themselves either. I really can't ever leave home again. Not for school, or camp, or my dad's house. If I don't find the boy, he will die. I look up at the watercolors painting over the blue sky. The night is fast-forwarding its heaviness and I feel it coming for me.

June 1981

Dr. Rivka Golod

<u>Summary of Test Results</u>

In the area of auditory perception, Amanda performed poorly on a test of sound discrimination. She consistently confused the high-frequency sound V, and the f. An audio metric examination is indicated to rule out a possible high-frequency loss, although clinically there does not appear to be any hearing acuity problem. As on other tests, the likelihood that anxiety is interfering is high, and should not be discounted.

If Time Were a Dog

WHILE I DON'T THINK I want to have a baby on my own, there's an urgency inside my thirty-nine-year-old body telling me I need someone to mother. I've been trying to write my second novel, and hoping my manuscript would be what I parent, but I can't stop thinking about making a human family. It's been six years since my first book came out. That's forty-two years, if time were a dog. My reading series has brought me many unexpected opportunities. One is that I got over my stage fright. I used to think the worst that could happen to me onstage if I did badly was that I'd die, but then I bombed onstage two shows in a row, and not only did I not die, I experienced a certain glory in surviving; and just like that, I was suddenly much less afraid. The second was the offer to write children's books for an editor who attended one of the events. Because I have failed, so far, to publish a second adult novel, and I am instead under contract for a nine-book series for kids called Frankly, Frannie—I have deemed myself less valid than the writers around me, despite the fact I love children's books, and their authors. This makes facing the second book harder. My "real" writing is what fills my life with purpose, and it's this specifically set-aside time a "real" writer utilizes to their advantage. However, I discover it's also the perfect time to binge-watch TV shows on an illegal streaming site that's probably infecting my computer with malware and stealing all my secrets, but who cares, because *Nurse Jackie*! Also, this is probably a good time to adopt a dog.

"You gave yourself three months to finish your novel," my therapist reminds me.

"I can do both," I tell her.

She shrugs. "It's your life."

I log on to Petfinder and scroll through all the cute dogs. I can already feel how much better my life will be. We'll play Frisbee in the park, race around the house, and collapse on the couch in a giggling out-of-breath heap of love. I apply for a gorgeous dog. She's part beagle, part shiksa, and I've decided to name her Pilot, and raise her as a Jew.

My friend Laurie drives me to New Jersey to pick her up. At the shelter, Pilot walks right over to me, without knowing who I am, and that means she's my destiny. I bend down to meet her face-to-face. She won't look in my eyes, yet there's something about her that's profoundly familiar, that calls to me.

In the car on the way back she sits on my lap. I cuddle her, but then I notice that as we drive away, she starts panting, like she's taking a brisk walk. Her nails dig through my jeans and her dry tongue hangs out the side of her stunned, open mouth. My lap looks like a bamboo doormat—shit, I didn't even think about shedding. As she hyperventilates, my own chest tightens, and I, too, start struggling for air. A dread creeps through me then, in the backseat of that car. The reason for her familiarity dawns on me. What have I done?

In my apartment Pilot takes a lazy jump onto the first chair she sees, and then she lies there—mouth open, tongue out, stress-panting, depressed and listless—for hours, then days. She won't move to eat, or drink water, or sleep in her bed. Toys don't interest her. Neither do treats. I spend a lot of time at her side, running my hand through her fur, talking to her, trying to soothe and calm her. I know what she feels. She's me at my dad's house; she's me as a child. After several days in the chair she finally gets down, only to shadow me. When I'm sitting, she stands on her hind legs and keeps her paws on me. It's incredibly sweet, and everyone thinks she must feel rescued, but I know it's not relief that's driving her to cling to me; it's her lack of relief, her uncertainty is what's drawing her so close, and this fills me with anxiety, and a deep unbridled sadness. When I get into bed, she needs to sleep so close that she practically burrows her way into my body, and this makes me want to cry. No matter how near she is, I know she feels like she can't get close enough. Instead of feeling needed, I feel only her existential anguish of needing.

Soon I will have to leave her alone, and I know she won't know whether or not I'll ever return; I know she'll feel I've left her to die. Her anxiety fills my body, which is already filled with my own. I cannot tell whether I am me or the dog.

I go to therapy; I'm gone for an hour and a half. On my way home I have a terrible image: Pilot, sprawled dead on Cumberland Street, having jumped out the window, trying to race after me. The image feels so real that when I don't see her lifeless body on the sidewalk I am genuinely surprised. At home, she's at the door, jumping up on me and grabbing at my legs just the way I used to do with my mother.

In the living room it takes a minute for me to register the overturned shelves, the books scattered across the floor. The window curtains have been pulled down, and above my desk there is a tear in the window screen the size of her body. It's a miracle she didn't fall out, four floors down. I am chilled by my earlier vision. Later I find dog scratches down the back of the front door. She was trying to get out of the apartment when I wasn't there. I burst into tears and worry that the former boyfriend from whom I'd inherited this apartment really did curse it. The day he'd moved out after we broke up I discovered toppled furniture, books and broken wine bottles flung across the floor, and the words "I HOPE YOU HATE IT HERE" scrawled across the hall mirror in Sharpie.

I call the rescue people who sound bewildered. The dog didn't have separation anxiety at their house.

"That's because at your house there were other dogs, here she's all alone when I leave," I say.

"Oh, we never thought of that," the rescue woman says.

She tells me to crate Pilot when I leave and not make a big deal out of coming and going. I tell her I don't think putting anyone with anxiety in an enclosed space is a good idea.

"Trust me," she says. "If you crate her, she'll get over this in no time."

I take her word for it. Shy of hanging posters of boy bands, I decorate Pilot's crate like a preteen's bedroom. I keep the door open so she can come and go as she pleases. Still, the idea of a crate doesn't sit well with me, but most of the world's ways strike me as counterintuitive, and this is probably one of them. I put food in the crate, leave the radio on, shut the crate door, go about my business at home, and ignore her when I leave.

When I get home, the crate is ten feet from where I left it, and it's filled with the white cotton innards of the crate cushion. Blankets have been pulled through the mesh and shredded. She's biting the bars in a full-scale panic attack. I rush to let her out, wrecked that the person who's supposed to protect her from her fears instead actively conjured this mental anguish. She has torn bits of fur off her own body.

As weeks pass, things get worse for her, and for me. I absorb her depression and panic. I cry, that I've taken her from her home where she was secure and am keeping her in a place she fears. Her harrowing, unendurable fear echoes as my own. Now I know something else, something I couldn't ever know—the helplessness of being a parent whose every effort to solve and fix their child falls short. I've failed both her and myself.

I have to make a choice. I can meet my own longing for connection by keeping her, guaranteeing her helpless misery, or I can sacrifice my own needs for hers. Pilot needs what I haven't yet been able to find for myself: a family. I have to find Pilot a new home. While liberating her was my attempt to rescue myself and give us both a family, I am not enough for her. I am not cut out to have a baby.

The rescue place finds a family in the country, away from cars and honking, away from skateboards. Before I hand her over, I bend down and sob into her face. We are the same, and I worry I'm giving up on us both.

INTELLIGENCE TEST: MAZE TRACING

See this little girl in the middle here? She wants to get out to the street and go home. Here is her home. You have to show me how she would get home without getting stuck. You see, she would get stuck if she took this turn. She cannot walk through a wall, can she? How should she go to get home? Make sure she doesn't get stuck.

This little girl is all by herself. All the way over there is her family. The little girl has to get to her family. You must find the shortest way there without falling off the sidewalk. If you fall off the sidewalk, the little girl has to start again. Don't get lost. Time is running out. Hurry, hurry. You only get three tries.

See if you can get out of this one. Start with your pencil here and find your way out without going up any blind alleys or crossing any lines. Do you understand? Do not lift your pencil until you have finished. If you fall off, you can't get back on. Find your way out. Are you lost? Look, you're stuck in a blind alley, see? You can't get out now.

You ran out of tries.

Oh How We Glowed

ALL MY EFFORTS TO stay home from camp have failed. Even when I explain to my mom that Etan needs me to keep looking for him, she says I have to go.

The bus to camp leaves from a cemetery, which is not a good omen. We take a taxi all the way up to Grant's Tomb, which is on 122nd Street—122 blocks away from our house; 127 blocks from Etan Patz's house. Ever since Etan disappeared thirty days ago, I've noticed that adults don't watch their kids as well as we watch our adults, and they make bad decisions, like sending us away for two months with grown-ups who are strangers. Just because they call it "camp" doesn't mean it's safe. My mom doesn't worry about the same things I do, and neither do the police, which makes them all bad watchers. If they worried as much as I do, they'd have found him by now. I'm one of the best watchers because I worry about everything. The newspaper said Etan's sister had a birthday party, but no one showed up because everyone is scared of them now. I'm not scared of them. I would have shown up.

When the policeman rang our doorbell, Deep Countdown for camp had just started, but the longer Etan stays missing, the more the news creates a new countdown I've never had before—Empty Countdown. This is the worst countdown possible. My other countdowns were about not knowing what's going to happen, but Empty Countdown is fearing what I now know *does* happen. Before Empty Countdown, I worried adults didn't know how to take care of themselves or of us, that they'd misplace us or get lost, but everyone said that was crazy. Now I know I'm right.

Empty Countdown cuts your breath in half and closes your throat tight every time you swallow. When I try to explain it to my mom, she gives me Dimetapp, or wonders if I have asthma like Kara. Empty Countdown doesn't let you get the same amount of air as everyone else, and what little air it gives you is frightened air, made from fire alarms that won't turn off, and smoke that never clears.

I've been in Empty Countdown for one month, half the time I'll be away. I cannot go. Even before Etan disappeared, I wasn't ready to leave, but now I know the world doesn't always return what it takes. How can all these parents, who are suddenly so afraid of having their kids go missing, choose to make us go missing? They're pushing us toward the very people they've been warning us away from—strangers.

If I leave now, when I should be here keeping track of everyone, people will die. Something very horrible is going to happen. I need to stay home and be the adult and stop the bad things from happening, but I keep getting moved forward, like a plastic game piece, toward Vermont.

It takes seven hours to get to Vermont. Seven hours is an entire day of school, three back-to-back movies, or an airplane ride to California. Seven is almost nine, which is how old I am, and also the same amount of hours that passed before anyone knew Etan Patz was missing, and that's a bad omen, too.

Kids and parents are sprawled on the greenery, laughing and hugging, like they don't see the two big buses waiting to kidnap us all away. The air carries the first-day sounds of a new school: children laughing, high-fiving, and neato-ing new haircuts, sneakers, and braces. Eddie and Kara whip out of the cab. A teenage boy takes our duffels. I have no control over what's happening. My body is moving past a blur of stripes: thick and thin bands of blue, yellow, and maroon tube socks pulled to the kneecaps. The boy throws our duffel bags down the throat of the bus, which I didn't know would happen. It is so far away. I hope the doors of the bus never open. Kara huddles in a circle with her friends, showing off her new unicorn earrings. What if Kara's bunk is too far from mine? A group of boys stand over Eddie and his new guitar. His red hair is orange in the sun and flops over his eyes. Not once have Kara or Eddie looked back to see if I'm okay. At home, when their friends are over, they ignore me. My stomach crumples. Will I exist to them at camp?

Inside my duffel are things I've never used on my own, like bug spray, a canteen, a penknife, and laundry detergent. My mom addressed all the envelopes for me and put the stamps where they belong so I could write home. I also don't know how to use sleeping bag straps, or what parcel post is, or how to call home collect. My mom does everything for me that I don't know how to do, but what will I do at camp when she's not there? She said people will do things for me if I don't know. I don't want to do this; I can't do this. I'm going to get everything wrong, and then everyone will see something is wrong with me and I'll die.

The bus is running; the engine is a countdown we can all hear. I am afraid my body will open and explode in front of everyone when it hears the bus doors open. My mom hugs a parent, and my nerves swing up. When no one else is afraid, I am truly alone. Everyone's backs are to my face, and I feel like the Egyptian vase I made in ceramics, with a handle too high, a spout too low, and an uneven, tilting base. The only way to keep it straight was to lean it against Imogen's. Imogen and Melissa are with their families this summer. They're so lucky. Why didn't Jimmy Alcatraz see where Etan Patz went?

I grip my mother's hand and stand as close to her as possible, pressing into her arm, hoping I might pass through her skin and make my way back inside her body where I belong.

"Manda, you're pushing me," my mom complains, stepping away.

Some other new girls nearby are talking to each other, which means they are not afraid. The space between them and me widens.

My mother inches me forward, urging me to interact with the others. Why does she want me to leave her? Isn't she afraid she'll die when her kids are away, just the way Jimmy's first wife died when their kids went to camp? What if my mom does die and Jimmy doesn't tell us until after we come home? We'll have spent the whole summer not knowing we should have felt dead.

My mom lets go of my hand. "You're Athena, right?" my mom asks the girl who has just appeared before me. Athena nods her head. When her lower lip trembles, I am soothed by her fear. "This is Amanda," my mom says.

"Hi," I say.

"Hi," Athena says.

"Do you have anyone to sit with on the bus, Athena?" my mom asks. Athena shakes her head. "Great, you can be seatmates!"

Athena takes a deep breath and nods, which rolls calmness through me.

"Perfect. Why don't you get to know each other a little and I'll be right back," my mom says, turning back to her friend. Athena and I stand there silently. My mom tilts her chin at me, which means, Say something.

"Which one's your mom?" I ask her. I feel like I am two selves. One self is talking to protect the other self, who is mute and unable to function or understand the world.

"She left already." Her voice cracks.

"Oh," I say. Her mom sounds like the meanest person alive. "I'm sorry."

Athena swallows and nods.

Then a woman with blond frizzy curls stands on an apple crate at the foot of the bus and the world suddenly fast-forwards around me. My lips go numb. The woman shouts instructions at us, but I can't hear them because the world has compressed and condensed, nestled and screaming, right inside my forehead. Things change fast; people are moving, greetings are over, and as the bus doors open, the sounds in the air turn mechanical and urgent. Athena pulls me. I turn and see that my mom is having a conversation, not paying attention to the fact she might never see me again.

I am in a line of disappearing children being devoured by the bus. I am the littlest; I might get trampled. I watch my own sneakers take the three steep black-treaded steps before I finally hear my mom behind me shouting, "I LOVE YOU!" but someone pushes me down the aisle. I slip into a window seat on the mom side of the bus. Athena slides in next to me.

My mother is looking for me, but the windows are too dark and she can't see. I stand and press my hands against the window and knock. I want off. She walks to the back of the bus, but I am in the middle. She walks to the front, but still I am in the middle. She's waving to someone else's child, not her own, and I start crying and want to freeze all the leaking flavors of emotion by stashing my fingers in my mouth, but I know I can't. Nine is too old to suck your fingers. The bus rolls away and I watch my mom, waving still to someone who isn't me. If she can't even find me on the bus, how will she find me if I'm being kidnapped?

I slump back down to my seat. I can't let anyone know how scared I am. My mouth makes small talk. Kara and Eddie are on a different bus and I didn't know that would happen. Out the window, the city world I know turns into a tree world I don't. The roads flatten wide and trees appear, thickening up the sides of the roads until they're a forest. Etan's mom was on TV asking that if a family took him to be their own child, to please send him back. What if he's here, in the woods, where they don't even have TV?

Eventually, the counselor and kids start singing camp songs. The music pushes up my heart and I begin to feel better, but Athena is just staring at the back of the bus seat, not swaying even just a bit. She is not a music person; we will not be friends. We don't say any more words for a long time.

Seven hours later, we arrive to green fields and log cabins painted orange-red. If camp were a person, cabin 4, where I am, would be the face, which feels too far away from Kara and Eddie, whose cabins are the knees and feet. I am given a bottom bunk that's pressed against a wall. This means I can sleep on my left side for two months and secretly suck my fingers without anyone seeing. The cabin smells unfamiliar, of mothballs, grass, and old wood. There are two doors to the cabin, a screen door and a proper wooden door. The screen door creaks loudly when it opens, which is a good sign. That means if someone comes to murder us, the squeaking door will give the murderer away.

Our counselor is a tomboy blonde named Sally. "All right, girls. We're going to make our beds and put things away, but we can't do that without doing this!" she says, bending over a cassette player. First we don't hear anything, but then a slow guitar build I recognize from the street side of our house comes out. In her Chuck Taylor sneakers, blue sweat jacket, and torn jean shorts, she starts singing, dancing a walk-strut with her eyes closed. "...'hey honey, take a walk on the wild side'...unzip your duffels!" she sings to us. We do. "Find your sheets!" She plays the song over and over until we're all moved in, and then we have a cabin meeting.

"Chicks, it's us against the world. Got it?"

We nod. My belly untightens. Sally is tough and warm at the same time. Even better, she's capable and safe. I can't wait to tell Imogen and Melissa about her. Some girls sneak looks at one another like they think Sally's weird. Maybe they'll think I'm weird, too, because I like her.

"We're gonna stick together as a team until we all find our place. Right on?"

We nod again.

"By the end of this summer, if you don't know every last word of 'Walk on the Wild Side,' then I'm a disgrace. Let's go get some bug juice!"

We walk as a clump down to the main house. No one knows what "walk on the wild side" means.

"Woodshop," Sally calls, pointing to a small cabin on the right. "Bike shed. Infirmary. Cargo net. Baseball field. Office. Bell. Main house. Seeger house." We follow Sally to a table lined with red plastic cups filled with something called bug juice, which is cold and tastes like Kool-Aid. A cloud passes over and covers the sun and my homesick hits me deep. I wish Kara's cabin were right next to mine.

The first few nights are like jail. I'm too homesick to speak and the asthma in my chest grows. At night when we walk through the dark back to our cabin, I wipe away free-falling tears that no one can see. In bed

I face the wall, fingers in my mouth, and cry myself to sleep. I know others can hear me because sometimes I cry so hard I can't breathe, but every morning I wake up amazed that I made it through another night away from my mother. When we reach eight nights, I forget to keep counting.

Athena, I quickly decide, is boring, but Stacia Moore is not. Stacia's duffel is filled with cool toys, like glow-in-the-dark light sticks. One night I wonder aloud what it feels like to glow, and Stacia says we should find out. Out on the porch, we crack the light sticks, cut them in half, and rub the sludge all over our bodies. We can hear Sally in her room practicing a Lou Reed song on guitar. Tracey turns out the porch lights, and I see gold winking sparkles on Stacia's chin, cheeks, and shoulders.

"We're glowing!" I shout.

"We're glowing!" Stacia is yelling too. The other girls come racing out of the cabin and everyone wants a turn.

"There are only four sticks left," Stacia says, which means not enough for everyone.

The porch lights flick on and Sally stands in the doorframe. "Whatcha up to, little chicks?"

"We're glowing!" I shout.

Sally cocks her head sideways. "What do you mean?"

"Tracey, the lights," I order. Tracey shuts off the lights and Sally gasps, then laughs, then gasps again.

"How did you do that?" she asks, awe-eyed and wondrous. Stacia holds up the empty wax sticks. "What are those?"

"Light sticks. My dad got them for me. He owns a paint store."

"Oh, hellish moment. We have to get you to Norma, immediately." Stacia and I exchange confused glances. Sally grabs Stacia's hand and Stacia grabs mine and we rush across camp to the infirmary. I feel like Madeline with a burst appendix, but I'm not sure why we need Norma the nurse when the only thing that burst was glow sticks.

Norma strips us down and rushes us into the showers to scour our skin with scrub brushes until it hurts. When we're done, she turns the lights off and Sally plays the ref, shouting: "They still glow!" It takes five showers before we're just regular human kids again. Wrapped in towels, we follow Sally back to the cabin, numbed, barefoot, and dull-skinned. On the tops of my feet I spy two luminous dots, and I smile at the part of me they couldn't wash away.

Stacia and I become very popular after that, which helps me be less homesick. Even Kara and Eddie hear about it. Plus, I get my first boyfriend. Gideon Kaplan and I are twins: little, sporty, and scrappy; but unlike me, he's not afraid of anything. Melissa and I have been writing to each other, but after I brag about Gideon she doesn't write back, and I worry I bragged too hard. I am trying not to think about that. When I do, I feel like I'm flipping and flying through outer space. Once I get home I will prove to her that I am not conceited about having a boyfriend. Imogen sent me a care package, so I know she's not mad.

My mom and Jimmy write me all the time, which just shows how boring their life is without me. Still, I check the return addresses just in case—as long as they match our home, I am safe. I write them back so they know that I've learned how to kayak, swim across the lake, play tetherball and tennis, make a leather bracelet, ride a horse, and shoot a bow and arrow as well as a rifle. I've also learned all the words to "Walk on the Wild Side." I don't know what I was so afraid of. Soon the kitchen and country smells that turned me sad at first become familiar. I feel stronger. I see Kara and Eddie all the time, and I know all the camp songs and everyone's names. No one teases me and when I am homesick, people make me feel better. Camp is a new world whose language I have come to understand. There's so much to do all the time and so many people to do things with that I feel the same sense of belonging I feel in New York. Camp Killooleet becomes another home where I am safe.

Then, one night late in July, someone taps me on the shoulder during movie night—*Lawrence of Arabia*, what a bore—and says there's a phone call for me at the main house. My heart belly flops. Phone calls are not good. Especially at night.

I peer toward the main house, which is a molar in the distance. There is a field of darkness to walk through alone before I find out that my mother is dead. I pray and beg and plead with the world and the phone company to reverse it. The walk is humid and damp. I want the thoughts to stop, but they refuse. These are the steps I am taking before the good part of my life ends. This is my fault and I know it. Had I been alert to my worries instead of letting my guard down, my mom would not be dead. Why did I let myself glow? How could I have been so selfish?

I see Kara and Eddie. They're crying. Even though Eddie is eleven and Kara is thirteen, they suddenly look much younger to me. Kara is holding the phone. My stomach puckers. For a brief moment, I realize a very small part of me is ready to be told my mom is dead so that the constant worrying about her death will end, but of course, that's not what I want. I squeeze the thought away as fast as I can.

"Is it Mom?" my mouth asks.

When Kara nods, I get dizzy. She hands me the phone. When I hear my dad's voice, I'll know it's true.

"Hi, pumpkin." Mom is alive! I nearly laugh with relief and gratitude. But why are Kara and Eddie crying?

"Baba died," she says. I feel my insides evaporate. Oh. Oh no. My wishes are even more powerful than I thought. That secret I'd forgotten, the secret nonwish that Baba would die: I've gone and done it. The more I worry about death and disappearance, the more it seems to happen. If this is a superpower, I want to trade it in for a weaker one.

I don't remember returning to the movie screening. My thoughts ran like their own movie, in an endless loop. I need to go home. I should never have left. Baba died because I had that bad thought. I am a jinx. This is the night Baba died. This is the night I learned I am a jinx. The fear I had before I left, the fear they said would not happen, happened. And then I came here and had fun. I never should have had fun. I will never leave again. I will go home tomorrow, and I will live there with my mother forever, because when I leave, people die, and now the poison is in my own family and crawling toward my mom.

My mom won't let me, though. We have no choice. So instead of going home for the funeral we stay in Vermont, and all the kids are extra
nice to me, Kara, and Eddie, and before I even know it, a few days pass,
and my old happiness creeps back in.

For the first time, a trip away ends too fast. Soon it's commando raids
and the camp banquet, then the buses come and I am crying because
I don't want to leave. But this is a totally different sadness: I am crying
like all the other kids. I am normal. I am cured. We go back the way we
came, seven hours by bus to Grant's Tomb, singing all the camp songs,
and every last word of "Walk on the Wild Side." My happiness is leaking,
oozing as nonstop chatter to Stacia. My sadness has reversed; I want to
go back to camp and away from home. This is the feeling I've always
chased. When I imagine next summer, nothing in me buzzes or pulses,
and I know my countdowns are gone. Out the window, trees turn into
buildings, and the city appears. I check with my body to see if being
back turned me into my old self, but no, I'm still cured.

The bus gets asthma and jolts, lowering. When the driver pulls the
doors open, I rush to Mom before Kara and Eddie and throw my arms
around her waist. "Did you have the best time?" she asks.

"Back to camp, back to camp!" I sing, and then run off to say good-bye
to my friends. I don't look back to make sure my mom didn't disappear.
Normal is the best feeling I've ever known. I survived camp. I even survived accidentally killing Baba. I am normal. Now I can do all the things
I never wanted to do before.

Our house is exactly where we left it, and I'm so glad to see it I wish I
could give it a hug. We whiz past the "Welcome Home" sign, to our bedrooms, to hug Jimmy, and then head to the garden to show everyone we're
home. Even new things—the umbrella stand, the lace covering the front
hall table, Marcel's haircut—none of these things push me out of my new
world. I wanted to carry my camp lightness all the way back home, and I
did. It's still with me; I am at ease. When the sun sets, nothing sinks in
me; and when I go to bed, I miss the sound of mattress plastic and the
smell of mothballs, and I sleep there all night, in my own room.

The next day we walk to SoHo to see friends. I unlink my hand from my mom's and hurry ahead, something I couldn't do before camp. Our narrow cobblestone streets, our clustered buildings, our borders and stoops, our bread shops and bums, our hippies, musicians, sculptors, and outcasts: Not once did I remember to miss them, and look— they're all still here. Jimmy Alcatraz, Vito, the Guardian Angels, Ciggy, Sasquatch, and even the lady on the corner. Everyone is safe, I think. Right where we left them. Not even the abandoned-seeming streets that used to give me chills haunt me.

I am happy right up until I see a "Still Missing" poster with a reward stamped across it: $10,000. Suddenly I bump into old me, and I feel a flood of shame for forgetting. I turn to my mom. "They didn't find Etan Patz?"

"No, sweetheart."

None of us say anything for a few blocks. Cafe Borgia took down their poster of Etan, and the row of missing posters that covered the scaffolding on Greene Street has been plastered over with concert posters and graffiti. I am furious. How will anyone recognize him and save him if people take his photo down? A block or so later we walk into a cold front, a stretch of emptiness and nobody. Broken windows, sharp panes hanging from the ledges. The buildings are black inside. Garbage bags and wood patch over the top floor windows, and graffiti colors the outsides. A pants-down bum is asleep on the sidewalk and we cross to the other side. Shadows of buildings cool the stone streets and spread thin the gloom, and the air smells musty, like spring, when Etan Patz disappeared. What if he's inside one of these buildings, and we're walking right past him? How would it feel to be so close to your mom knowing your mom didn't know? My arm rises, my hand slips and locks into its old position in my mom's palm. My dirty Pumas land soft, and with no one around I can hear all our steps, like we're in a movie and the sound is the signal to the audience to be scared.

But when we hit the other side of Houston Street I feel safe again, and my fear slips away as I run after Eddie. At camp I was scared until

I wasn't. I went away and didn't come back at the first sign of trouble, which means I am brave. My body made a callus around my feelings, and now I know that being scared doesn't mean staying scared. I'm tough enough to withstand anything. I'm not going back to how I was. I am brave now. I am cured. I am normal.

*   *   *

It isn't until a couple of days later, when my mom and I are back-to-school shopping, that I ask when I can see Melissa. My mom goes silent. At first I think she didn't hear me, but then she stops walking. I don't like the look on her face.

She didn't feel any pain, my mom says. It happened in her sleep. What? What do you mean? Now I am sitting on the curb, my feet in the gutter, staring at my knees. I can't stop crying. What about our piggy bank? Who will break it open and count all the change? Melissa would never die before the change reached the top. She would never die without telling me first. And if she did die, she would call to tell me she died, even though I know that's not how death works, but Melissa would have done that for me, just like I would have done that for her.

When my knees become my knees again, the world feels different. My body has been replaced with an exact replica of my old body, and only I know this new body isn't actually me. When other people look at it, they'll think they're seeing me, but they'll be wrong. I don't feel close to myself, and worse, I don't even feel close to my mother. Nothing is the same. This is the opposite of cured.

As the new me slips off, I know that I'm not the old me either. I'm a new old me. A worse me, a bad-luck me with power I don't want. I am a killer of people. I left home when I didn't want to, and once I stopped being scared two people died, and that is my payback for not worrying. Worrying keeps people alive.

"When did she die?" I ask.

"A week before Baba," she says.

"Why didn't you call and tell me?"

"I thought it was best to wait and tell you in person," she says.

But she didn't tell me. I had to ask. She knew when she called me at camp. For an entire month she knew that Melissa was dead, and I didn't. For an entire month I thought Melissa was mad at me for having a boyfriend when really she was dead. For an entire month, I was happy, carefree, when I should have been devastated and in mourning. I am a bad person.

Every draft of air tells the new story of me. The beep and grind of morning garbage trucks, plastic bags caught and panicked in the wire bones of fences, the smell of blood from a freshly scraped knee, the hard striped candy in bowls at my grandmother's, the flapped-open lip of a broken sneaker sole. Every signal, every layer, gesture, flavor, texture— I feel separated from it all. I am cardboard in the shape of a person. I feel nothing. How could my mom let me laugh, play, have a boyfriend, sing, jump, kayak, swim, make friendship bracelets, and drink bug juice while Melissa was dead? If I had known she was dead, I would have come right home. I wouldn't have made myself glow, or learned any of the camp songs, or gotten a boyfriend, or laughed.

The rainbows on my laces have faded; they're almost gone. Everything disappears. I know that every day is someone's birthday, and now I wonder if every day someone dies. Someone could be dying right now, and we're doing nothing to save them.

"But you said she wouldn't die," I say.

"I didn't think she would," my mom tells me.

"You said what she had wouldn't kill her."

"I had hoped it wouldn't," she says.

"But it was possible? She had something that people die from?" I ask.

"Yes," she said. "She did."

Nothing is safe anymore. I am angry, in a way my mom can't make better. I want her to apologize. I want her to admit she made a mistake, that she should have told me the truth from the start and let me stay home. There was a funeral I didn't know about. I was getting ready for school when Etan disappeared, and I was watching a boring movie when Baba died, but what was I doing at the exact minute Melissa died? Was I sleeping, too? I didn't even know she needed saving. My mom said Etan would be found. She said Melissa wouldn't die. My mom knew, and she lied.

"Why didn't you tell me she could die?" I ask.

"I didn't want to upset you," she says.

Now how can I trust what my mom tells me? Does everything I worry about come true and she's been telling me I'm wrong about the world just to keep me from getting upset? If I don't know what does and doesn't happen, how will I know whether to say yes or no, run or stay? I am nine years old and I still don't know the rules for anything. I don't want to be protected from the truth. I want to know what can happen, and what to do when that thing happens, but she won't tell me. Although my heart and brain feel betrayed, and I feel more alone than I've ever felt, my body still needs my mother, and this is confusing.

Before I left people were blurry and I worried everyone would get blown away like skywriting, but then I got cured and everything seemed fine. Now the cure is gone, and so is Melissa. My mom doesn't understand what I need, and I fear she never will. Maybe she never did. Instead of telling me how to handle a bad thing, she always said there'd be no bad thing, and now Etan, Baba, and Melissa have all disappeared from life—that's three bad things in a row—and I don't know what to believe anymore, or whom. Things don't mean what they did just ten minutes ago. I can't be the new me. I will never get another boyfriend, and I will make sure never to be happy again. I will always be this old bad me, hatched and abnormal, like no one else.

The wind presses hard against me, a private warning telling me not to move forward into the future, pushing me back to the beginning before I was born, before I had days. Somewhere, there's an original world where I haven't killed anyone. One day I'll be dead, too, but I don't know when that will be. I could die at any time. I could die now. Maybe I am walking toward it; maybe it's walking behind me, trying to catch me and tag me out, dead.

My mom says, "I don't know." I don't know what she looked like. I don't know what she thought or felt or smelled or tasted while she was dying. I don't know if she knew she was dying. I don't know if dreams turn into death, or your breath forgets to come. I don't know if her mother found her in the morning, or whether she was awake when it happened. I don't know if she was on her side or her back, wearing her bandanna or not. I don't know if she was scared or smiling.

I was right all along, but no one listens to me, and no one tells me the truth. I feel grief for every moment that passes. I feel time as it leaves me. I don't need to read clocks to understand. I feel time as I walk through it. Soon, time will grow its gravity-hours and push down the light, burying today, like Melissa. I am always walking toward my next separation. I am always walking toward someone's death.

I don't want to go to sleep again. I don't want to go back to school. I don't want a new classroom, or new friends. Why does the world invent kids if it's just going to throw us away?

"An unlucky bicycle rider fell on his head and was instantly killed; they took him to the hospital and fear he cannot get well. What is foolish about that?"

"He was already dead so he couldn't get well," I say.

"I have three brothers, Paul, Ernest, and myself. What is foolish about that?"

"You can't be your own sibling."

"The body of a young girl cut into eighteen pieces was found yesterday. People think she killed herself. What is foolish about that?"

I don't like these questions.

"You can't cut your own self up like that," I say.

"There was a railroad accident yesterday, but not a serious one; only forty-eight people were killed. What is foolish about that?"

I feel scared and want to leave. "It's very serious when someone dies or gets killed. Especially forty-eight people." I use my strict voice so she knows I mean business and she shouldn't try to kill me.

"A man said, 'If I should ever grow desperate and kill myself, I should not use Friday for the purpose because Friday is an unlucky day and might bring me unhappiness.' What is foolish in that?"

I don't want to be an adult, I don't want to grow up in a world that doesn't take death or accidents seriously; where adults test kids by asking what's foolish about being murdered or killing yourself. Did Dr. Rivka write these questions? If she thinks there's something foolish about death when I know there's not, why am I the one being tested?

Scapegoat

I AM NOT DOING well in school and the teachers call my mom and set up meetings. They want to know if I can see the board and hear the teacher the way the other kids can. How can I know if what I see and hear is different? I know this is my chance to get hearing aids, but now that it's an option, I'm not sure I want to be deaf. If I can't hear, how will I stop the person who sneaks up from behind to kill me? I'm so disappointed in myself. I thought by now I'd be over this. That I'd be able to leave my mom without feeling like I'm dying, and do what everyone else can do. Everyone else is worried about not doing well in school, but I don't care about that. I'm starting to wonder if anyone can even hear me when I try to explain.

Siobhan calls on me when I don't raise my hand and asks me to define a word. Everyone turns toward me and I can hear them waiting for me to get it wrong. All the letters in my head shake apart like a Boggle tray; I feel noisy and blank at the same time. I'm being timed and I can't think and my feelings are a marching band across my body.

"I . . . I . . . I have to go to the bathroom. I'll tell you when I get back," I say, hurrying out of the classroom. Outside, I'm breathless, humiliated and shaking. I look for Kara, but she's in science class with her head down.

But then I have a genius idea. I'll write it down. My mom will read about my problem and explain the answer; even better, she'll finally realize that I'm not working correctly and need some sort of medical equipment that makes people do things for me because I'm too broken to do things for myself.

"I'm in trouble with Siobhan. I ran out of class today because I didn't know what the word 'scapegoat' meant," I write to her in a note I leave on her pillow.

"I'll call Marie tomorrow." She leaves the note outside my bedroom door.

She calls Marie for everything. When I'm scared about going away on a field trip, didn't do percents for my math homework, forgot to learn about the galaxy, or couldn't memorize a sonnet I was supposed to recite—Marie. Even though she works for the school, Marie gets me out of everything: trips, homework, tests, and memorizing poems. It's like there's a secret channel between my mom and my school, my tutor, and my pediatrician. I know it's about me, but no one will ever tell me what gets said. And afterward, it turns out I still don't know what "scapegoat" means, how to do percents, what makes up the solar system, or the meaning of iambic pentameter.

Still, I'm sent for testing.

The doctor's waiting room is the same as all my other doctors' offices: plain and brown. The only magazines are for golf and sailing. I take it as a good sign that there is nothing for children here. It means they are serious about deafness. In the waiting room I practice cat's cradle with my new babysitter, Margie. I know I'm here so they can test my hearing, but a small part of me wonders if they'll be able to hear the inside of me, and then call my teachers and parents and even my pediatrician, Dr. Fine, for a big meeting to present the findings. People, this doctor will finally say, we have discovered the problem with your daughter and I know how to fix her. Here, have a listen. Then he'll press Play on a tape recorder and everyone will hear the pinball sounds of all my worries crashing into one another and all my organs.

Soon a nurse comes out to fetch me. She makes Margie wait outside, which I don't think is very friendly. In the next room, there's a big brown chair facing a wall of glass windows. They tell me to sit, so I do. A doctor arrives but doesn't say hello; he just juts a magic wand into my ear and makes it vibrate. I try to pretend I'm not surprised. He vibrates the wand in my other ear, too. Then he writes a note. When he pushes a piece of foam into both canals, I can hear the outside layers of the room at the same time I hear the inside layers of my brain. Then, finally, he says something.

"When you hear a sound out of your right ear, I want you to raise your right hand. Do the same with the left. Okay?"

I nod, but I immediately go blank inside at the words "left" and "right." I look down at my hands, which look the same to me. I can write with both hands exactly the same way. The first time my mom saw me do that, she freaked out and made a phone call. A few days later a woman came over to our house and made me hop across the room on one foot and then the other. I showed her my right hand, right eye, right knee, right ear. I touched my right ear with my left hand. She asked, "Which hand do you eat with, lift with, throw with, draw with?" Then she wrapped tape around that hand and said, "From now on, you must always sit on your left hand." But I can never remember which hand is left. She told my mom I was ambidextrous, and we never saw her again.

The deafness doctor leaves the room and goes behind the large window facing me, but I don't hear any sound.

"Are you ready?" he asks. His voice sounds like it's speaking from inside my brain. I hear it on both sides, so I raise both hands.

"Don't raise your hand to my voice, only to the sounds you hear," he says, adding, "And only raise one hand at a time. The one that correlates to the noise, not both."

Shame spreads up my torso, into my neck. I don't like getting things wrong. Isn't a voice a sound?

A slow, glowing shriek is growing in my ear, higher and louder until it actually hurts my canals. I've never heard anything like this before. Did my head explode from being scared and now my brain is leaking? I look at the doctor, terrified, but when I see his expression I realize this is the sound. I throw my hand up. Soon the noise shrinks and I nearly cry with relief. Now there's a new high-pitched sound in the other ear. I raise that hand. Soon notes are being flung at my ears over and over, and the high sounds linger behind like echoes circling around my ear hole. Sometimes there is no sound at all, and I sit waiting for one and when I look up, the doctor is waiting, too, and then he writes something down and I worry. It's getting hard to keep track, because the old sounds stick, and I have to listen underneath the leftover sounds for the new ones coming in.

Am I supposed to keep my hand raised for as long as the sound plays? What did the person before me do? My hands are shooting up one after another after another. A couple of times when I raise one hand the doctor looks at me, surprised. My brain is getting tired. I'm feeling confused about sides. Once the noises are totally gone, the only thing I hear is the noises that didn't erase.

"Now I want you to repeat the words I say as well as you can," he says. "She."

"She," I say.

"Fahrenheit."

"Fahrenheit."

"Sister."

"Sister."

"Twins."

"Twins."

"Can you say twins again, please?"

"Twins."

"One more time."

I pause and swallow.

"Twinssssssssssssss," I say, holding the *s* to show him I know how to say the word, so he won't ask me again, and this can be over. I hold it until it whistles.

"One last time, please."

I imagine that when someone hears or sees or finally understands what is happening inside my body, they'll worry about me, but this doctor is not worried about me. He is making me repeat words because he has found something else. Just like at the eye doctor, where I went thinking nothing was wrong but came out with two wrong things, there is something new the hearing doctor has found. Why else would he keep making me repeat all these words? I am swept by a sick realization—no one has discovered my wrongness, not in all these years, and it dawns on me that they may never, and I'll be stranded by myself, in my worry dungeon, without anyone to help me. Instead, I will just keep adding on other, extra things that are wrong. My hands feel like spaghetti in a strainer, and my mouth tastes like dirty rain. All the regular world sounds have been replaced by an endless hum, the dead bodies of all the noises he sent to me.

"Amanda, can you say twins for me, please?"

I look at the clock, whose big face and numbers once meant nothing to me, and although now I can read the numbers and say what they mean, time in the world never lines up with my pace. I never match anything, not time, or test answers, not even height or weight for my age, and now maybe not even my own wrongness. From now on, I will be like Etan: trapped somewhere in this city, a place known only to him but unknown to everyone else, and unable to be discovered. I am below the world; in the secret place broken kids are dropped. The people standing above don't know how to save me.

"Twinssssssss," I say. "Twinssssssssss."

Frankie Bird

I'VE ALWAYS HAD A name obsession because mine never quite fit me. Even my mom agrees I was misnamed. When I ask what she'd name me if she could do it again, without hesitation she says, "Fiona." Amanda is the name for a girl who wears Laura Ashley dresses and cares about hygiene. "Amanda" helps her mother with domestic chores, wears pink tights on her head pretending it's a veil, and practices walking down the aisle. I knew my name was wrong for me, just the way I knew I never matched the "normal" student those tests were testing me against, and I never got placed alongside the rest of my peers on the growth charts and percentile curves—I've never been where I was expected. Even now, in adulthood, the trappings other people seem to so effortlessly find continue to elude me. My internal has never matched my external and my external has never matched the world.

Since I was small, I've kept lists of favorite names I've loved. With my worn, broken-in clothes, my proud scrapes and scabs, and short mop of curls, Ramona was closer. Even Pippi. Or a boy's name would have worked, too. Billie was good. Andy, also.

My pregnant friends always come to me for ideas—by the time I was in my thirties, I'd already named ten babies, not one of them mine. Once, at a writer's colony, I told a table full of new friends that I was a veteran baby namer, while confessing the belief I'd been misnamed myself. A fellow writer said, "You're a Frankie." I remembered instantly that when I was twelve I had read *The Member of the Wedding* by Carson

McCullers and immediately recognized Frankie Addams's name as my own. Frankie is a name that matches my identity, one that stretches easily between feminine and masculine. Had it been mine from the start, I'm convinced I would have been better able to match the version of me others imagined. Which is why I want to pass down this name to my own child, a preemptive strike to remind myself to love the child who exists, not the child I expected. If she's girly, she can be Frances, and if she's boyish she can be Frankie. Frankie Bird. Maybe just Bird. My girl.

In the process of naming people's babies, a process that's spanned more than a decade, I've given away some names I love and then watched them grow too popular for me to use (Oliver, Declan). I've lived through at least three trend cycles, watching my secret list of coveted names pass by on embroidered knapsacks (Atticus, Scout, Mathilda); called out on the street (Vera! Milo! Arlo! Simon!); introduced to me in baby announcements (Agnes, Lulu, Iris, Maeve); and used in my own family (August, Charlie, Nico). All the names I've loved have been taken and used by others, but never Frankie. Frankie is mine.

And yet—I'm still no closer to having a real, human Frankie Bird of my own. It still feels like a joke that I'm forty. How can I be this old and feel...not grown-up? I'm waiting to feel the way everyone else my age seems to feel: capable enough for marriage and parenthood and career stability and mortgages. Almost all of my friends are married, even the ones I was sure never would be. Some are divorced and into their second marriages. A few have stepchildren. All my closest friends have children, even those who didn't want them. I've sat through every pregnancy announcement, always happy for them and sad for me. Even if they're pretending, even if some seem entirely incapable of being parents, spouses, or homeowners, they're doing it. They're either brave or stupid, jumping in before they're ready, but I can't. I don't want to accidentally fuck anyone up. I almost ruined Pilot's life, but not quite.

I'm not ready for another dog, and unlike some of my friends, I have no eggs in the freezer, but the drive to have a family isn't going away, and that's why I check the search box for "has kids" on OkCupid.

I write to a guy with a young daughter. He's so handsome, I decide I can forgive him for living in Jersey City.

Jersey City and I exchange emails and he sends me another photo of himself, one with his daughter, who's nine and very cute, but she looks sad. I forward the photo to my friend Laurie with a subject heading "Too old?" and she writes back that he's cute but looks like he might have a ponytail. I feel a splash of disappointment, but Jersey City and I decide to talk on the phone.

Jersey City's name is Javier. He has a type of accent I can't place; it's not exactly British, but it's not not-British. He's hilarious, and we make each other laugh instantly. When he tells me about himself, though, it's a NASCAR race of red flags flying everywhere, and I walk to the other side of the room, as if I could somehow sidestep them. He's forty-six, divorced from a woman he married impulsively, who left him with their daughter for a year. He doesn't have a steady source of income. Right now he's a cinematographer, although he really wants to be a filmmaker, maybe even a photographer; he's not sure. He's thinking he might even write a novel, although, of course, playwriting also appeals. My gut says to move on, and when I tell my friend Polly, she makes a face and says, "Hmm...not great for a forty-six-year-old man." But that's not what I want to hear, from Polly or my own gut. Besides, who am I to judge someone for not having his life together?

He calls me twice the next day and twice the day after that. It's a lot, and it's hard to concentrate on my own writing when he's calling and emailing so much. But then, on the fourth or fifth phone call of the week, it all clicks into place, and I know I should never listen to my gut again. He tells me his daughter's name: Frances. Frankie, for short.

*   *   *

Javier and I spend weeks talking on the phone. He's been at his summer house in Maine this whole time, but now he's coming in to meet me in New York. I'm excited but nervous. To make our meeting memorable, we decide to walk toward each other across Fourteenth Street. He'll start at Seventh Avenue and walk west, and I'll start at Eighth Avenue and walk east. When we think we see the other person, we'll stop. The idea is absurd and hilarious, and so right up my alley that I worry I'm setting myself up for a huge disappointment. I've looked at his picture a million times and concluded that his face is so excellent that, unlike mine, there's no wrong angle from which to look at him. Plus, his eyes squint when he smiles, and his smile reminds me of something embedded deeply in my subconscious that I can't access. Our phone conversations have levity but are satisfying, and although I have questions that gnaw at me, my overall sense is one of certainty that this could work out. But I know my pattern, and it's this: Out of the scraps of information I have before we even meet, I create a person who is perfect for me—and then when we do meet and he doesn't match my unrealistic expectations, my disappointment unglues and debilitates me. In other words, I do to others what was done to me all my life—I expect the person I've imagined, rather than getting to know the person who arrives.

We text beforehand:

> **Javier:** I'm almost there.
> **Me:** Me too.
> **Javier:** What if you hate what you see?
> **Me:** What if you hate what YOU see?
> **Javier:** I won't.

I'm sort of laughing as I walk toward Seventh Avenue, praying that this ugly dude isn't him, hoping that hot guy is. I keep walking, absurdly nervous and excited. Sweating, mildly shaky. Someone is about to walk into me, and I'm annoyed, looking over his shoulder and about to walk around him when he stops, smiling. I almost keep walking, but then: "It's me!" he says.

Oh no.

"Oh my God!" I say, forcing a smile. This can't be him. Why can't I ever meet someone my body doesn't reject on sight?

I force myself to hug him to hide my disappointment. His profile said "5′6″," but there's nothing five foot six about him. He's barely any taller than I am. It feels like they sent the wrong guy. He's dressed like a college kid: pageboy cap, checked short-sleeved button-down, jeans, and dark brown huarache sandals. He's wildly skinny. But the superficial concerns aren't the real problem. There's something worse that I'm preventing myself from acknowledging.

Clearly, he's not having the same reaction. "It's you! It's you!" he keeps saying as we walk toward Eighth Avenue, grabbing my arm and letting his fingers linger. When he touches me, something spoils in my belly. I am flushed with mistrust. Can't I just let myself meet someone I like? No matter whom I choose, my body never tells me what I want to hear. Besides, who says my body's even right? I try to ignore it.

We decide to have lunch, but before we go inside, he wants to kiss me.

"Right now?" I try not to flinch.

"Yeah, let's just get the first awkward kiss over with," he says.

I have no idea how to say no. I wonder if kissing him will help knock this terrible feeling out of me. "Okay. Awkward kiss, here we go."

We kiss and it's not terrible. Were he a bad kisser, I'd have no problem ending things now. So long as you have a tongue, there's no excuse for bad kissing. But he seems to know what he's doing, and now I'm stuck. I feel nauseated and disappointed and yet, oddly, I'm drawn to a certain sexiness about him.

During lunch, he's excessively affectionate, as if we're already a couple instead of two strangers weighing the possibility of a second date. He makes weird kissing faces at me, like he's suffering from affectionate Tourette's.

"How's your burger?" I ask.

"I've had better," he says, then proceeds to explain everything the cook did wrong. I don't own the restaurant, I just chose it, but still, I take the critique personally.

"You cook?"

"Well, yeah, I owned a restaurant."

"You did? I thought you were a cinematographer."

"I am. But my ex, Meredith, decided she wanted to own a restaurant, so that's what we did. When 9/11 happened, and Frankie was born, Meredith didn't want to stay in Jersey City anymore, so we moved to Maine, and opened the restaurant there."

I tried making small talk about the restaurant, and received instead a full rundown of Javier's codependent relationship with Meredith, who had apparently—after insisting on an open marriage—run off to Florida with Earl, one of their customers, leaving Javier alone with two-year-old Frankie.

"Whoa. That's brutal."

"Yeah, Frankie cried all the time, wailing that she missed her mama. I just let her cry and cry and told her it was good to feel her feelings and yeah, it was brutal." My feelings for him advance with this image, and for Frankie, a child I've never even met. There is an empty maternal space that my body wants to urgently fill. "Then Meredith came back, wanting Frankie, and I was like, no fucking way."

"So what now, do you even speak to Meredith? Does Frankie ever ask about her?" Even as I say it, I recognize the answer I am fishing for: that all he and Frankie want is a mama person.

"Oh yeah, we're on great terms. She's an amazing mother." I blink at him in disbelief. But he's not joking. "She wasn't then, but she is now. When Earl got a job in L.A., he and Meredith moved there, so Frankie and I followed." Does this man have no will of his own? "After a couple of years, Earl lost his job, so we all moved to this small island off the coast of Maine, where she spent a lot of time as a kid, and where my family has a house. But then Meredith left Earl for our friend Leo, and Earl moved out and now Leo is moving in. Great role model, huh?"

"Wow. That's a lot of information."

"Too much?" He looks worried but keeps going. "Now she's a clothing designer. You should check out her blog."

I hold my eyes before they roll of their own accord. "Maybe I will."

Since he has traveled all the way down from Maine to meet me, I feel obligated not to ditch him immediately, so when we leave the restaurant we walk around the Village for a while. Besides, he's not all bad. I like his energy. We can be friends, I think. Not what I'm looking for, but still. We go to Art Bar, where I haven't been since my early twenties.

With a drink in me, I am better equipped to handle his overly tactile nature, and by that I mean I ignore it. He tells me about a documentary he wants to make in Peru and invites me to come with him. I laugh it away. "I can't wait for you to meet Frankie," he says at one point. "You guys will love each other," he says at another.

It's too much, too fast, and as much as I'm not interested in him, Javi comes with something I want: a family. So instead of leaving, we order another round. We giggle and poke fun at the other awkward people on their first dates.

"Do you have time for a relationship?" he asks me, suddenly serious.

"Yeah," I say, because although I'm not certain he's for me, my insecurity doesn't want him to rule me out. "Do you?"

"Yes," he says. "Maybe. I think so. I don't know."

What kind of answer is that? Does he need to phone a friend? Now it's dark and I'm ready to go home, but because I'm drunk and don't want to hurt his feelings, I find myself making out with him.

As we say good-bye on the street, he gestures to the building behind us. A church. "Let's get married," he says.

"Ha-ha," I say. "Funny."

"I'm serious. Let's do it. It'd be fun."

Alert, alert, red flag, code red, alarm, alarm, abort mission. "I'm Jewish. My rabbi would be very mad."

This fast-forwarding reminds me of Peter, and I know it's a danger sign, though my drunk brain can't remember why. Isn't having someone who wants to commit a good thing? That's the problem with red flags, I think to myself. People tell you how to spot them, but they never tell you what they mean. We part with a promise to see each other again, one that I promise myself I won't keep.

At home, I hop onto Petfinder to cheer myself up. Dogs don't lie about their height and talk only about their exes. Dogs aren't uncertain about their ability to make time for you. Dogs don't say all the right things on the first date, though I suppose dogs will try to marry you within hours of meeting. I pull out my notebook to keep track of the dogs I like and I come across a message.

"You are so super cute and I feel blessed to have met you." He must have written it while I was in the bar bathroom. Oh, man. This guy is not boyfriend material. But it sure is nice to feel wanted. And Frankie—isn't Frankie a sign?

June 1981

Dr. Rivka Golod

<u>Summary of Test Results</u>

Her written story was excellent in terms of organization and content. She was asked to write a story that started with "If I lived on an island…" Amanda named the island "Isolation Island." She enumerated all the activities she would do on this island, and wrote that if she got lonely, she would peel birch bark off a tree, build a raft, and float home. I wonder if Amanda feels separate from other kids for some reason.

Jinx

WHEN FOURTH GRADE STARTED, Etan had been missing for four months, and Baba and Melissa had been dead for two. Although, to me, Melissa had been dead only two weeks. Everyone kept giving me copies of *Bridge to Terabithia*, even my mom. It's a good book, but I don't know how I'm supposed to feel about it, since the girl who dies is a tomboy like me and nothing like Melissa.

I keep finding out information that no one told me about my best friend. My mom says she missed most of third grade because she was sick. She had a brain tumor, which was what Holly, Daniel, and David's mom had. Why hadn't anyone told me this? Melissa died while I was at sleepaway camp, *just like their mom did*. How was I supposed to protect her if I didn't know what was going on? I would have forced myself to sleep at her house and save her from dying in her sleep.

If I don't learn how to make myself brave, I'll never be able to save Etan or any of the other people who need me. I decided my first brave thing was going to be telling my friends and teacher that Melissa died, but then the night before school started, my mom called and told everyone, and then told my friends not to mention it because it would upset me. Now everyone knows, but no one will even talk about it with me. When I'm at school, Melissa didn't die, but when I'm not at school, she did.

I didn't want to start fourth grade knowing I'd be leaving Melissa behind, but I didn't know how to stop any of it. I stuck by Imogen as often as our schedules allowed. Even though I was away at camp all summer, Imogen and I still had the same taste in boys, and we still wore the same tomboy clothes and liked to climb trees and eat french fries and tell each other funny stories; but even now, a few weeks in, there is a part of me that is still sitting on the curb, staring at my knees.

I count how many times I see Eddie during the day and turn it into good luck. Kara is in seventh grade now, which is in a separate building a few blocks away. I miss her. I go to Marie between every class because I don't feel well. She lets me lick envelopes and put stamps on them. Melissa's death isn't softening into old news; I feel it over and over again, hitting me fresh a hundred times a day. Even when I'm telling Imogen about my camp boyfriend, and the night I glowed in the dark, I am realizing that all that time Melissa was already dead. How do I apologize for not knowing? Or get rid of the flashes of shame that splash when I think of how carefree I was while Melissa was in bed dying? Imogen wishes she could have gone to camp with me, but I can't say she should come next year, because I know I am never going to camp again.

Our classroom looks right into a playground, which was a gift from the parents of a sixth grader who died. I watch the fifth graders play in it, tense when they jump and roughhouse, concerned at their unconcern for the dead boy. There is a plaque and a bench with his name, Joshua, and the dates of his birth and death. We don't get to play in the garden until fifth grade, next year. I don't know why it's a privilege to play in a dead boy's garden. No one should play in it. They should leave the dead boy alone, but no one ever does. No one but me seems to even remember it's his.

People say life continues, that you move on, but I don't want life to continue, and I don't want people to move on without me. If I'm not here, I want them gone, too, but here I am living, continuing on, right under Melissa's and Baba's noses. I should not be alive because I have killed people. I left and people died and now I am a jinx and also a murderer. I never want to leave again. Seasons pass through the garden every year, and we get older, but the dead boy stays the same age. Time swats the days, one faster than the next, and Etan turns seven and then I'm ten. Two years older than Melissa, who is still eight. My stepmother has a second baby, Rebecca, and now I'm no longer the youngest girl uptown. Even though I'm afraid of weekends with my dad, I still want him to love me. I don't want to be replaced, but I can already feel it happening. I feel jealous of the new baby, of the way my dad looks when he talks about her. Does he make those same eye faces when he talks about me? I want to tell Melissa all of this. I want her to know that I'm sorry. I waited for her, but time rolled me up with the days and dragged me along; I couldn't stop the clocks from running, or my birthday from coming, and I feel guilty. I still don't know what she looked like when she died. Everything is moving, and life goes on. Is that true for Etan, too, even if we don't know where he is? Does he know where he is?

Now I am in fifth grade, and our new classroom looks down onto the dead boy's garden. They arrest a man named Calvin DeVyer, who had kidnapped two boys, but it turns out he didn't take Etan. I wonder what happened to Joshua. At recess, we clank down the stairs to play. I try to run softly in case Joshua's buried under my feet. When we play tag I worry I'll accidentally breathe his death into my lungs. No one ever talks about Joshua, not the teachers, not the older students who knew him. All I know about him is the playground. I don't know what he looked like or whether we'd have been friends, but still it makes me sad that all that's left of him is a bench and trampled dirt.

My desk is next to the window and sometimes during Expression and Health I daydream down onto the dead boy's flowers. His death takes up the whole garden. Soon I will be older than him, too. Time is counted for all the years you've lived, and it's counted for how long you've been dead, but I don't know how much time exists between missing and dying. Etan has been missing for so long, it's become who he is, and people seem to accept it, like it's a broken arm that will mend and not a mystery no one has solved. If I had made the world, I would stop everything from continuing until he's been found. I would stop school and learning. I would stop playdates and recesses until the world is returned to the way it was before Melissa died and Etan disappeared, but nothing stops. Am I accidentally erasing people by continuing on?

I try to pay attention to what the teacher is saying. Something about geography, something about continents and borders. The world is not the same as it was, so why do we act the same as we did before? Something about founders and government. Even my mom moved on. She still shops and laughs and lives her life like it's okay that her father died. If I died, would she forget and carry on like always? Something about flags and history. When I left people died, but I was here when Etan disappeared and I still couldn't save him. What if I'm not a saver at all? What if I'm only a killer? Suddenly, a new worry takes hold: What if Etan is dead? Horror drops a cloth over my head and for a minute the world goes black. Maybe other people are moving on because they think he's dead, too. Or worse, maybe in the same way my mom knew all along that Melissa's sickness could kill her, people know Etan is dead and just aren't telling the kids.

*   *   *

The kids in my class are changing and growing, forming cliques that Imogen and I aren't a part of, and my body is staying still, the same as it was last year and the year before. Maybe my body is staying behind like Melissa, Etan, and the dead boy even though I'm alive. Maybe my body stopped growing as punishment for not saving anyone. My mom and Jimmy start going out a lot, now that we're older and my siblings can watch me, which is why I start leaving her notes on her pillow. She answers them and leaves them outside my door.

"I'm always the smallest one in the class and I don't like it!" I write.

"I'll make an appointment with Dr. Fine," she writes back.

Dr. Fine, my pediatrician, weighs and measures me, then pulls out the growth chart to mark where I am. The last two times I've been in the same place. Four foot two and sixty-four pounds. The chart, Dr. Fine explained when she pulled it out years ago, is where all the children of the world are measured. It says who's average, below average, or above average. Right in the middle is where the lucky kids land, but I'm not even on the chart for kids my age. I'm all the way down in the seven- and eight-year-old sections. What I wouldn't give to be average. There are other sheets for other things that tell her how a person should be, but right now, I care just about the sheet that means average. "Am I close?"

"You are exactly the same." This is what she always says. I don't know how to ask her if not growing could be a curse for being a jinx. When I ask if I'll ever grow, she just says, "That's the hope," but that's not an answer. Time moves everyone forward, but it's always forgetting to bring me.

"Is there anything we can be doing?" my mom asks. "Is there something she can take?"

"Is she eating her vegetables?" Dr. Fine asks my mom. My mom's face carries the question as she turns to me, as though she doesn't know the answer.

"Yes, I eat my vegetables." I am annoyed my mom doesn't know that. It means she's not paying attention.

Dr. Fine sends me to get a lollipop near the waiting room, but instead I wait outside and cup my ear to the door while she and my mom talk in private. It's all a low mumble. I can hear my mom asking questions about glands and thyroids, endocrines and hormones, but I can't hear the answers. Am I ever going to be average?

That week our teacher, Zola, gathers us together to explain about a test that fifth graders across the country all have to take simultaneously. Now I am paying attention. I do not like tests and don't want to take one, especially in a room with every other fifth grader in America. My eye starts pulsing like a little heartbeat, and suddenly I can't breathe. I am not getting enough air. The room spins, and Imogen slices her hand across her neck, which means she can see I'm dying.

The test is called the ERB and is three days long. I don't want to sleep at school! We shouldn't forget our number 2 pencils, Zola is saying. If we can bring more than one, that would be good. Everyone nods their heads, like they know what a number 2 pencil is. Is this information everyone but me was born with? Even Imogen seems to understand. What if I accidentally bring in a number 4 pencil, or a number 7? What if my mother doesn't know where to buy them? I am so worried about the pencil that I miss everything else.

"You want to score very high on this test. If you score below a certain number, you could get left back a grade, and you don't want that, do you?" Zola asks with an eye grin.

I didn't know being left back was a real thing. I thought it was just one of my own fears, the ones everyone tells me will never come true. The bad things they say can't happen keep happening.

I can't take this test. If staying back is something that can happen, I know it will happen to me. My body is being held back, so the rest of me will be also. What if I open the test and the words are in another language? What if they aren't words at all, but shapes or symbols we're supposed to turn into words, and I don't have the right number 2 pencils? What if I'm the only one who doesn't understand?

When you're left back a grade everyone moves on without you, and you stay in place like a dead person. Your old classmates will see you sitting through the exact same lessons, still with Zola as your teacher. You'll be the oldest in your class, and at birthday parties you'll say, "I remember when I was your age." You'll have nothing in common with anyone anymore. No one will be your friend. I press my fingers into the side of my head. What if this test tells the truth about me, that I'm a part not of this world, but of another?

My mom says not to worry—no one is holding me back a grade, and Zola was exaggerating and doesn't know what she's talking about. Even so, there is a halo of dread staticking off me the morning of the ERB as I walk to school. My pencil case is filled with number 2 pencils—ten more than I need, just in case. I try not to think of all the things that came true when my mom said they wouldn't.

While Zola leads us single file down to the cold auditorium, and the other kids rush to find their names, I am still upstairs in our classroom hanging my jacket in my cubby. Zola was too fast. I still don't know what this test is about, why we're taking it, or what it means. How will I know what to do? Zola introduces us to a man named Proctor, and now it's just us and Proctor, who is not a friendly-looking man. I browse the room for Imogen, to catch her eye for comfort, but she's up front. A thick flutter pushes up beneath my skin, wedging my ribs, making it hard to breathe. Before I can pass out or have an aneurysm, someone calls for a taxi. It's Proctor, who removes his whistle fingers from his mouth.

"Every section is timed. You are to follow the instructions carefully and listen to everything I say. I will not be answering any questions. The test is not difficult. You should be able to figure everything out quite easily. Is that clear?"

My classmates mumble yes.

"You must think hard and you must think fast. What you're entitled to, you'll get. Do you understand?" I don't nod.

Proctor sits on the edge of the stage. "You may begin."

Hundreds of hands flip over the short stacks. On the other side is something I've never seen before. Bubbles. Each row with a different letter of the alphabet. I don't know how to use this form. All around me, my classmates are rubbing their pencils, massaging fresh squeaky tips into the circles. Proctor strolls up and down the aisles, hands behind his back. Kelvin and Manu turn one way, then the other, trying to make eye contact with Pietro, who seems to have no questions, because he's filling in the forms like he uses them all the time. What am I supposed to do? Fill the circles in, or not? And which ones?

Proctor claps, startling the entire front row. "Pencils down."

I put my pencil down without having scratched out one lead mark.

"You may open the test booklet. When you are finished reading the paragraph, please look up."

I wait until everyone else has done this, just in case I didn't hear correctly and then I open mine, too.

ANALOGIES

    1. Blue : sky :: _____: grass
    2. Leg : knee :: _____ : elbow

"You may begin."

I have never heard the word "ANALOGIES," but it seems like ANALOGIES are words that want to be sentences but aren't. I glance at Kelvin, hoping to find him flopped and weeping, rocking back and forth, but he stays calm, pencil tapping against the ruled paper in his blue book, thinking and considering. Kelvin is the dumbest person in the grade, but maybe now I'm the dumbest person in my grade. Maybe I have a brain tumor.

I turn the page quickly, to see what's next, and it's one long stretch of ANALOGIES like dead animals on the highway, bloody and endless until "STOP" appears, three entire pages later. I look at the clock. I have thirty-nine minutes left. I circle the first words I see and vow never, ever, to think about this test again. Zola said this is a test to see how much we know.

I don't know anything.

STOP.

Why don't I know anything?

The next test is thirty minutes, and we are to think hard and think fast.

STOP.

Something in my chest feels sticky. No matter how many times I wipe my hand on my corduroys, they won't stop sweating. The number 2 pencil slips from my hand. Everyone turns to stare at me. I have forgotten how to breathe.

1. How many cents will 8 oranges cost at 3 cents each? Answer: _____. Maybe I should go to the nurse.
2. David earned $3.50 in June, $2.25 in July, and $1.50 in August.

How much did he earn in all? Answer: _____. Maybe I have the flu or leprosy. I need to call my mom.

3. Frank bought 3 two-cent postage stamps and 13 one-cent stamps. How much did he pay for all? Answer: _____. I am so tired. I just want to put my head down and rest. Just sleep until this is done. If I'm left back a grade, does that mean I'll come to school tomorrow and be sent to fourth grade, or does it mean that next year I'll start fifth grade again?

I think I need to go to the hospital.

"Pencils down!" Proctor says. "You have thirty minutes for the next section. You may begin."

I put my hand on my heart like I'm doing the Pledge of Allegiance, but I'm telling my heart not to turn off. Now we have to put words in missing spaces. There are right words and wrong words and we need to think carefully, which means guessing, but how am I supposed to know what right word they were thinking of? I am not a psychic or a mind reader! I can feel every second crawling against my skin.

Eventually, it's pencils down. There's a near stampede, everyone is racing away, out of the auditorium, to the cafeteria, and quickly, before Proctor changes his mind about the lunch break. During lunch, everyone is saying how easy the test is, and you'd have to be a moron to do badly. I am a moron. Pam says she was well-prepared, and a few other kids say they were, too, and Marlo pulls out flash cards. How did I miss that part of school? I am not hungry. I am curled inside a very small room inside myself, hoping no one can see that I don't know anything.

After lunch, it's back to testing. Words switch places with one another on the page, and the room is growing dark at the edges. How did everyone prepare, and when? The smartest kids hold their arms around their blue books, afraid their right answers will slip off and roll to the feet of the wrong-answer kids.

I am alone.

*   *   *

A month or so later, we are decorating the stage for the middle school production of *Oliver*, when Pilar comes racing in.

"Did you guys hear about Kelvin?" she asks.

"Was he kidnapped?" I stand, worried.

"No. He has to stay back a grade," Pilar tells us. I can't believe she's laughing at him. "He did really badly on the ERBs."

I'm about to ask how she knows, when she begins bragging about her score.

"I should skip a grade, because I scored really high."

"I scored high, too," Imogen says, proud.

"I'm in the eighty-ninth percentile for math and ninety-fourth in verbal," Pilar counters. "What'd you get?"

I don't even remember a test called verbal, and I have no idea what those percentiles mean. How do they know their scores?

"Eightieth percentile in math and seventieth in verbal," Imogen says.

Pilar rolls her eyes. "I thought you said you did *well*." She turns to me. "What'd *you* get?"

"I don't know," I say.

"How could you not know?"

"I didn't know we got results."

"It was a test; of course there were results, you retard."

I look at Imogen, confused and hurt by Pilar, but she just shrugs.

"I'm not a retard," I say to Pilar.

"You might be. Why else wouldn't your parents tell you how you scored? Maybe you got zero percentile."

"I did not!"

"How do you know? You didn't even know there were results!"

"My mom didn't say anything," I tell her.

"That's because your mom coddles you like a baby. That's what my mom says."

"She does not!"

"Does too! No one else's mom sits with them in the classroom, no one else's mom gets them out of school overnighters, or out of slumber parties. Your mom does everything for you."

Now I'm infuriated, and also mortified. I always assumed no one else could see my fears, or tears, or even my mom sitting in the classroom with me, and now I am humiliated and angry that other people—and their parents!—know my secrets and are judging me for them.

"I'm not a baby," I tell Pilar.

"Your mom probably thinks you are, and that's why she didn't tell you. You're a baby *and* a retard!"

Why doesn't my mom tell me the results for anything? Is Pilar right, and my mom thinks I'm stupid? Does she think I won't understand my own scores? Suddenly, I'm furious at my mother for protecting me from things she doesn't want me to know.

Imogen's head is traveling back and forth between us, but she doesn't defend me. I know she'll say she couldn't read our lips fast enough, but her face is red and I can tell she's embarrassed for me. When Pilar leaves, though, and I finally look at Imogen, she's holding back tears.

"What's the matter?" I ask.

She's staring at her shredded Adidas. "I stayed back a grade."

"You did?" I ask, just as I remember her telling me that first day of third grade that it was her second time with Faith.

She nods. "I'm not a retard, am I?" she asks.

"No," I say. "One hundred percent definitely not."

I'm overcome with anger and resentment at my mother for doing everything for me instead of showing me how, for protecting me from the realities of the world instead of telling me the truth. I'm going to go home tonight and ask her for my test scores. Except: I'm angry and resentful at myself, too, for needing it. The more I think about it, the more I realize I can never get a straight answer from my mom that has to do with my own self. When I ask her why she and my dad divorced, she says it's none of my business. When I ask her what Dr. Fine says after a visit, she says I don't need to worry about it. She didn't tell me

Melissa died until I asked her. She probably won't tell me my scores even if I do ask.

Then again, she has always known when something was the right thing to do. And she's hardly ever wrong. So maybe telling me bad news *isn't* the right thing to do, and it's Pilar's parents who are bad parents. Maybe other people's parents don't know how to do the right thing.

June 1981

Dr. Rivka Golod

<u>Summary of Test Results</u>

    While it may sound like Amanda has a block to learning and thinking, I'm not sure this is the total picture. My feeling is that it is truly difficult for Amanda to do certain kinds of cognitive tasks and that this was probably more the case when she was younger. Moreover, it does not appear that Amanda developed adequate compensatory mechanisms for learning, possibly because it became convenient and/or satisfactory, for whatever reasons, not to be so "smart," so to speak.

Yes, No, Maybe, I Don't Know

I START DATING JAVIER. Despite the fact that I've vowed to not repeat the mistakes of the past, to listen to my gut—which says Javier is not my guy—the rest of me can't decide. My plan is to keep it casual, refuse to be exclusive, but I am unprepared for the speech he gives me on our third date.

He doesn't want to see anyone else, just me, and don't I want that also? I do not. Yet it's also unthinkable that I would tell him anything other than what he wants to hear. I am convinced that any rejection, no matter how small, will catalyze in others the same thing it sets off in me, a pain so deeply personal that it sends me to bed for days. I say yes because I am terrified to hurt someone else so profoundly.

My hyperaccommodation of other people's feelings is a deeply wired reflex that feels impossible to unlearn. Separation anxiety fills me with such grief that I am pained on behalf of others; I refuse to cause someone else anxiety. And so, when Javier asks to be exclusive, although neither of us knows to whom we're committing, I say yes when I really mean "I have no idea." I was taught it's charitable to protect people from their feelings rather than help them face them.

One evening a few months into our relationship, Javier and I are in his apartment in Jersey City, where he's cooking dinner. His apartment feels like we're on a small boat, inside of a secret world, and I love the sense of containment, though it's hard to completely relax into it with a massive painting, created by his ex-wife, looming over the dining room table.

"So listen," he says. "I don't think Frankie wants to live with Meredith after this year. I have an idea: What if I sell this place and use the money to buy a house upstate for all of us to live? We'll find her a school, have another kid, and I'll shoot movies while you hold down the fort."

I look at him. "I have to hold down the fort?"

"Yeah. I have to make the money."

"I have to make money, too."

He offers an indulgent smile and waits.

"Okay, fine. I'll hold down the fort!" I say, ever easygoing. "That sounds great."

Do I really believe that? I don't think so; I'm not at all sure Javier is really right for me. But he makes me laugh harder than anyone. Something about him feels comforting, familiar, enough that I disregard the red flags. Do I care that he's forty-six without a stable source of income? That he's passive and ambitionless and controlled by his ex-wife and also maybe afraid of her? That he's hard to engage in conversation? That he's vaguely New Agey and says "blessed" and "love and light"? That I've never met his child, who is one of the reasons I chose him? In our best moments, he's sexy and funny. Everything he's saying is something I want to hear: He wants to put down roots, to have another baby.

Besides, I'm forty. My eggs are probably so old they have neck wattles. So I pretend to him, and to myself, that this is the most amazing idea I've ever heard.

He's beaming. "Is it time to meet Frankie now?" he asks. He's been asking this since our first date, but I've always hesitated. Kids usually love me, and I love kids, but I don't want to take this leap of meeting his child without first being serious about her father. I've been a stepkid, and though I loved Jimmy, the dynamics are fraught. I love the idea of having a baby with Javi, but then again I love the idea of having a baby with anyone. I'm about to tell him to wait; I don't think I've thought this through all the way. But then he smiles at me again, pleading.

"Yeah, I think so."

Next thing I know, we've made plans to go apple-picking upstate.

A couple of weeks later, we meet at Eddie's house to pick up Lili, my nine-year-old niece, who will join us on the excursion. I'm more nervous than I thought I'd be, since I really want to get this right. I've bought Frankie "I'm so happy to meet you" books (*When You Reach Me* and *Mrs. Frisby and the Rats of NIMH*) and a card that took me much too long to compose. It reads, "I'm so glad to finally meet your dad's favorite person. I hope you haven't read these, but if you have, please don't throw apples at my head." As soon as she walks in I can see that Frankie is small like her dad, with wide-set eyes, full lips, and straight, caramel-colored hair. She's both beautiful and soulful, but when I try to greet her there's a look in her eye that makes me anxious. Is she bratty, contemptuous, or just shy? I can't tell what's wrong, but I know it's me.

At least the card makes her laugh. I try to relax as she and Lili giggle happily together in the backseat, instant friends. Javier tries to catch my eye as he drives, but I don't know how to fake an appreciation for Frankie that I don't feel. At the apple farm, we get our baskets and start picking. Frankie is serious and quiet. She climbs up into the trees and yanks apples down, inspecting them carefully. She walks ahead of everyone, even Lili, and when I try to help her reach a branch, she turns on me and snaps, "I can do it myself."

I choke back my disappointment. When Javi told me about her, he presented her as a bucket filled with love and affection, said that she climbs onto the laps of everyone who walks through her front door. Clearly, I don't qualify. I remind myself that I gave Javi extra chances, so I need to do the same with Frankie. But what if she and I hate each other? Even though I chose Javi in part to have a child in my life, now I worry that she's going to come between us, prevent Javi and me from starting the family I so desperately want. I bat away my dread, but it's too late. On the drive back home, Javier turns to me.

"I'm so glad you two met. Isn't she magical? Isn't she the most incredible kid ever?"

"She's pretty great," I lie. This is a fucking catastrophe.

We finally reach Javier's sister Valentina's apartment in Manhattan, where we're dropping Frankie off to spend the night. Valentina is lovely: earthy and maternal. She embraces Frankie and Javier, and even Lili and me, and insists that we make ourselves at home, though we plan on staying for only a moment. In the living room, Frankie and Valentina huddle together and then turn to us, smiling.

"Frankie is showing me the books and your card," Valentina says.

Frankie is beaming up at me. "I didn't throw any apples at her head!" She doubles over with laughter. I'm thrilled that my card meant something to her after all, that she does think I'm special, the same way her dad wants me to think she's special.

But even so, I'm confused by her, or at least by the difference between Javi's description and my experience of her. She's not sunny and lighthearted; she's intense and thoughtful. How does he see such an opposite version of his own child? This incongruence stirs another flash of anxiety. When I was little there was a version of me that felt out of alignment with who I really was. The adults' version had me learning disabled, and the other version—mine—had me devoured by mental anguish. Do Javi and I look at the world and see different truths? Will this always be true with the people I depend on?

When it's time to leave, Frankie throws her arms around me and squeezes hard.

"I liked meeting you, Amanda," she says. "You're a good girlfriend for my dad. Perhaps we'll meet again."

I laugh. "Perhaps we will."

*   *   *

Two months later, Javier invites me to spend Christmas with his family in Massachusetts. A regular Jewish Christmas at my mom's in the garden is regularly fun, but each year as my siblings' families expand and take on their own traditions and the garden kids marry and procreate,

I grow more self-conscious about appearing to others as though I have not broken free from my family of origin, mortified that they can see my child-self got her wish to never leave home. When the day ends and I return home to my apartment, I throw myself onto my bed and cry myself to sleep in my clothes. I'm excited to experience a different version of me during the holidays, in another town. Frankie will be there and so will all seven of Javi's siblings. He and Frankie drive in from Maine and pick me up at the train station.

"You're going to meet my whole family, even Abi and Abu!" Frankie greets me, excited. "Are you nervous?"

"I am," I admit, taken off-guard by the degree of her empathy.

Javier's parents' house is lively and festive. Music is playing and everyone is chattering affectionately in Spanish. They welcome me like an old friend. People roll in and out of the kitchen; food is cooking and Abu is sitting on the couch strumming the guitar with a crooked hand. Frankie takes out her trumpet and screeches "We Three Kings." We all cheer.

"Frankie told us about the books you bought her and the card you made," Abi says, coming out of the kitchen. Frankie is bobbing her head up and down, yes yes yes, and we beam at each other.

We drink, we laugh. When Javier goes outside to smoke, Frankie and I talk about how we can get him to quit and then come up with an endless stream of nicknames for each other. Dinner is a feast, and everyone is trying to teach me Spanish phrases, and everything I imagined for my family of choice is occurring right now at this moment. I feel equal. And I feel at home. I want these people as my in-laws. I want Javier and Frankie as my family. I want this.

That night, the family gathers around while Abu plays guitar and they sing Christmas carols and Argentine songs, and I'm in heaven. After some drinks, and people have gone to bed, it's just Javier, Abi, Abu, and me in the living room.

"Javi," Abi says to him.

"Sí, Mama?"

"I hope this is your last girlfriend ever."

"Me too," he says.

"Me three," I say.

"Good!" Abu says. "You're the one we want."

An ecstatic glow radiates inside me. To hear how wanted I am, by all these people, two of whom I've just met, feels like concretized peace. The family I've just realized I want is saying it wants me, too. But now that I've identified the people with whom I want to belong, I become terrified someone will change their mind and take it all away.

Javier tucks Frankie into her bed on the couch and reads her a story, then calls me over to say good night. I perch next to Frankie's pillow.

"I think my family really likes you," she says. "You fit in well. Do you like them?"

"I love your family, Frankie."

She smiles and then gives me a hug. "Good night, Amanda. I'm so glad you're here."

I kiss her forehead and walk back to Javier, glowing harder than I ever did at camp.

"Told you," he says. "She's magic."

"You know, I think you may be right." The whole family might be magic.

*   *   *

On the way back to New York, we stop at a café and Javier runs in to get us coffee and breakfast. Frankie is playing with her brand-new iPod Touch in the backseat, and suddenly a wretched, foul-garbage smell settles in front of my face. I cough, horrified.

"Oh my God. Frankie! Was that you?"

"Silent but deadly. Better get used to it." She laughs.

I laugh, too, harder than the occasion calls for, because I know she's telling me that she wants me to stay, and she knows I will.

Listen Carefully and Say Exactly What I Say

AFTER ERBS AND THE hearing test, I get another eye test, and then my mom makes an appointment with a special doctor on the Upper West Side. I don't know what the hearing doctor said, but I assume he played the tape of me for everyone, heard all the wrong things in me, and finally called an expert to tell us the name of what is wrong with me. Dr. Rivka is the expert. My mom says she's a specialist who is good at solving problems. For the first time since the hearing doctor, I let myself feel hope again that someone is finally going to locate my worries and find the pill to get rid of them. I don't even mind if the hearing doctor did find things wrong that are worse than worries, because I have a meeting with an expert and she will cure all of me.

The waiting room is small and beige. Everything is one color, and it feels like we're sitting inside a mushroom. My babysitter, Margie, and I sit down on the couch and wait. She pulls out a pad and a pen and starts a game of hangman. I can barely contain my excitement at the new me. I know that solving my problems won't make me look any different, but I still imagine the fixed, calm version of myself as taller, with straight, glossy blond hair that swings when I walk.

Dr. Rivka is short and bosomy, and we're not that far into the game when she comes out and shakes our hands. I follow her down a short hall, reminding myself that when I walk back down this hall after my appointment, my worries won't be clouding up my heart any longer. I'll be able to hear people when they talk, and go to slumber parties, and I won't be afraid to leave my mom. When I'm solved I'll be able to stay an entire weekend at my dad's without making my mom rescue me. Then I can have a life just like everyone else.

I don't know how long it will take, or what's going to happen. My mom didn't tell me that part. I just know that soon, maybe even in ten minutes, I'll be cured, the way I was those few days after camp, but this time it will last forever. My excitement feels like Christmas on the inside of me. Even if it's two shots in the arm, I'm going to be brave. Even if it's medicine that tastes like the Son of Sam's diarrhea, I'll drink it. There's no examining table in her office, no scale or even a table with medical supplies. That's when I realize that Dr. Rivka doesn't have stethoscope ponytails hanging down either side of her like my pediatrician, Dr. Fine.

"Take a seat there, Amanda." She points to a low, white table.

I sit as she unzips a soft leather briefcase with gold-embossed initials that say "WAIS-R," which are not the initials for Rivka Golod. Strange markings cling to the dry-erase board, and a tang of worry zippers through me. How can a person who isn't careful enough to wipe all the letters off a board find and erase all the wrong things in me? She can't find what she's looking for and starts emptying the briefcase onto the table. Behind her, I notice a long wooden table lined with different dolls. On the table now, she's stacked thin navy blue boxes, a straight ruler, pencils, scrap paper, a stopwatch, and a cardboard cutout of a little boy. She settles into a chair across from me. One leg over the other, glasses on, and then she's still, staring at me. I don't know why she isn't saying anything. Am I supposed to say something? Should I ask her how she is? A fever of sweat breaks out on me as I realize I'm supposed to know what to do, and I don't. The longer I'm quiet, the more uncomfortable she'll get, and soon waves of sweat will break on her, and she won't know what the terrible feeling inside her means, or how to get rid of it. But I'll know. The feeling is that she's embarrassed for me that I don't know something I'm supposed to know. She takes a deep, loud breath, and after she exhales she leans forward.

"Are you ready?" she asks.

Soda bubbles boil and fizz in my belly. How can I be ready? Ready for what? But she is waiting for an answer, so I make a tiny nod. My insides begin to burn as a very skinny crack splits me down the middle, peels me apart like a fingernail separating two stuck pages, making two me's. One me doesn't know what to be ready for; the other me pretends she does.

"Very well. I am going to ask you a series of questions, and I want you to answer them as best you can. All right?"

I nod. Leaving Mom, going to school, sleeping over anywhere, night-time, bedtime, going to my dad's, going on class trips, leaving New York, when my mom goes out to dinner or on vacation, getting a brain tumor, dying of cancer…Why didn't I write all my worries down? She can't fix ones I can't remember. I don't see a needle, which is good. Maybe she'll just say magic potion words, wand a stick over my head, and poof, I'll be normal! She opens one of the books and turns over a Boggle timer.

"Are you a little boy or a little girl?"

Surprise knocks everything out of my brain, numbing my face. Does she not know the answer or does she think I don't know the answer? Could she be mistaking me for someone else? Should I tell her she's made a mistake? If I say nothing, then when Dr. Rivka realizes for herself she's been giving the wrong person a test, she'll wonder what's wrong with me because I didn't correct her. But if I humiliate her, she'll never fix me. What should I do? She looks at the sand timer. Oh no, she's timing me!

"A girl," I say.

"How many days are in a week?"

This is a school question. I'm not here for school questions; I'm here for worry questions. Did she forget that she's supposed to take my worries out? Did my mom forget to tell her to fix me?

"Seven?" I ask. Oh no, it might be five! Maybe she's not counting weekends!

"How many seconds in a minute?"

Wait, was seven right? She looks at the sand timer. Allegra's time game flashes in my head.

"Sixty!" I say.

"How many minutes in an hour?"

How many questions like this is she going to ask me? Why is she asking me school questions, from way back in first grade? My mom is going to be "absolutely furious" when she finds out that Dr. Rivka did not do her job. My mom does not like when people make mistakes, which is why I try hard never ever to make a mistake. That's why I don't put away the dishes, or help with dinner—because I never cut the carrots the exact way she showed me. She gets very frustrated because now she has to cut them herself. I can't do anything right. I want to do only right things. Sometimes even when I wait until I am positive I know how to do something, my mom says I did it wrong.

"Sixty?"

"What is a month?"

This is the most terrible appointment I've ever had in my life. This is not why I'm here. She should be draining out all my blood and giving me new, better blood, listening to my chest and giving me vomit potion to drink. She's supposed to be fixing the feelings part of me, not the school part.

"A month? A month is like February or March."

These questions are sounding like she thinks I'm dumb.

"What is a year?"

Does she think I'm dumb? Is that my problem?

"Do you want me to repeat the question?" Dr. Rivka asks.

"A year is like a stretched-out month. A year is a very long time."

Does my mom? Did Zola? Do all my teachers? I am mortified. Embarrassed for myself that I didn't know I was dumb until now.

"What time of day is p.m.?"

My butterflies turn on. I don't want to think about the night.

"The time of p.m. is when you have to go to bed."

"What time of day is a.m.?"

"That is when you have to leave your mom and go to school."

I don't want to know who thinks I'm dumb. Imogen? Did Melissa? Is that why I couldn't tell time? I thought my worries were covering up my brain, but maybe really it was dumbness that was getting in my way.

"Are you normal or a reptile?" Dr. Rivka asks.

I'm not normal. This is why she's asking me this question. People don't think I'm normal. I'm dumb and abnormal. If I say I'm normal, will she laugh, slap her knee, and say, "No you're not, you fucking idiot!"

"Do you need me to repeat the question?"

"I . . . I . . . Am I normal?" I ask, floating away so that only the body of me hears her answer.

She smiles and stifles a little laugh. My blood burns around my bones.

"No, mammal. A mammal or a reptile?" she says.

Now, instead of relieved, I'm embarrassed for mishearing her. "Oh," I tell my laces. I feel myself lift because I know we learned this at school, but now I can't remember what each one means because I'm so mortified and also there is too much pressure in my brain and now all I'm worried about is the pressure and making a mistake in hearing her, and hoping my body is not going to die in front of her if I make another mistake.

"Am I a mammal?" I ask.

"Let's move on," she says.

Am I a mammal?

The questions keep coming, and she never tells me the answer or says yes or no; she just keeps holding up cards and pulling out puzzles and mazes and asking questions. Here is the first card. Can you tell me what is wrong with this picture? I can't believe I'm so dumb that all this time I didn't even realize it.

I look at the clock and feel a flump of dread and fear.

"What about this one?"

How is it still 3:55?

Time is changing outside and soon the sky will grow older and darken with age, but in here with Dr. Rivka, time stands still.

"All right. Are you ready to try something new?"

I nod. Does everyone know I'm dumb, or is it just the adults?

Out the window the sky is being blinded by night and I swell with early-day darkness, that terrible late-afternoon longing. The questions come at me, one after another. What do you do with a stamp? Why do people have stoves? What do thirsty people do? Why should people take baths? The questions melt into one another, word-lava oozing without sense. Why do doctors and nurses give people shots but don't read the newspaper about traffic signs for farmers not needed in cities who picks up the garbage at school for fire drills why people spell trouble the dictionary reason for one paper or public education for free houses in the country?

I am homesick at school, and even when I am home I ache for my mom, missing her terribly even when she's right there. I know this isn't normal. A person can't miss what's there. Something is very wrong with me. What if Dr. Rivka never lets me go home? What if Margie got fed up waiting and left? What if she went outside and got lost and now she's dead? My worries tangle like paper dolls.

"Listen carefully," Dr. Rivka says, "and say exactly what I say."

I lean toward her so that I can hear even the pauses between letters. I worry I won't hear her, even though she's not far from me. What if my ears break off when I need them?

"The string on my kite is broken."

"The string on my kite is broken," I say.

"Big horse," she says.

"Big horse," I say.

Go to the store. See the funny clown. The circus came to town. I am a mother. These are my children. Dr. Rivka closes the book, looks down at the thin boxes and scrap paper, and when she does that, I know she cannot cure me.

"I think we've done enough for one day," she says. "I'll see you next weekend."

Next weekend? I have to do this again? How many tests like this do I have to take? Dr. Rivka stands and walks to the door. Maybe next weekend comes the fixing part. Maybe this was just the appetizer of things. Or maybe there is no fixing me.

Normal-Sized

LIKE REAL SUPERHEROES, THE girls in my class are turning into women overnight. We're in sixth grade now, and everyone except Imogen and me is getting their puberty. Dr. Rivka couldn't fix me. I saw her for four entire weekends in a row, and then I never saw her again. My mom didn't say a word to me about it, so I know it's true that I'm too broken to fix. Only I don't know what part of me is the broken thing; maybe it's all of me. What I do know is that I'm an incurable jinx who exists outside time and space, which explains why I'm not growing out of my tomboy phase and still can't figure out how to care about Jordache jeans, Secret deodorant, shopping, halter tops, or wearing lip gloss. During recess the girls won't play sports anymore. Instead, they sit on the bench braiding each other's hair. Now it's just the boys and me. Omar James says I'm talented at sports, so I show off for him.

Imogen and I keep a journal charting the growth of our breasts. After school she comes over and we lift our shirts and I measure myself, then her, record the numbers, and then next to the numbers draw the levels of bump that are there, which in our case is none. Maybe she won't get boobs either because she's deaf. But unlike me, she has hope. Nuar says that people who are tall get their puberty first. Also people who are fat. I'm not either of those things, but maybe when I'm taller. Only I'm not getting any taller. What if I never get my puberty? I'll have to sit on the sidelines of life forever.

But it's happening to my friends, and they've turned into people who wear flowered spaghetti-strap summer dresses and hair barrettes, which is not who I am. Kara's at a new school, and it's fancy. There, they get to wear uniforms, which means everyone matches and no one is wrong. I want to be with her, but she says it's not a good school for me; that it's really hard, and there's a lot of pressure and I wouldn't like it. It takes her four hours to do all her homework; sometimes she cries. But if I got to wear a uniform, none of that would matter. Maybe nothing would bother me ever again. Besides, I do my homework really fast. Sometimes I don't even do it at all, and my mom writes a note saying why I couldn't do my homework. Other times, when it's just too hard, and I'm crying and hyperventilating, she just does the homework for me. I have the best mom.

People are having more slumber parties, and because I am too afraid to sleep over, I'm getting left out of more things, even with Imogen, who isn't afraid to sleep over. My siblings ignore me, so I'm left out at home, too. Sometimes Vito cheers me up by making me fun drinks, which is why I sometimes go in there after school. Vito wasn't there a few weeks ago, but Tony was. He said he had a surprise for me in the back and I followed him, but then he just sat down.

"It's a pony ride," he said, slapping his knee.

A pony ride is not a surprise, it's a dumb thing uncles do. But you have to do what adults say, so I climbed on his knee, which he jumped up and down. The surprise happened when he put his hand down my pants, trembled, and something made my lower back sticky and wet. He pushed me off him and yelled, "Look what you made me do." I went home and changed my clothes and tried to forget.

Now when we go across the street to eat at Joe's Restaurant, if Tony is our waiter I fall asleep at the table. Everyone loves it there, and I don't want to ruin it by telling. Also, I didn't make him do it, but I know no one will believe me because everyone says I'm overdramatic.

Most days I come home from school crying.

"No one talks to me anymore," I tell my mom.

"Why not?" she asks.

"Because I'm never at the sleepovers!"

"Well, then you should go," she says. Just like that, like she doesn't understand me.

"No! I can't! I can't do that!" I feel like a steering wheel after someone lets go. I can hear my voice crackle.

"Have it your way."

"They all have secret jokes without me, and I'm always left out of stories and things."

"That's not very nice," my mom says.

"No! It's not nice at all!" I say.

"I'll call Marie tomorrow," she says, as if Marie has any control over my social life at school.

"No! Don't call Marie! That will make things worse."

"Well, then I'm not sure what you want me to do."

"I want you to fix it! I want you to tell me what to do!"

"They're just jealous of you," my mom says. "Maybe they want to be more like you."

"No, they want to be less like me. I want *me* to be more like *them*."

"They sound jealous, if you ask me."

I'm so frustrated. "Just forget it! You don't understand anything!" I yell and storm upstairs to my room, throw myself down on my bed, and sob. After a while she comes up to check on me.

"I don't want to go back to school," I say into my pillow. "Everyone is so mean to me."

"What can I do to make it better?"

"Send me to a different school," I say. "I hate it there. I don't want to go back."

"Do you really want to switch schools?" she asks.

"Yes!" I say.

"Where do you want to go?" she asks.

"I want to be with Kara, and I want to wear a uniform."

"Okay," she says.

This picks me up off the pillow. I peer up into her face. "Really?"

"Of course. If switching schools would make you feel better, then that's what we should do. I'll call Mrs. Maynard and make an appointment for a tour."

I nod and then hug her. "You're the best mom in the entire world."

*   *   *

That night I lie in bed, thinking about how much better things will be, how all my problems will be solved now that I'm going to a new school. Except—I scramble for the pad and pencil.

"Dr. Fine never said why I was so short!" I scribble in a note to my mom.

"You're right! If you're really worried, we can go to a growth doctor."

"I'm really worried!!!!!! What's a growth doctor?"

"A doctor who can tell us whether you need to take something to grow."

"There's something you can take to grow?????"

"Of course! There's a pill for everything," she writes back.

I can't believe what I'm reading. Why didn't she tell me about this sort of doctor earlier? She knows I've been hanging from my chin-up bar for weeks; but also, if there's medicine for everything, why didn't Dr. Rivka give me one for my worries?

Before school starts the next morning, my mom drops me off at Eric's office. He's the assistant of someone I can never remember. Eric sits on the edge of his desk and plants one foot on the ground; I can tell she's told him kids were making fun of me for my size.

"Amanda, I want to tell you a secret," he says.

"Okay," I say. I like secrets.

"What I'm about to tell you will change your entire life. It will turn all your worries upside down." I am getting chills on my actual organs. "Amanda," he says and stands. "Men"—he turns to the window, pulls in as much nostril air as he can, and then faces me—"don't like tall women. I want you to burn this into your memory. You are lucky to be small. Tall women are too masculine. No man wants to be with a woman who reminds him of a man. Trust me on this one. Don't worry about your height. Your height is perfect. Men love small women. Got it?"

I blink. Does he know about Tony at the restaurant?

He leans into me. "Now, don't tell anyone. This is just our secret. You don't want other small girls knowing what you know, right? Then they'll go steal your men."

I hesitate. "Right." But I already know men like small women, because they also like small girls. I am not interested in keeping any of them for myself.

"You're welcome!" He stands up straight, beaming, and returns to his seat at his desk.

I hurry back to my classroom in relief, until I see Imogen standing near the window and notice something new: buds.

A Beautiful, Gorgeous Life

NEW YEAR'S EVE IS tomorrow, and Javier and I are throwing a party together in my apartment. Frankie and I have been inseparable since the Christmas visit a week earlier. We tear open the decorations, blasting the radio, and hang New Year's banners and streamers on the wall, and dump 2011 plastic glasses on the table along with hordes of other 2011 items that will be of no value by 12:01 a.m. Javier isn't joining us, and eventually I find him on my bed. "You okay?"

"Yeah, I think so," he says. "Nothing's wrong."

"Except you're lying in bed staring at the ceiling while we're in there hanging things up and having fun. You don't want to join us?"

"Some friends of mine are having a last-minute New Year's Eve dinner party upstate."

I can feel the heat of disappointment sweep across my face. "You want to go?" I ask.

"Maybe," he says. "I don't know. Do you?"

He never seems to know what he wants or how he feels, and this is making me increasingly nervous. "We have twelve people coming over tomorrow for our own dinner party," I say. "Lili and Frankie are having a sleepover."

"Can't we just cancel?" he asks.

The party is in twenty-four hours. I can't believe he just asked me that. Or that he'd rather be with his friends than do something domestic with his daughter and me. Even though a week ago I was wondering if I

should leave him, now that I feel him leaving me, I'm unglued. I'm trying not to pirouette into panic. Why does this relationship make me feel
so off-balance? One week I know where I stand, and the next I don't.
What is wrong with me?

Finally, he glances at my face. "No. No, I don't want to cancel," he
says. I breathe out in relief. "...I don't think." Oh God, why is he doing
this? At this point, I don't care what he decides—he just needs to make
a decision. His equivocating makes me more anxious than anything else.

I pretend I'm going to the bathroom, but instead I duck into the
pantry and open the party whiskey. I take a long pull and then return
to Frankie, who's done an excellent job of decorating. The whiskey does
what I needed it to do: lower the volume on my apprehension. We wrap
up, turn off the radio, and then lie on the couch to read books. Finally,
Javier comes out. He picks up my guitar and starts playing and singing
"Wild and Blue," and for a moment I am happy again. I long for these
minutes to be my entire life, instead of just one turbulent drop on this
unpiloted relationship.

Over the past two weeks, I had thought things were finally solved.
For the first time in years, I hadn't felt anxious. Instead, I had been
flooded with calm, a surety that time had finally opened its door to me,
was allowing me to step through and get what I've wanted for so long: a
family of my own. This sense of certainty—the faith that I'm adequate,
capable, and seen—is what I've been chasing my entire life. I've felt
it once before—with Peter; but as soon I felt sound and certain, he
changed his mind. The idea that I could lose this, too, terrifies me.

Later, when he finally says, "Let's have the party," he doesn't look convinced. My stomach is in knots. So much for that whiskey.

"Great," I say.

Lili comes over the next afternoon, and she and Frankie play while
Javier and I cook. I'm trying to tell if Javier would rather be upstate with
his friends, but he's not revealing anything. It doesn't matter, though.
The fact that he had been willing to cancel our party is something I
can't un-know. Inside his waffling is another story I can't extract, but I

recognize it's an old threat, a story my body knows about being rejected in favor of other people. Like sleeping in the maid's room so my dad's new-and-improved children could have their own, glorious bedrooms. At Rebecca's bat mitzvah, I watched my dad give a speech about how proud he was of her, and I cried silently, jealous that she got my dad in a bargain neither of us made. What I feel now is similar. The central place Javier's ex-wife's painting occupies in his apartment, his following her and her boyfriends across the country, wherever they moved...I don't want to be anyone's remainders. I go sit on the floor of the pantry to try to stop this spiral of panic.

"What's going on?" Javier's head pops in.

Before I can stop myself, I let it all burst out: "What if none of this happens?"

"None of what?"

"This, us. Upstate. Living with Frankie. What if Meredith won't move, or won't let you take Frankie? What if the Jersey City house doesn't sell? What if I can't get out of my lease? What if you change your mind about me, about all of this?"

"You want to come out of the pantry and we can talk about it?"

"No, no. I don't want to come out of the pantry," I say. I'm unstrung and ashamed of having a panic attack in front of him, traumatized by the chance that he'll think I'm crazy and leave me.

"Can I come into the pantry?" I nod. Javier gets a chair from the kitchen, pulls me onto his lap, and rubs my back. "We can do whatever we want. No one is going to stand in our way," he says.

"But what if you change your mind? What if you decide you don't want this, or me, or a family?"

"That's not going to happen. I want to have a baby with you. I want a family with you. You're the one. You're it. We can do whatever we want. We can get married if you want."

"Really?" I ask. Do I want that?

"Of course. We'll live upstate; it will be a beautiful, gorgeous life. You have to be optimistic about it. You have to look on the bright side of things."

"I know, but ... you change your mind all the time. You almost bailed on our party."

"So what? A party isn't life. It's not good to see everything in a negative light," he says.

"This isn't negativity. It's worry."

"Well, it seems sort of negative to me," he says.

He knows about my anxiety—I've even named it for him—though he's never seen me having an actual panic attack. But now he's rejecting the identity I've shown him, assigning me a new label to match a problem I don't have. I know this game. It makes me shut down entirely.

"You okay now?" he asks.

I know he's not going to help me. "Yes. Thanks," I lie, feeling deadened.

"Good, because ... brussels sprouts." He points to the stove with the spatula. He kisses me and returns to the kitchen. He has dismissed my actual feelings and given me new ones he can understand. How can I make a life with someone so determined to misunderstand me?

Lili and Frankie have been writing fortunes for everyone to pull out of a hat at midnight. It isn't until I inspect their work that I finally see the difference between Frankie and Lili, and perhaps identify the thing I sensed in Frankie early on: darkness.

Lili: "This year you will find a new nail polish color and get a beautiful new hairdo."

Frankie: "You will (probably) not die this year."

Lili: "You will find a million dollars on the ground and you'll get to keep it."

Frankie: "At the end of this year, only four people will exist. You will not be one of them."

"Frankie!" I say. "You can't put that in there. Write positive ones," I add, feeling instantly like a hypocrite, and sounding too much like her dad and my mom. I wonder if Frankie is being overlooked for who she is, erased in favor of a preferred and easier child, and that's when I realize what rubbed me the wrong way was our sameness, like Pilot.

Despite its rocky beginnings, the party is a triumph, and for four hours I am upbeat and untroubled. I feel necessary and loved and known, and I finally understand what my role should be in Frankie's life: to be the adult who can see her for who she is and protect her. In bed later, I turn to Javier.

"I have something to tell you," I say. "For years and years I've known the name I wanted to give my daughter someday. I've been so sure about it I even made my friends promise they wouldn't use it."

"Okay?"

"The name is Frances Bird. Frankie for short. Bird is the middle name."

Javier sits up and looks at me. "You know Frankie's middle name?"

I shake my head.

"Bette. Frankie Bette."

The names are so close that cold creeps up my arms. "I think your Frankie is the Frankie I was meant to have."

"Me too," he says. "Me too."

A Stay-Behind Kid

A FEW DAYS LATER I'm standing on a dark gray carpet at Kara's school uptown, watching girls in uniform with books under their arms, studying their braces, middle parts, and glasses. The younger girls wear headbands and barrettes. Instead of "Hi," they say "Hello." I appreciate their manners. Our tour guide, Jorie, wears pearls, has thick black arm hair, and wears white gloves "to keep her manicure." She apologizes for running late, but it's "review week" and she "doesn't dare miss a word." My mom nods and smiles.

Jorie shows us the entire school—all five floors. We ride the elevator—a privilege, Jorie tells us. Only seniors, faculty, and visitors are allowed. Friday privilege is for everyone. That's when students can wear their own clothes, which doesn't feel like a privilege to me. We see the middle and upper school, and we meet uptown-named girls: Vandy, Miven, and Bellamy. Every time we step into a classroom, the girls stand until they're told to sit. When Jorie finishes the tour, I stay with the sixth graders and learn *amo, amas, amat, amamus, amatis, amant* in Latin. Everyone thinks it's cool that I live downtown, in the Village.

After lunch, Jorie takes me back to Mrs. Maynard's office and shakes my hand good-bye. When I go here, I'm going to start shaking hands also. Mrs. Maynard opens her office door and signals me inside.

"Hi, pumpkin. Did you have a nice time?" my mother asks. I nod a big yes, even as a warning goes off in my gut; something is wrong.

"I'm glad to hear it," Mrs. Maynard says. "Your mom and I wondered whether you might like to spend the rest of the day here."

"Yes!" I say. Maybe they like me so much they're going to let me switch schools right now.

"Great. Winifred will be your guide, and you'll spend the rest of the day with her and the fifth graders."

The fifth graders? I look at my mom, who smiles like Mrs. Maynard didn't say anything weird. Is it bad manners to correct a headmistress?

"You mean the sixth graders?"

"No, the fifth graders." The room shifts to the left.

"But I'm in sixth," I say.

"I wonder if you noticed that the sixth-grade girls are quite developed. I worry that with your stature you'll feel left behind."

"Left behind?" My scalp feels tight.

"Developmentally. We think it's a good idea for you to spend the day with the fifth graders and see how you like it."

I look at my mom, but she's quiet. A flash fever scampers under my skin.

"But I'm in sixth grade," I repeat, not knowing what's left to add.

"I understand, but we thought it'd be a good idea to give your body a chance to catch up," she insists.

This is really happening. I have to repeat a grade and my mom isn't saying anything. I failed the ERB test; that's why she never told me the results even when I asked.

"Winifred will escort you to the fifth-grade classroom, where you'll spend the remainder of the day. She'll bring you back here during the last class, and we'll all make a decision together."

All I can do is nod. I feel helpless, and my mom isn't coming to my defense. Winifred appears, her body dusted with a thin downy platinum, even on her face, and I follow her. I look around the fifth-grade classroom. White, small faces clot the room. In the back, off to the side, two black girls sit together. A skinny blond girl with an upturned ski-slope nose and dried whiteheads on her chin sits cross-armed, her face fixed in teenage hatred and boredom. Her body hasn't come in either, but still, there's something oddly adult about her. Maybe it's because she looks like she's from an L.L.Bean catalog.

I look carefully at everyone and notice that even among the fifth-grade girls I am still the smallest. I sit with them through math, gym, and English. They are nice and all, but still—babies. There's no way I'm staying back.

At the end of the day, Winifred walks me back to Mrs. Maynard's office and hugs me good-bye. Then she gives me her phone number, which I'll never use but makes me feel special. I join my mom in the office.

"They're a lovely class, aren't they?" Mrs. Maynard says. I agree. "Do you feel like you fit in a bit more?"

"Not really. I mean, I'm still the smallest," I say, regretting it instantly.

"Your mother and I have been talking, and we really do think it's best that you stay back a year. You are much better suited to that grade."

I don't understand. I thought we were going to have a discussion and decide together. Why am I always left out of conversations about me?

"So, if we're all in agreement, you can start Whittaker in the fall, repeating the sixth grade. Or, you can remain at your school, and advance with the grade you're in."

I am going to be behind, always—for the rest of my life.

"But I learned sixth grade already."

"Well, think how smart you'll feel when you already know all the answers," my mom says.

This isn't a choice.

*   *   *

There is a way to be and I'm not being it, and I don't know how to change. Is there someone I should be the exact copy of, and they've forgotten to introduce me? Or maybe a person is supposed to be a fact, like an answer that doesn't change, and I'm more like an opinion, which the world doesn't want?

The growth doctor has X-ray machines and lots of nurses walking around. Just like all the other doctors, he looks only at my mom when he talks, not me. They put a heavy apron on my body, and my hand on a cold metal plate, and then X-ray my wrist bones to see how tall I'll grow. We go back into his office and he lectures us about glands and pulses. He says stuff about lowering blood sugar and insulin and then a terrible thing about a seizure, but don't worry because that's rare. I do not want a seizure. I'd rather be short. He tells us about growth hormones, which they give to horses, and leg extension surgery, where they cut your legs off, add more leg, and then sew you back together. I don't like how any of this sounds, but my mom is taking frantic notes and nodding. She asks questions about how long things take, and what hospital we'd use and who would do the surgery, and I do not want to do any of this. When he asks if I have any questions, I raise my hand.

"Will I be taller than Gary Coleman?" I ask.

He looks at my chart and says, "It looks like you'll be five feet tall, exactly."

I smile. That number is good enough for me. I don't want to take horse pills, have seizures, or get my legs cut off. My mom shakes his hand, but I am already out the door, leaving as fast as I can before my mom says yes to the horse pills. My after-doctor treat is ice cream, and as we walk I realize something that stops me in my tracks.

"If we know I'm going to be five feet tall, then I don't need to stay back a grade," I tell her. "Tell Mrs. Maynard what the doctor said. You'll see; she'll let me continue on with my grade."

"Sweetie, I don't think that's an option."

"But if I'm going to be normal-sized, why would I have to stay back?" I ask.

My mom doesn't know what to say, although there is something she wants to say. I can see her eyes trying to figure out what to do, but she hails a cab instead. I know there's something she's not telling me, like the reason I'm staying back is that she knows I'm never getting my puberty and she's just too afraid to say.

June 1981

Dr. Rivka Golod

Summary of Test Results

Amanda's greatest difficulty in the language area was on a test of story comprehension where she failed at the 7 year to 9 year level. This stands in direct contrast to her excellent ability to comprehend verbal absurdities and pass the verbal reasoning tests given at the 14 year old levels. On another test of verbal reasoning, Amanda obtained a high average scaled score of 11. This was the same subtest on which she obtained a defective scale score of 5 only a few months ago when it was administered on the ERB. I attribute Amanda's poor performance on Standardized Testing to performance anxiety linked to her fear of failure and difficulty extracting meaning from silent reading material. The vast un-evenness in her overall scores should be interpreted with caution.

The Bright Side

WE'RE IN A CAR, flying up some fast highway on a drive upstate: Javier, Frankie, and me. Frankie makes a surprise attack from the backseat with the caterpillar legs of a scalp massager and I scream while she laughs hysterically. Javi says, "Look, I'm driving with my eyes closed," and closes his eyes. I scream again, and he turns to look at me, grinning, his right eye closed, his left eye wide open. Frankie is doubled over in the back. "You're so easy to scare!" she says. If she only knew. It feels like practice for the life we'll have next year. I see the three of us in the car like I'm watching a movie, just a regular, happy family driving upstate.

The relief, if only for a day or two, from being the only one in a room without the main trappings of an adult life is powerful. When we stop to get some lunch, I know that when other people look at us, they'll see an actual family, and it feels amazing. I take Frankie to the bathroom and when we come out Javier is at the counter paying, and Frankie sits next to him and I leave them alone to have some dad-daughter time. At the magazines, a woman says, "You have such a beautiful family."

I look over at Javier and Frankie, who seem like they might be arguing. "Thank you so much." I grin. Maybe Javi and I will give Frankie a sibling and one day this really will be my own family.

I feel like an insane person. I'm being a hypocrite. In the midst of my family contentment, I'm perpetuating the very misconceptions about single people that I wish didn't exist. No one should feel shamed or evaluated based on a single set of standards that not everyone wants, and yet here I am, not only wanting it, but acting like I have it, so I can feel like I belong. I want strangers to think I've been chosen by someone and I am the same as everyone else.

I've written my first short story in a long time, about a little girl who finds a baby on the street and her mom lets her keep it. It's not until I'm done, and have given it to Javi, that I realize the story is about my own craving. I am embarrassed. Worse, he's had it for two weeks and hasn't said a word.

Did he read it and hate it? Has he forgotten about it? Does he not care to read it because he doesn't want to know more of me? Or is he embarrassed by how much I want a family? I remind myself that he's slow to act on anything: His website is years out of date, and although he says he's going to update it, he doesn't. Months passed between when he said he wanted to read my first book and when he ordered it on Amazon. He still smokes, though he told me on our first date that he was quitting. He said he was actively looking for work that would keep him in New York, but that doesn't seem to be happening because he keeps taking jobs that are out of town. Everything he does is languorous; he operates from the point of inertia, moving only when he's forced. That's not my way, but I remind myself not to judge him by my own standards.

*   *   *

When we arrive upstate I meet Javier's friends, who are all married with kids, interesting, and smart. We sled and talk and play music and it's fun and we cook a big meal for dinner. I'm relieved to discover how much I genuinely like them. Javier and Frankie go to the butcher for meat for the stew, and I stay behind, helping out with kitchen tasks.

"This is the happiest I've ever seen Javier," his friend Richard tells me. "I think you're good for him."

I feel like a glow stick. "How so?" I ask, fishing, I suppose, for some compliments.

"Well, you know, Javier's a floater. He operates like he's still moving from town to town, the way his family did when he was a kid in Europe, but with you, he seems more grounded. Maybe this time he can stay anchored. It'd be good for him to have a home base."

"Also good that you're his age," Natalia adds, then sees my face. "Shit, you don't know about Anastasia?" I shake my head, sensing a looming threat. "Um, his last girlfriend was twenty-four."

"Yikes," I say.

"Yikes is right."

I had been so happy, only to suddenly be slammed with nerves. Maybe he can stay anchored, Richard said. It's true that he lives out of a suitcase, always going between Maine, his TV shoots, and Jersey City. I have told myself this will all change when we live upstate with Frankie.

Afterward, a group heads outside and returns reeking of pot. It bums me out that Javi has a kid and still smokes pot. What if Frankie needs him and he's too stoned to help her? We stay up late talking, playing guitar, and telling stories none of us will remember. Soon we're exhausted and make our way to bed. In the morning, after breakfast, Javier says he wants to talk about my story.

"Yeah? You read it?"

"Of course I read it," he says. "Let's go to the kitchen."

We sit at the kitchen table and he tells me he thinks it's amazing.

"Really?" I ask. "You're not just saying that?"

"Seriously. I think it's incredible."

"Wow. Thanks. Anything I should fix?"

"I triple-love the ending, but it's too upsetting. Anyone with a kid who reads this is going to find the ending too dark. It might work against you."

"Okay. That's good feedback. Thanks. I'll come up with alternative endings."

"Great."

We're quiet for a minute. Either I'm being too sensitive, or something weird has come between us while we've been up here, but I'm not sure which it is.

"I like your friends," I offer.

"They like you, too."

"Are you . . . okay?" I ask. "You seem kind of . . . off." I feel preemptively worried, and there's only one answer I can bear to hear.

"I'm just trying to figure some stuff out."

That was not the answer. "What sort of stuff?"

"Us stuff," he says. He glances at me and can probably see the tissue on my organs starting to crumple. I can't hide it. "Don't freak out. It's nothing to freak out about," he says.

"I'm not freaking out. I'm listening. What are you trying to figure out?"

"I'm not sure what I want," he says.

I force my face to stay even. "Meaning?"

"I'm not sure I want to plant roots upstate," he says.

I relax, my organs soften, blood flow resumes, and my heart returns to beating. "Oh. Okay. Well, we don't have to live upstate. That was your idea."

"I don't know if I want to plant roots or make a family again. I don't know if I want to stay in one place."

He's not sure about me, he means. Everything he said he wanted just a few days ago, he's taking back. Gravity holds my body in place while the rest of me hovers to the side, just TV static in the shape of a body, waiting until it's safe to reunite.

"But . . . you said. Just the other day . . ."

"I'm just trying to figure out what shape I want my life to take. I need to figure out how to have you in my life."

"Did something happen?" I ask.

"I don't think so."

I'm a flipbook of emotions: enraged, devastated, disappointed, heartbroken, and monstrously confused. "Then why are you changing your mind?"

"I don't know," he says. "Well, maybe I know. I'm not sure."

His waffling is torturing me. I cut him off before he can say something more permanent.

"Okay, well . . . we don't have to make any decisions right now."

"Great," he says and leans across the table to kiss me.

The next day we all go for a hike. We follow behind his friends in the woods. Frankie is up ahead walking with a little girl named Eliza. Javier takes my hand.

"Let's do it," he says. "All of it. Let's be a family."

"Yeah? You really want to?"

"Yes, I really do," he says. I squeeze his hand. "At least I think I do," he adds.

I stop. "Oh my God. You're killing me."

"What do you mean? I just said I wanted a family with you."

"And then you added, 'I think I do.'"

"Right. Right now I think I want that," he says.

"Which implies that tomorrow you might feel another way." He looks sheepish and shrugs.

I can't live like this, but I don't want to let go and be without him and Frankie. She shows me the sad, dark poems she writes in her journals; we play games on my iPad, watch movies, read books, and have a connection that never has to be restarted after periods apart. Frankie fills me with purpose. I'm awed by her, by the way she grapples with her own truth at such a young age. I'd happily sacrifice my own time, my precious writing time, to be with her. I'm quiet for the rest of the hike, and when we return I lie down in our room and take deep anti-anxiety breaths. I cannot endure these small breaches of intimacy. Every time Javi vacillates on our future, I am thrown out into a vast black bottomless universe. Any kind of separation has always done this to me. I can't live with the undecided. There is no one to swoop in and fix the situation for me.

Ten minutes pass before Javier comes in and sits down on the bed. He's stroking my arm.

"Everything will be fine."

"You say that now, but then in five minutes you'll say something totally different."

"Maybe, but I'll land on something," he says.

"But why do I have to be pulled through this with you? It's like you're thinking out loud."

"I am thinking out loud," he says.

"Well, don't. I don't like it. It's not fair to me."

"It's not fair to keep it from you either," he says.

"Yes, it is. Just make a decision. This is unbearable for me. I can't be trapped inside this uncertainty. I can't breathe."

"Try to look on the bright side. You don't have to go right for the negative all the time."

"That's not negativity, it's anxiety."

"Well, I want to live my life going toward lightness and love. Not complaining and negativity," he says.

My stomach hardens like I accidentally swallowed a kettlebell. How does he keep mistaking my anxiety for something it's not? I feel defensive and demeaned. At least my anxiety is honest. Aiming to only go toward lightness and love seems like the worst way to hide from who you really are. I worry that no matter what Javi and I look at, we'll both report seeing different things. Being rejected sends me into bed and under the covers for days, but having my anxiety rejected this way is splitting me apart. For the first time, I feel the urge to fight back on behalf of my emotions, to get them the recognition they deserve after a lifetime of being ignored.

June 1981

Dr. Rivka Golod

Summary of Test Results

Amanda's fine motor movements of her fingers are excellent. There was some mild awkwardness, by contrast, in the area of speech praxis (eg in repeating multisyllabic words). Laterality is well established. She is right sided for handedness, footedness and eyedness, although she has trouble distinguishing left from right, and is equally as comfortable writing with her left hand as she is her right. Orientation is not entirely secure; she must think carefully before she locates body positions and must reposition her body in order to locate positions in space.

She has a poor understanding of spatial and temporal concepts. It is difficult to understand history, or read a map, without a spatial and temporal framework on which to anchor ideas. She specifically needs to understand geographical relationships, and can only do so if taught visually and kinesthetically. For instance, instead of asking her to follow directions on a map, she needs to first experience the route by taking it.

The Drainpipe Man

THE FIRST DAY OF sixth grade for the second time is cold pins and needles. I wake up damp on my mom's couch, eyes burning. It's chilly and dark outside, and I soft-walk past Mom and Jimmy, climbing the stairs back to my room to glance at my new uniform, drenched in regret. By the time I discovered the fast one they pulled, it was too late to stay at my old school. It's not until seventh grade that the good uniforms kick in. Until then, it's tunics. The kind of uniform *Little House on the Prairie* kids probably wore. Had I known from the beginning, or at least paid better attention when I was visiting, I would not have agreed to stay back. Even altered, the uniform is too big. It goes past my knees, and the straps keep slipping off my shoulders. Tunics are for babies.

I love the blazer, though. While it doesn't signal that I'm broken and they better take care of me, it does something better. It says they need to take me seriously, that I'm important. I get dressed, pull my socks to my knees, and slip on my new L.L.Bean bluchers. In the kitchen, the table is set for breakfast with notes from Mom and Jimmy: "GOOD LUCK! WE LOVE YOU MORE!" The dark, quiet kitchen reminds me of being awake after lights-out, and my body lances with boiling worry that something will happen to my mom while I'm gone. My brain sizzles, too, with the dreaded realization that I'm too old to still have this fear. I look at the clock: 7 a.m. The school bus will get here at 7:15.

I can't eat the cereal; I don't even try. But I force a slab of white bread into my mouth, realizing on my rush to the bathroom what a terrible mistake I've made. I brush my teeth, but it doesn't take away the smell of vomit. I spray myself with something I find under the sink. Now I smell sticky and sweet, like an old lady. I go outside and wait for the bus, hoping to air myself out.

Vito stands across the street, outside Joe's, arms crossed and ready to watch us kids go to school. Jimmy Alcatraz is long gone. Where the mafia hangout was is now the Figaro Café. The air is fresh, the slight coolness in front of each breeze carrying the smell of change and beginning, except I'm not changing; my worries keep repeating themselves, just like the rest of my life. If I were going into seventh grade the way I should be, Kara would be four grades ahead of me instead of five, and I'd be one floor below her at school instead of three. Now she's a junior. We'll overlap for only two years before she goes to college, and then I'll never see her again. I wish Kara and I were going to the first day of school together, but high school doesn't start as early.

I'm the only one on the school bus, and I watch carefully to make sure the driver doesn't trick me and drive to a secret location where he'll chain me to a furnace in the dungeon and feed me to alligators, but I recognize the route. It's the way to my father's house. As we near the Pan Am Building, and the "Karen Silkwood was murdered" graffiti, my body goes into countdown. When will this feeling ever go away? Why haven't I outgrown it? We pass it, and the countdown subsides. Soon my new school comes into view, and I realize I've been holding half my breath and my shoulders are at my ears.

In front of the school, chauffeurs in suits release uniformed girls from the backseats of Cadillacs and Rolls-Royces. Nannies wave before strolling their carriages to the boat pond. The street is clogged with girls hugging, shrieking, and jumping up and down. I overhear girls talking about European vacations, au pairs, exchange programs, new dogs, and boyfriends. No one speaks to me. Mrs. Maynard is standing at the front doors, shaking all the girls' hands. Everyone is wearing a blazer, and whatever authority I felt it gave me disappears in this surge of sameness.

All my classmates from Little Red are going into seventh grade today.

Most of the kids went to the high school five blocks away, and I imagine them now, in their regular clothes, not even noticing my absence. I miss Imogen, but when I saw her over the summer, she was wearing colored lip gloss, tight high-waisted jeans, and a tube top, and she had feathered her hair. She bragged about hanging out with Pilar and some new girl named Constance. Constance wears a C cup. Constance used three bottles of Sun In on her hair. Constance was already smoking. Constance sounds constipated, is what I wanted to say. Blood rushes to my face when I think about Imogen and Constance together all the time. Maybe this is my chance to start over again and get things right.

But these girls do not look like the right people to start over with. They are my opposite: blond and pale, with symmetrical features and a haughtiness that looks steamed into their tight skin and crisp clothing. A dull ache begins to thud inside my temples, and I press them back with my fingers. Please don't be a brain tumor on my first day of sixth grade for the second time. I catch my sudden urge to suck my fingers and swap it out for a calming chomp on my nails.

My homeroom is in a hidden nook on the second floor. Stenciled on the door is "VI," which I find out later is the roman numeral for six. Mrs. Smyth, the homeroom teacher, has a scoop of blond-white hair, a tan, and wears a colorful flowing island caftan. She comes right over to greet me. Her necklace is made of oversized turquoise beads that clack when she moves. I am homesick for my mom.

The girls are all nice to me, and their kindness offers me hope. They gather around my desk to interrogate me. Where do you live? What school did you go to before? What did you do for your summer vacation? Do you have a boyfriend? I can't let them sniff out how vulnerable I am. A blond girl with an upturned nose, a popped collar, and a flush of whiteheads on her chin pushes through the small crowd.

"Anyone ever call you Mandy?" she asks. Her mouth doesn't open wide when she talks, which makes her look like a ventriloquist.

"Yes," I say. "But none of them survived." I sound like my dad.

All the girls laugh, and even I take myself by surprise. Scent thrown.

"You're funny," she states, staring at me without a smile. She walks away.

"That's Bree," a girl named Magda whispers. "Stay away. Madison too."

I memorize three names. Bree and Madison are popular. Magda is not.

The first class is called Western Civ, which I've never even heard of, and Mrs. Smyth spends the lesson telling us about what we'll learn. No one even opens their notebook. What was Kara talking about? This school is a breeze. Later, when Mrs. Smyth mentions the books we'll read for English, I nod because I've read them already, in last year's sixth-grade English. No one knows that this is my second time, and I feel like a genius. This is why they can't ever discover that I'm an idiot who has to do everything twice because I don't get anything right the first time.

When the bell rings, Mrs. Smyth tells us to single-file at the door, smallest person in front. Much to my despair, that's me. My tunic keeps falling off my body. Why am I so small when I'm the oldest? Maybe I should take those hormones or get that leg extension surgery. Downstairs, girls and teachers file into an auditorium. I'm between two blond girls who lean over me to talk to each other like I'm not there. They giggle about a teacher named Mrs. Plump.

This is "Prayers," which I guess is also church, and strange since I'm Jewish. I feel like a crasher for being there. After we all say, "Amen," Mrs. Maynard welcomes everyone, and then there's a school song everybody knows and announcements about committees and groups. Everyone nods, murmurs, laughs, claps, and raises their hands for things I don't understand. When we file out, I feel arms cross over me and note the smell of Breck shampoo. Kara! She snuggles her face in my neck and whispers to me.

"I just got here," she says. "How's it going?"

"Good," I say. "I made some girls laugh this morning."

"Of course you did. You're hysterical," she tells me.

I am?

"I'll find you later!" she says and darts ahead, entwining herself with her friends. My breaths come easier and deeper now. All I wanted was to be at the same school with her again. And a uniform. No matter what floor I'm on, I know Kara is somewhere near. If I get scared, I can find her and she will save me from dying.

The second half of the day is different. Mrs. Smyth says it's time to "get down to business" and "take careful lecture notes." I've never taken any notes before, lecture or not. She has suddenly begun speaking very quickly, too fast for me to copy down every word she says. I get half of them before they trail off.

I notice that when Winifred writes, she first leans back to listen before hunching over to jot stuff down. How is she going to learn everything if she's writing only ten of the words? I realize that out of everyone in my grade, I'm the only one (almost) keeping up. They're failing and I'm succeeding! When Winifred, or anyone, asks whether they can borrow my notes, I'll say, yes—of course! I'll be happy to let everyone copy them. I look up at the classroom door where Kara is grinning and waving wildly at me. I can't wait to tell her that I'm smarter than I thought. I hope she checks on me every day.

When the bell rings, we pack up our books and I glance over at Winifred's notes, just to get a sense of what she's doing wrong so that I can offer my help. But her paper's been divided into sections resembling a type of chart, full of roman numerals. There are indentations and underlines and it looks very well organized and clean. How did she do that? I have pages and pages of sprawling text, but Winifred has a clean, well-laid-out chart. As she leafs through her notebook, I see dozens more just like it. What the hell?

Other kids' notebooks look the same. Some have even pulled out rulers to ensure their rows are perfect. Where are they getting these charts from? Mrs. Smyth didn't even draw on the board. Is there another part of the world that exists that I can't see? Everyone always seems in on something I'm not. As the day progresses, I become increasingly alarmed at how little I understand. This was a huge mistake. I followed the wrong path, led by a false belief that uniforms had power. This wasn't what I meant to ask for.

The girls in my class, while friendly, are too young for me. I watch the girls in the seventh grade, the grade I should be in, but they seem, weirdly, too advanced. They're developed and sophisticated in a way I can't ever see myself being. They're not my people either. I am stuck somewhere in the middle, in a place that doesn't exist. I'm embarrassed that I wasn't allowed to advance with everyone else. All my fears are coming true.

Outside, girls yell their good-byes. Some take off in pairs; others run toward Jackson Hole for after-school Cokes and fries. I stand alone, hoping someone might say good-bye to me, or ask if I had a good first day, and do I want to join them for fries, but no talks to me and I stand alone and still at the curb. Kara has Curriculum Committee, so I have to go home by myself. I'm taking the Fifth Avenue bus for the first time, alone. I know I'm old enough to do this. Eddie is fourteen and he's been going to the East Village by himself, where bums set garbage cans on fire to get warm and cars are bombed out like there's a war on, but still, I'm afraid. I remind myself that I'm twelve, twice as old now as Etan was the morning he disappeared. But what if the person who took him waits at all the bus stops? The news a few weeks ago said a man was arrested for luring some boys into a drainpipe. They found pictures in the drainpipe of little boys who looked like Etan Patz. What if the Drainpipe Man is the person who took him? After they arrested him, they discovered he used to date Etan's babysitter. What is wrong with babysitters?

My mom drew me a map. A big box squares HOME, and the gridlike streets that make up the distance between Eighth Street and HOME look very short. When I get off at Eighth Street, I just have to follow the drawing. Even though it pulls up mere feet in front of me, I scramble onto the M15 before it can leave without me. Gratefully, I flash my bus pass.

"You're going to Eighth Street and Fifth Avenue, right?" I ask, just to make absolutely sure.

He nods, and I walk to the back where it's empty, worried because he didn't say yes. A nod could mean he wasn't listening. I watch Central

Park fall away, The Plaza, and FAO Schwarz. The wind is strong and brown lunch bags roll down sidewalks, past the fancy Fifth Avenue department stores, disappearing behind us. The backward tumbling reminds me of my own body when I'm trying to fall asleep. With a defeated exhale, the bus stops and lowers, like my grandma's electric bed, for a woman in a wheelchair. Leaves and napkins fly up from the sidewalk in circles. A plastic bag catches in the weave of a metal garbage can and thrashes against it, trying to escape, but it's caught, held hostage.

My mother said the bus will drop me off on Fifth Avenue and Eighth Street, and all I have to do is walk straight, right through Washington Square Park. Easy-peasy. Once we're at Fourteenth Street, I realize I'm the only one on the bus. Marci Klein was on a bus when she was kidnapped. I stand and check that we're going in the right direction. My breath is starting to thicken. But then the arch for the park's entrance comes into view, and I calm down, ring the bell, and stand near the door.

But, instead of stopping where he's supposed to on Eighth Street, he turns left and keeps going, away from the park. My colon spasms and a noose lassos around my neck. I feel the slipknot tightening into the hollow of my throat; I can't get air. I am being kidnapped. No one can save me. I start swallowing at the air to get some into my lungs, pulling whatever I can through my mouth and nostrils to keep me alive. Please let me off the bus. I will do anything you want. I will be nice to Holly, I will not think bad thoughts about other people, I will... Is he slowing down? He's slowing down, oh thank God thank God.

He stops, but the moment between stopping and opening the door feels like a lifetime and I worry that he's changing his mind, and he's going to look in the rearview mirror, spit out an evil laugh, press the gas, and steal me away, but then I hear the deep wheeze and the door accordions open. I fly out, entangled in relief and terror, and having no idea where I am or how to get home. I don't know where the park is. I was paying attention only to being kidnapped, not to where the bus was going. The bus did something different from what my mom said it would do, and I can't adjust for that difference. I can stay true only to the directions as they are, and only from the place I'm supposed to be, not wherever I am.

Maybe if I walk straight, I'll still hit the park. My mom is always right, so even though there was an error, she'll still be right. I walk straight, but the park does not appear, and the neighborhood starts feeling shady, and I become more lost. Now the fear that hit me blocks ago turns crippling.

I turn and look behind me. What were buildings and sidewalks on my way here now look like shapes and textures. Windows are rectangles, two-dimensional drawings. I'm hit by an ominous, tumbling sense that I've fallen into some replica of reality, a world flattened into two dimensions. Colors are beige and muted and stretch into one another. As everything starts to double, I feel myself rise up, above it all, vibrating.

I'm lifting above the city like mist, and all of a sudden I know what's really going on. People are just game pieces being played on a city-sized board. Everything looks fake, like it's been illustrated. Even the bricks look drawn on; roof shingles are rectangles darkened by charcoal. The cars look like paper cutouts, and cracks in the sidewalk are drawn on by chalk. Everything is a farce; nothing is true. Abruptly, I have seen life for what it is. We are all objects without meaning. The meaning comes only from the giant invisible hands that are playing their game with us. An early fall chill. Someone is lowering the sun, and immediately I know my entire family has gone on without me, not noticing I'm even missing. I imagine my family doing things they don't even do—sitting around a campfire, reading aloud from a book, playing guitar, laughing at jokes— now that I'm gone. Kara's bracey grin; the boyish glint of Eddie's squinty laugh. The things I'll never see again.

I walk fast toward the nearest store, determined to make them save me. The cool sweeping mist of each big breath puffs in dragon blasts through the inside of me. They didn't have enough information to keep him in jail, so they let the Drainpipe Man go. Now I know that anyone who passes me could be the Drainpipe Man. Little kids dash zigzag in a burst down the street toward me. Little darting faces. Their carefree laughs, squinting eyes, uneven mouths, baby teeth, and crooked little chins look suddenly both ominous and in danger. I duck into Bolton's, where the women on staff wear white stockings and pleated blue skirts. I don't realize I'm crying until someone calls for tissues. They coddle me and give me a lollipop. When they talk baby talk I realize they think I'm younger than I am. This is a common problem. Sometimes I wish I *were* still nine. Not the bad nine where Melissa and Baba died, when Etan disappeared, but the nine where people tried to protect me from the real world. Usually when people do find out I'm older than they thought, they gasp in disbelief, and I feel like apologizing. I am not being who they expected me to be.

When my mom rushes in, she thanks the women who work there and I'm relieved she looks as worried as I feel. Out on the sidewalk, I expect her to ask someone where we are, or hail a taxi, but instead, she walks down the block and there, in front of us, is the park. I don't understand. It was right there the entire time? I try to explain what the bus did, and how hard I tried to follow her map.

"I wonder if your ambidexterity caused the problem," she says.

"It didn't," I say.

"I'll find you a tutor," she says, walking fast as we approach the park.

I don't want a tutor. I just want someone to help me inside my body. If I can explain what happened, maybe she'll finally hear me, but I don't know the words.

"I . . . I got overwhelmed," I say.

"A tutor can help you with your problems following directions," she says. "They can work with you after school." She clutches her purse to her chest, pulling me behind her.

I have problems following directions? "Maybe if someone walked the route with me? From start to finish? Then I'd know how to do it the right way," I say.

"I'll draw the map so it's clearer for you. I should have labeled the stores and restaurants and not just the streets," she says. "I'll make the letters bigger. Maybe they were too small."

"I don't think that was the problem," I say.

"Can you walk faster?" she says, her face pinched and drained of color. I hurry behind her through the park, passing a guy on a unicycle juggling pins, a man blowing giant soap bubbles toward the little kids who chase them, a musician singing James Taylor songs, and my-age kids dancing for change next to a blasting boom box. Those people don't seem scary, but I must be wrong. My mom pulls on my hand. There are so many things to fear in this world; I am even starting to fear myself.

I am a growing constellation of errors. I don't know what's wrong with me, only that something is, and it must be too shameful to divulge, or so rare that even the doctors are stumped. Whatever the case, not knowing is making everything worse. Is there some truth about myself no one will tell me? Whenever I ask, the answer is always the same. I have problems learning. When I push for more information, my mom gets flustered and says, "I can't explain it." She's keeping something from me, I can tell. I try so hard to shake away the images, but I feel them coming—trouble learning how to tell time, bad grades, failing tests, the ERB, Dr. Rivka, staying back a grade, the notes the other kids took, getting lost—my heart sinks at the realization of the absolute horrid truth: I'm dumb. The adults lied to me; my mom lied to me. I didn't stay back because I was little. I stayed back because I'm stupid.

That's how I know that no matter how many tutors she hires or maps she makes, I won't get it right. I don't understand how to do things. Other people know facts that I don't, and not knowing, even things I never learned, is dumbness. Everyone else's brains have information my brain doesn't have. I don't want anyone to know this truth about me. It has to stay hidden.

On top of being stupid, though, I know there's something else, the source of my worries that no one seems able to find. If the world discovers that I have a weird extra flaw on top of being stupid, who knows what grade they'll put me in. Who knows what will happen to me. Who I am is a secret I have to keep forever.

As we rush home through Washington Square Park, I smell the hotdog carts, the pretzel stands, the fall pollen, new clothes, the faded perfume—and our fear. The sense that we're just a board game has stayed with me, and I feel like I know things about the world no one else does. The map is crumpled up and grimy in my hand; I am crushing the very streets I am racing through, even HOME. Every smell cements this one terrifying experience inside me, and the truth about myself I now understand. From now on, all perfect New York City fall evenings will forever call up in me this specific terror, and an exquisite sadness, every September for the rest of my life.

A Word Never Means Only One Thing

THE NEW TUTOR CAME, but Mom didn't like how he dressed, so we got another, but I still can't read a map. I sit all the way in the back of the class because I don't want to be called on, ever. I never figured out how to take notes like the other girls, and now I'm too afraid to ask. Whenever Mrs. Smyth so much as looks my way, I get dizzy; I bend over my notebook like I'm too busy documenting her very important words to be called upon, though most of the time I can barely follow what she's saying because I'm so worried about being too dumb to understand. The rare times I'm able to listen and do know an answer, I don't raise my hand, in case I turn out to be wrong. If I'm called on, all the blood rushes to my skin and I grow light-headed and have no idea what I've said. It takes anywhere from five to ten minutes for the trembling to subside. After class, I sit in the front for a few minutes, pretending I'm scribbling some deep follow-up thoughts, when *really* I'm copying down from the board what I can't read from the back of the room. Not that it helps.

This school is as hard as college. All the girls, even in the grade below me, know more than I do. When they talk about papers we have to write, and they reference their fancy, charted notes, they talk about thesis and evidence, college words I haven't learned. At Little Red, I learned how to make a stool in shop, play piano, marbleize paper, paint scenery for school plays, and make papier-mâché. Capital letters still confuse me. Why do they have to go in some places and not others? And commas: They say put it where you would take a breath, but whenever I put it where my body breathes it's always the wrong place. Am I breathing wrong?

Don't get me started on "parts of speech." In "The dumb girl is thinking," for instance, "girl" is a noun because it's a person, but "girl" also describes what gender someone is, so why isn't it also an adjective? A word never means only one thing, but no one seems to understand that but me.

It's getting harder to pretend. For the entire first semester, I'm required to attend every after-school lab, and when I return home there's a tutor waiting. Soon I'm scheduled to leave school to see a tutor during the middle of the day, and while the teachers know, the other students don't, and I sneak out when no one is looking. I don't know what I'll say if I'm caught. Just imagining it mortifies me.

Then, in the middle of all this, I find myself spending four weekends in a row taking the same sorts of tests I took with Dr. Rivka in fifth grade. This time I go alone. I must have failed that test and that's why I'm taking it again. Or maybe they're hoping I've miraculously gotten smarter. Knowing I got it wrong the first time makes taking it a second time even more stressful. How am I supposed to know the right answers this time, when no one ever told me?

But the questions she asks are harder, the timer has less sand because it always runs out before I can answer, and the first questions come: What is the Apocrypha? What is the main theme of the book of Genesis? Who wrote *The Iliad*? Who cares?

I float inside an endless stretch of cloudy, white eternity and the not knowing turns into time itself, caught in the sticky fabric of the universe, like spider webbing to my body and face, making it hard for me to see and hear, swaddling my brain in a gauzy wrap. I worry that I'll never hear anything again. I feel turned inside out. What is a catacomb? Name the two countries that border the United States. Here is a sentence whose words are all mixed up so that they don't make any sense: For the started an we country early at hour to ask paper my teacher correct I my. Suppose you are going south, then turn left, then turn right.

Suppose I planted a tree that was eight inches tall. Suppose she never lets me leave? Suppose I can't be the things I want to be in my life because I'm so stupid?

The world feels like an enchanted forest filled with hidden riddles, stairwells, and doorways through which my peers and siblings advance, while I just continue on, walking past secret passages I can't see. I feel sorry for my mom because I'm this way. Kids are a reflection of their parents, and I don't want to reflect badly on her. If I keep sitting in the back, don't get called on, and figure out a way to never do things that are too hard for me, then maybe she won't be embarrassed by me and no one will catch on that I'm an idiot. She has kept it a secret all this time; now I will, too.

*   *   *

The only place I feel comfortable and accepted in the whole school, in all of uptown, is the art room. Up there with Basi, the painting teacher, and Mr. Indresano, the ceramics teacher, I don't feel stupid. I feel a belonging I don't in the rest of the school. No one tests me or makes me do after-school labs. Mr. Indresano gets my sense of humor, lets me curse, and teaches me how to do magic tricks, which I'm good at—unlike Latin, history, and biology. Also, Basi thinks I'm special. She is impressed that I can name the artist of any image she shows me, even if I've never seen the painting before. I like having that magic.

The air is different up here on the fifth floor. When I'm walking up from the fourth floor, the minor accelerations of my heart that mark the time of day begin to roll smoothly again. It's cool and smells of clay and it's like a private world just for me. Sometimes a few of the upper-school kids are here, but they are cool, with short spiky haircuts and lots of black plastic bracelets. I'm always the youngest, and Basi and Mr. I. give me attention and teach me things I can learn how to do like paint a still life, make a bowl, juggle, and describe a drawing so people can see it without looking. Plus, I have a crush on Mr. Indresano and I like that I always know where to find him. Mr. I. lives in the East Village; he and I are the only two people in the entire school who live below Fourteenth Street. The art room is like being in the Village while being uptown.

The social scene confuses me almost as much as the academic one. Whenever I talk to one of my classmates I feel like I'm a weirdo. My hair is short and frizzy, my nose is too big, my lips barely close over my braces, and my ears don't seem to stop growing. The other kids are perfect: all clean lines; no smudges. We have nothing in common, and I feel overwhelmed by how many of their references I don't understand. What is Frost Valley; what are rope lifts, Vail, and the Jitney? I can't be caught not knowing something.

Everyone except me lives uptown. Their houses are sprawling and shiny, like someone is always cleaning. Madison Spencer wants to be my friend because I'm funny, even though her parents don't like Jews, and she thinks Mr. Indresano is dirty. She even thought I was kidding when I met her joke's punch line "Because he's a kike!" with the words "I'm Jewish." She's the first popular chubby girl I've ever met. The first time I go over to her house, she shows me all the books her dad has about Nazis. I know not to bring up this information at home if I want to hang out with her again. Even though I feel out of step with myself at Madison's house, split from who I am, like when I'm at my dad's, and afraid if I'll ever get home, I've discovered that one of my separated selves is a stronger version of me, and I use her as a shield. She knows what to say and how to say it in order to keep the attention off what I'm really feeling, to keep the defective me from being witnessed by people my age.

Madison and I watch sitcoms and talk on the phone. I tell her about Adam Ant and David Bowie, but she thinks they're weird. I don't tell anyone else. Through Madison I make more friends, and soon I have an entire community of people who like me; finally I can breathe easy. But even though I now have a safe, home feeling at school, no one will actually visit me at home because Tory Fitzpatrick said downtown is where bums and poor people live, and everyone believes her because she's related to a famous designer I've never heard of. I feel sorry for her that she thinks this, because the Village is amazing and I wouldn't trade my bums or poor people for their lives, ever.

*   *   *

Seventh grade arrives, and we're finally in skirts. I'm so little I have to roll mine over four times just to keep it from falling down. There are two new girls that Madison and I become friends with, Tatum and Amelia. While Madison is the only popular chubby person I've ever met, Tatum is the only beautiful nerd I've ever known. Amelia is Jewish like me, and buoyant, always up for adventure. They are unafraid of the world, ready to separate from their parents and explore the street side of life in a way I'm not. Even as I feel comfortable with them, I'm always hiding a part of myself, pretending I'm cool when I'm tortured by a constant, unrelenting anguish. I'm thirteen, I still have countdowns, and my body still trembles for days leading up to any separation from my mom. Even though people think I belong, I know I don't. I thought my wrongness would go away—whatever it is—but it's not. It's getting worse.

Amelia, Madison, and Tatum all have the straight, bouncy hair I've been craving all my life. They have boobs; they shave their legs. They aren't afraid of growing older, of becoming women. They want boyfriends—they even think Eddie is cute—while I'm just pretending. I'm funny-looking: tiny, underdeveloped, with braces and hair like a clumpy mass of wool, and my features are too large for my face. I'm afraid of sex. I don't want anyone so close to me they might see who I really am. But we have dances with the nearby all-boys school Allen-Stevenson, and they all get dressed up and wear makeup and flirt and dance. There's a boy with bright red hair named Josh I like. He's the class clown, which is what I am becoming, and the odd one out in the bunch of blond kids. He lives in the Village also and he's really cute. We dance together at all the dances. When we catch Tatum, Amelia, and Madison all making out with their dance partners, the two of us laugh and make fun of them. I want to kiss him, and I am terrified that he'll kiss me.

Sometimes, though, I catch Madison and Tatum off to the side whispering. What are they doing without Amelia and me? The uncomfortable feeling turns into a threatening flicker in my chest, tinting the window my eyes look out of with a feeling I can't name. It's not the same as when I leave my mom, but it's related. Something about needing to be seen, something about being left.

The only reason I want my period is because it seems like one of the only markers in life that will tell me I'm normal. Otherwise, I don't want it, ever. I'm afraid of growing up. It seems that the older we get, the more the girls around me know, while I don't know anything. I don't know how to french-kiss, or what to do if a penis drops on my lap. Amelia, Madison, and Tatum know all about tampons and pads, but my mom hasn't told me about any of that stuff. I just pretend I know and nod along. Now that there are boys involved, my nodding has taken on a life all its own.

It is 1983, and the world is expanding and shrinking: We get a TV; my uncle Stanley dies, which makes me cry for days; we get an allowance; AIDS starts infecting the men in our neighborhood, though I don't understand why it's just here. Madison's family gets cable and we all go over there to watch Duran Duran on a channel called MTV—it's the greatest channel in the world. We dance to the endless music videos and watch ourselves in the mirror that hangs behind the couch in their TV room. Sterling, Madison's older sister, joins us. At one point Sterling starts french-braiding Tatum's hair. I'm surprised, but Tatum doesn't even react, like they've done this millions of times.

"Wait, hold the end," Sterling says. "You left your scrunchie in Southampton. Let me run and find it."

Sterling scuttles out of the room, and Amelia and I look at each other. None of us have ever been to Madison's family's house in Southampton before. Or so we thought. Sterling returns and secures Tatum's hair and she looks in the mirror and smiles.

Sterling lies on the couch and Amelia and I sit on the arms of the leather club chair, feeling defeated and confused.

Why does Tatum get in, but I don't? Is it because she's so pretty? All this time, while Amelia and I thought we were safe and secure in our friendship with Madison and Tatum, we were wrong. Now all I feel is secondhand embarrassment. The same kind I feel when I remember I'm dumb, and have been dumb all this time, starting from the beginning.

"So, you guys went to Southampton together?" Amelia asks them, trying to sound casual.

"Yeah, a few times," Tatum says, like it's no big deal.

"I would have invited you guys, but I was only allowed to bring one friend," Madison says. I'm jealous they did something without me, but my body is splashed by a nervous dread: I'd never have gone to Southampton, even if she'd asked. Have they seen who I really am, and is that why I wasn't invited? Have they realized I'm not good enough?

"That's okay," Amelia says fast, then looks at her Swatch. "I should go. I don't like taking the bus at rush hour."

I look out the window and am caught off-guard by how dark it is. Normally I go to Madison's only on the Fridays I stay at my dad's, but tonight I have to get back to the Village. If I take the subway at this hour, I might get raped or killed. If I don't, then there's the long walk from the 6 train home, another place to get raped or killed. I imagine myself on the back of a milk carton, just the way they started doing with Etan Patz's picture. Plus, I don't have money for a cab. I can't go to Amelia's because she lives on the Upper West Side, and I'm definitely not taking the bus. I suppose I could always walk over to my dad's house, but I don't feel welcome to just stop in unannounced. Though I'd been fine just a minute ago, the news about Southampton, seeing that the sky died before I was home safe, and that I don't know how to get home in order to *get* safe, builds swiftly inside me. My breathing goes heavy, and a spray of tingles warps through my body. My brain is overcrowding with words, and my heart is overcrowding with beats. My face flushes with sweat, while my fingers are freezing. When I look at my friends, their bodies are taking up more space than they had been moments before. There's an emergency feeling telling me to get out of this room immediately. Something very bad is about to happen to me.

"Just going to the bathroom," I say, trying to walk across the room as casually as possible, afraid for some reason that Madison will block me, or Tatum and Sterling will tackle me and stuff me in a closet and never let me out. Nothing this weird has ever happened before. I speed walk to Madison's bathroom, where I feel my body start to close down. I'm dizzy, then instantly hot, sweating hard by the time I throw up. I'm shaking and crying and I don't know what's wrong with me, but my heart will not slow down and I think I'm having a heart attack. I force my throat to swallow, because it doesn't seem to be doing that on its own. I do not want to die on the bathroom floor of a Nazi's Park Avenue apartment.

There's a knock on the door. Amelia is calling good-bye.

"Bye, Am!" I manage before puking again. I am mortified and worried she heard me. My face is soaked with sweat, and I stand at the sink feeling my entire body shake as I splash water on my face and run a dollop of Madison's toothpaste over my teeth and tongue with my finger. I look swollen, like Melissa. She had something wrong inside her, just like I do. I have a bad feeling. I try to block it out, but I can't. It's grabbing me and whispering in my ear things I don't want to know: No one in the entire world has what you have. You are defective and stupid and something is wrong with you, a wrong that is so bizarre it's never been discovered. You are going to be the person inside whose body they discover this medical weirdness. That is how you will be remembered. You are a shameful, ugly, little being.

Not ever knowing what will trigger this bizarre reaction inside me fills me with dread. This thing is ruining my life. It's always ruined my life, but now it's branching out into my friendships. How can I ever be happy if even the smallest things, like not knowing how to get home, or learning my friends didn't invite me somewhere, are so overwhelming I throw up and have heart attacks? I can't live like this. It's too hard.

No one's in Madison's room when I come out of the bathroom, which is a relief. I hurry down the hall.

"Bye, thanks for having me over," I say from the doorframe as I feel my body get stick-pinned like a voodoo doll.

"See ya!" Madison calls, waving without looking at me. I walk down the hall and pass Madison's mom's bedroom. Just like my mom, Mrs. Spencer is always in her bedroom. I pass it, thinking that moms are safe, and I backtrack and stick my head in.

"Mrs. Spencer?" I ask.

"Yes?"

"I'm a friend of Madison's and I don't know how I'm supposed to get home."

"What do you want me to do about it? Where's your driver?"

"I don't have a driver."

"Hail a cab."

"I don't have any money."

"Oh, for fuck's sake. Call your mom, then," she says, holding the phone out to me. When my mom answers, the ache I get right before I cry grows stronger in the back of my throat. I tell myself I can cry later; I can't cry now.

"Hi, Mom. I'm at Madison's, but I don't know how to get home."

"Can you put Mrs. Spencer on the phone?"

I look at Mrs. Spencer, who is glaring at me. "My mom wants to talk to you."

"Hello? How much? And who will pay me back? And when will that be? Are you kidding? I can't trust Madison with my money. You really don't have a driver?" Long pause. "Now that seems like a better plan."

She hands the phone back to me.

"What a bitch," my mom says. "Have the doorman get you a cab, that's their job. When you get here, I'll pay the driver."

When I hang up, Mrs. Spencer is aggrieved by my existence and exhales heavily. "Are we done?"

"Yes, thank you."

"Okay. Now, out, out, damned spot." She waves me away with the back of her hand. I bolt out of the apartment. As soon as I'm in the back of the cab I worry. How will my mom know that the cab has arrived? There's no way she can know unless I get out of the cab and tell her, but what if the cabdriver won't let me out until I pay, and he traps me? I worry all the way home. I worry when he lets me out of the cab to ring the bell, I worry waiting for my mom to answer the door, I worry as she counts the money, and then, once the cabdriver is gone, my worries disappear because I'm safe at home with my warm, loving, opposite-from-Mrs.-Spencer-mom. Whatever else happens, even if my friends all abandon me, I know I'll always have my mom.

June 1981

Dr. Rivka Golod

Conclusion:

  While this evaluation finds Amanda's cognitive abilities to be highly variable, it's my opinion that emotionally based factors are making her under-achievement appear even more dramatic.

A Sense of Rightness

WHEN HE SHOULDN'T THINK out loud, he does; and when he should, he keeps quiet.

Out of the blue Javier says, "You know, it's okay that sometimes we don't like things about the other person. Sometimes your partner will just rub you the wrong way, but that's just the deal, and you have to live with it."

"What things about me don't you like?" He won't tell me.

I try again: "What if I can change those things, wouldn't you want that?"

"You can't change them. Besides, I'm sure there are things about me you don't like," he says.

"There are, and I'm happy to tell you." In fact, I want to tell him, because I do believe people can change.

"Well, I don't want to know what they are."

When he falls asleep that night, and I am left alone with my imagination, the field of things to not like about me suddenly expands. I feel vulnerable and held hostage, as if I'm being kept from a part of my own self, a part I want to know, deserve to know; a part he has the power to show me. The feeling is too familiar. My entire childhood I felt kept from my own truth, as though who I am is too dangerous for me to know: Should I be afraid of myself? Is it how I look? Is it my body? Is it my anxiety, that I'm in therapy and take medication? I want to wake him and ask, Which of the million unlikable things about me are the most unlikable things? I can't let it go. But I've learned enough in the last few months to keep my worries to myself.

The other thing keeping me up is the baby conversation. Now that I have someone I could see myself having a baby with, I need to figure out how to make that happen—the sand timer on my ovaries is running out, and the more time I spend with Frankie, the more I want a baby of my own. Yet, in order for that desire to be realized, I need Javier on board, but whenever the topic comes up, he deflects, which makes me think he's not interested in having another child. He's invited me to spend a month with him and Frankie in a gorgeous island house off the coast of Maine, and I want to go, badly—I'd love to spend more time with him and Frankie, to have a quiet place to work on my stories and my next children's book—but there's no point in continuing our relationship if he doesn't want another kid. I need him to give me a straight answer, one way or another. I'm almost forty-one. I can't waste any more time.

In one of our long phone conversations, I try endlessly to frame a question in such a way that he'll have to answer. Finally, I just ask: "Are you morally opposed to having another child?" I am thrumming with dread at his response.

"No," he says. "I'm not morally opposed."

Not exactly an answer, but it's the best I've gotten. "Does that mean I should come to Maine?"

"Yeah, I think you should come," he says. Relief. There is still a chance.

I fly to Portland, Maine, and then take a bus. As I get closer, I picture our reunion. I haven't seen Frankie since New Year's, and imagining her face makes me smile. I wonder if she'll be looking for me, too, the same way I used to scan the crowd for my own mother's face. As we pull into the station, though, I can see immediately that they're not there, and I am slammed by a sudden splash of dislocation, until a motion to the side of the bus catches my attention. Javier and Frankie are running down the street, trying to get to the station before we do. I wish I didn't read all of his actions as symbolic nods to my standing in his life, but I can't help it: I've taken a plane and a bus to get here, and he's the one who is late.

Frankie gives me a huge hug and shows me the bag of baked goods Javier picked out for the ferry.

"Want a cheese Danish?"

"No thanks, my sweets."

She scours through the bag. "What about a croissant?" I shake my head.

"You're not hungry?" she asks.

"I am, I'm starving. But I'm allergic to dairy."

Javier smacks his head. "Goddamn it! I totally forgot," he says.

"That's all right," I say, reminding myself that in families, no one keeps score.

On the ferry, Frankie wants to show me everything we pass, so I can see the island as we pull into the harbor. Dots in the distance have names, and Frankie knows them all. She's excited for me to meet her mom; she keeps telling me so. She wants to show me her bedroom and hang out in her house and stay for dinner and have a sleepover. It's sweet that she considers me a friend, but I wish every mention of her mother didn't make me want to vomit. In photos Meredith looks like a French new wave "It" girl. She's so skinny and straight that in comparison my own small body looks like someone's zaftig Bubbe. I sense that Meredith is a monumental threat; Javier is patently afraid of her, which means he's unresolved and still under her sway. Although he has promised he's on my side, I worry he doesn't understand my feelings. I think Javier enjoys my jealousy, as though it means something more than that my feelings are slippery. His fear makes me afraid of her also.

The ferry edges close to the harbor, and I don't know how we'll get through the thicket of fishing boats. The island is foggy and gorgeous.

Frankie darts off the ferry, pulling me behind her. "Lobster traps!" she yells. She races ahead, pointing wildly. "Candy store! Post office! Library!" I smile and laugh, while Javier lags behind us.

The smell of low-hovering clouds and wet rocks feels like a secret all my own, as if I'm walking not on the island, but inside it. The coastline is ragged, and the oat-colored linens and cream undergarments clothes-pinned and sun-drying on front lawns have a decidedly French feel. A woman with a headscarf is working in her garden, listening to the radio. She waves her spade hello to us.

"Lichen! Spruce tree! Moss! Our favorite hike is back that way! The swimming quarry is over there."

We pass rambling colonial and Victorian houses. The gardens and the surrounding woods are wild and perfect, nothing manicured. Cars pass slowly; drivers lift their palms up off the wheel, an erect flag of fingers in a lazy salute.

"Blackberry bush! Dragonfly! Sumac! Perennials!"

We start up a hill. Frankie points ahead. "That's Abi and Abu's house, where you're staying. My house with my mom is over there," she adds and points a bit farther down, but I don't look.

Javier unlocks the door and we walk into the kitchen, where Frankie starts narrating the kitchen appliances. Javier finally starts laughing, too.

"Let's show Amanda where she's going to write," he says.

"Ooooh yeah. You're going to love this!" She zips ahead and Javier and I follow her up the stairs, through a bathroom, and toward a door, be-hind which she reveals the most dreamlike writing carrel I've ever seen. A sanctuary of wood: beams, floor, desk. A faded army green, vintage metal index-card box sits on the desk, which rests in front of a window overlooking the forest, or what they call "the backyard."

"Are you sure this is okay with your dad?" I ask Javier.

"Yeah, he's really excited that you're writing here."

"Amazing. This is totally amazing. Thank you," I say and hug him. A stacked tower of books waiting to be reviewed for the local newspaper, where Abu's a critic, are waiting for his eye. I'm inexpressibly happy. This is the life I've always wanted, where I could be a writer and a mother. They show me the rest of the house, and, strange as it sounds, with every room a sense of rightness grows in me. Somehow this is-land feels like a place that has always belonged to me. We unpack, and

Frankie goes over to her mom's. Javier takes the car to get groceries, and I stay behind to set up my writing space.

At dinner, Javier and Frankie hold hands, and then reach for mine. Oh no, are they going to expect me to say grace? I put my hands in theirs.

"Every night at dinner we say what we're grateful for," Javier explains.

My voice box seizes up. This feels like a test. I'm as nervous as a seventh grader. But they offer normal, bland statements about togetherness and good food, so I do, too, even though my heart is pounding and I feel weirdly naked, but then it's over. I didn't say anything wrong.

"Will you come pick me up from school tomorrow?" Frankie asks me.

I'm opening my mouth to say how happy that would make me, when Javier interjects. "Amanda has to write. You can see her when you get home."

Frankie looks disappointed, so I add: "I'm sure there will be some days I can pick you up, Frankie."

"Will you come to my school and do an assembly? All my friends know who you are and love your books."

"They do? That's crazy. But yeah, I'd love to!"

"I'd love it, too."

"Frankie, stop talking with your mouth full; it's disgusting," Javier tells her.

"Sorry," she says, mouth full. Big swallow. "Maybe you can come watch me when I do my trumpet lesson." I nod enthusiastically. "Then you can meet all my friends and I can point out all the kids who don't like me because they think I'm weird."

Javier kicks her chair. "Frankie, sit like a normal person, please."

Frankie unbends her legs and sits properly, but he continues to pick on her. I don't like it.

After dinner I make tea and we sit around the table. It's only 7 p.m., but I'm exhausted and ready for bed. "Island time," Javier explains.

In the morning, Javier and Frankie are already gone, so I make coffee and begin writing. I am the most productive I've been in a long time.

Something about the carrel makes me take myself more seriously. I make a sandwich; I make more coffee. At some point in the afternoon, the carrel door swings open and Frankie's sweet little face pops in.

"How many words did you write today?" she asks.

I look at my computer. "Two thousand!"

"Wow! That's like a hundred pages," she says.

"Four, but close enough." We grin at each other.

Frankie leaves to visit her mom and returns at dinnertime.

"Look what Leo made me!" Frankie yells, barreling through the screen door, wielding a sword.

It's wood, carved intricately and painted silver. "Holy cow, that's beautiful," I say, awed by the craftsmanship.

"Papa, look!" Frankie holds up the sword to Javier, who barely looks.

"Nice," he says.

Frankie and I exchange looks. Hers says, I'm worried. Mine says, Don't worry. She is disappointed, and she doesn't understand that Javier doesn't want to hear about Meredith's boyfriend. I know the feeling.

At dinner, I lean over to Frankie. "What was the best part of your day?"

"When my teacher said I was a natural at trumpet!" she announces, proud. "What was the best part of your day, Amanda?"

"When you came into my office and asked how many words I wrote," I tell her. "Because seeing you made me happy."

She giggles, happy and embarrassed. "Papa, what about you?"

"The best part of my day was cooking you guys dinner and the worst part of my day was having to tell you to stop talking with your mouth full."

Frankie looks down at her plate.

*   *   *

While island time slows things down, the month seems to speed past. One afternoon we make a picnic lunch and take it to one of the island's preserves. Through dense woods, the two of them scramble up the path, much faster than me, and I can't help but notice that Javier, having promised to take care of me on this trip, doesn't look back to make sure that the branches and brambles haven't locked his city girlfriend in a half nelson. I follow them out across slabs of granite to the flat surface where we eat and look out onto the bay. Frankie goes to collect rocks, and Javier and I sit quietly. I can't tell if this is his normal station, or if he's just being inordinately quiet. Though we've been dating for eight months, we haven't spent enough time together for me to even know. I get up and walk out onto the rocks by myself to see how far I can get just jumping. I'm pretty far out onto the bay and I turn to wave at Javier, but he's not looking at me. Even when I'm in his sight, I feel out of his mind.

Being here is worth it, though, since Frankie pops her head into my office every day after school. As soon as I'm ready she grabs her sword and we go for girls-only walks, where, in between times of her pretending she's a ninja, she confides in me things she doesn't reveal to her parents.

"That's my dad's house," she says, pointing her sword at a large, rambling white house. "People rent it from him during the year and we use it during the summer. I don't have my own bedroom, though."

"You don't? Why not?"

"I have to share with my cousins. But it's still my house, right? Don't you think I should have my own room?" she asks.

I know better than most people how important it is to have a bedroom at your dad's house. But I don't want to step on anyone's toes, and I certainly don't want Frankie racing back to either Meredith or Javier and telling them I was criticizing their parenting. While I'm the least diplomatic person on earth, Frankie has brought out in me a different, more measured person—when I'm with her, I feel like I know what I'm doing, like a real adult.

"You know, I think it's hard for people whose parents never divorced to become divorced parents themselves. They don't know what it feels like to be the kid shuttling between two places, so they don't quite understand what matters and what doesn't. That's why you have to tell them what matters."

"I have told him, but he doesn't get it. He says we're only there for the summer, so what do I care?"

"Could your mom talk to him about it?" I ask.

"I've asked, but she always forgets!" Frankie runs toward an abandoned house. There's a bicycle on the roof, which makes her laugh, and we try to see through the windows. "Did you have your own bedroom at your dad's house?" Frankie asks me, her face pressed to a window too dark to see through.

"I didn't," I say.

She pulls away from the house and starts stabbing the ground with her sword. "Did that matter to you?"

"Very much. Especially because my dad and stepmother had two kids together, who had big, beautiful bedrooms, on the same floor as my dad and my stepmother. Eddie and Kara and I were downstairs all the way in the back, off the kitchen, stuck in the maid's room. A room so small you could barely open your suitcase."

"Like Cinderella," she says, pulling up her sword and skipping ahead. "Were the maids mad about sharing a bed with you?" she asks.

I smile and explain while we pass a low wall built of rocks. She climbs up on them and starts walking. She keeps one hand on my shoulder and we walk in sync.

"I'm the only person in my entire family whose parents are divorced."

"Really?" I ask. "That's surprising."

"You're the only grown-up I know who understands about this stuff."

"Well, I bet you that's not true, but I'm glad you have me. If you want me to talk to your dad with you, I will. Just say the word, okay?"

She smiles, but her eyes look glazed, like she might cry, and she jumps off the rocks and bolts ahead, then down into a squat, cutting the air with her sword. "Death to my enemies!" she yells. Frankie is uncertain about her father's love, and I realize that's another thing she and I have in common.

We make ice pops, we play Boggle, and she reads me her dark and beautiful poems that are beyond her years. Javier spends his days painting someone's house, and one of those days, it's just me there when the phone rings.

"Meredith?" a guy asks.

"Uh . . . no. This is Amanda," I say.

An awkward laugh. "Woops. Sorry. This is Earl. Is Javier there?"

Earl is the guy Meredith left Javier for. "No, sorry. Can I take a message?"

"Yeah, tell him to call me when he can. Sorry I called you Meredith," he says. "Weird for us both, I guess."

When Javier gets home I give him the message. "That's Meredith's Earl?"

"Yeah. He's staying in my Jersey City apartment."

"He's staying in your apartment?" Something about this creeps me out.

"Yeah. We're friends."

Later, Leo, whom Meredith left Earl for, comes over to help Javier move a table. There is too much line-crossing here for my comfort. Where are their boundaries? How is this even appropriate? It all rubs me the wrong way and makes me feel disoriented, like one of us is improperly interpreting the world.

The next day, my iPad goes missing. Javier hasn't seen it, but I hear giggling coming from Frankie's room. I knock on the door, but she doesn't answer.

"Frankie?" I call. No response.

I push the door open and see Frankie and a friend, giggling on her bed, playing a game on my iPad.

"There it is! I've been looking for that." Frankie pretends I don't exist. "Frankie, can I have my iPad back? I need it for work."

She continues to ignore me. This is unlike her, at least the her I know, and it reminds me of the beginning when I wasn't sure about her. But now I think I get it. She's got a mini teenager living inside her who is mad as hell. I am still hovering in the doorway, unsure what to do, when Javier barrels past me and grabs my iPad out of Frankie's hand.

"Not cool," he says. I follow him downstairs, and he's fuming. "What the hell! There are scratches all over the screen."

"Lemme see."

He hands it to me, and, sure enough, there are tons of tiny fingernail scratches in semicircles fogging up the black mirror. He turns around and shouts Frankie's name and is about to storm upstairs.

"Javier!" I snap. "Don't. This is my battle. Not yours."

He stops. "She scratched your iPad."

"I know, but let me deal with it."

"Suit yourself."

I do some work and after Frankie walks her friend out, she tries escaping back to her room.

"Hey, come here for a sec, okay?" I ask.

Frankie comes over and sits on my lap. Javier steps in from the kitchen to watch, and I become aware that what I'm about to do is as much for him as for her, and I pray that this new approach works.

"I love sharing my iPad with you, but when you take it without asking, it makes me not want to share it with you anymore." She looks at me, stunned. "And that feels terrible, because sharing my things with you makes me feel close to you. So if you like sharing my things with me, you have to ask me before just taking it, okay? That's what sharing means." She nods.

"And if you'd asked me, I could have told you how sensitive the screen is, and that you need to use the pads of your fingers and not your fingernails when you play games because your fingernails scratch the screen, making it hard for me to read. Scratches don't go away."

Her face turns red. "I'm sorry."

"You are forgiven. But you get where I'm coming from about sharing, right?"

She nods, gets off my lap, and then looks at me for a long minute. "I really like how you handled that," she says.

This kid cracks me up; she makes my face detonate into idiotically large smiles. "I'm so glad."

I look at Javier, who looks kind of shocked. "How did you know how to do that?"

"I don't know," I say. "I just explained things in a way I wish people had explained things to me as a kid."

But that's not all of it. I wanted Javi to see that I'd be a good mom, that if he decides he's on board for another kid, he's doing it with someone who knows what she's doing, even if I'm just winging it for now.

"That was awesome."

I smile, proud of myself, and then realize that I just did something easily with Frankie that I've found painfully hard with adults: set a boundary. She didn't push back and try to turn my no into a yes; rather, she accepted it, and the entire exchange leaves me with an unfamiliar feeling: grounded.

I can do this. I can be someone's parent. Or maybe it's Frankie who makes me a good parent because she's the very person whose parent I want to become. I never considered how happy another person's child might make me, but here she is, filling and overflowing the empty mom part of me. Frankie is enough. She's more than enough for me. If I am lucky enough to help raise her, maybe I wouldn't need to have my own child. I'd already have her.

*   *   *

One day Frankie invites her friend Cecilia to sleep over, but the afternoon she's supposed to come, there's a terrible rainstorm, and Cecilia doesn't call. When she's a half hour late, Frankie calls her, but no one answers. She tries every ten minutes for the next hour— nothing. By 3 p.m. the weather is clearing, and Frankie is beginning to spiral.

"Let's take a walk," I say. "We'll get ice cream."

On the walk to town, Frankie is distraught. "She doesn't like me. She doesn't want to be friends with me anymore. She never wanted to sleep over in the first place and now she's avoiding me."

"You know, I don't know much, but I do know this. Our worries are almost never right. When we assume someone is thinking or feeling one way about us, usually the worst and most personal, our assumptions are almost always wrong."

"Well, what else could it be?" she asks. We come up with some ideas: Maybe the power went out, or the phone lines are down, or her parents had other plans.

"I'm telling you, there are a million reasons for things and guessing never works. When you find out the truth, you'll be frustrated at how much time you wasted worrying needlessly."

Poor Frankie is on edge all day, getting worse and worse as the hours go by; even making cookies and playing Boggle doesn't help.

It's 6 p.m. by the time the phone finally rings. As soon as Frankie hangs up, she skips into the kitchen, beaming with relief.

"You were right," she says. "Cecilia's phones were knocked out. Her dad's bringing her over now."

"See?" I say to her. "What did I tell you?"

"But how did you know?" she asks.

"A lifetime of overthinking," I answer with a wry smile.

Every day with Frankie little explosive pockets burst open with revelations. Being able to give her what I needed someone to give me when I was her age feels like a course correction, and every exchange leaves me feeling a bit sturdier in the world.

I find myself falling more in love with this little girl. I am less certain about Javier, which is a problem, but the thing I am most certain about is this feeling inside me, a grounded calm, of being a member of a family where I'm not the frightened child, but the knows-what-she's-doing mom. One night when I'm walking out of the carrel, I stop, halfway through the bathroom, hypnotized by the sound of Javier's and Frankie's laughter floating up from the kitchen, which arrives at the same time as the smell of simmering garlic and the sizzle of lamb chops. The family feeling I have is powerful, and I'm struck hard by the sensation. My entire life I thought I could never get anything right, that every effort would result in failure, but here I am, in an actual house, with a child and a partner, and a sense of purpose unlike any I've ever had. To raise a child with someone—to raise *this* child with someone—feels like my calling. I'm so overcome by emotion that I sit down on the toilet and tell myself that even if this doesn't work out, even if I never have a family of my own, I'll have had these four weeks to experience what it would have felt like, and for that I will always be grateful. When I stand up, I am convinced I will do anything it takes to make this last.

Once Frankie is in bed, I ask Javier whether he's talked to Meredith about next year, about our living upstate. He says he and Meredith haven't talked yet, but they will, they will. I am frustrated. It's becoming clearer that Javier doesn't really want to make plans for the future. He doesn't like clarity. He likes living in the in-between, the whatever-happens. The metaphysical space Javi relishes is a place I dread, and I bat it away every time it nears. This, I think, is the definition of incompatible, but I do not want to know this. Not right now.

The next day, Frankie asks me to pick her up at the Arc Cafe, but when I get there she grabs my hand. "I want you to meet someone."

On the way up the stairs, I realize what's about to happen, and my mouth dries. In an office, down a short hallway, two women are seated at computers. I recognize the skinny, vaguely French one as Meredith. I smile and shake her hand. She doesn't stand up.

"This one likes you a lot," she says drily.

"I like her a lot, too."

"You getting a lot of work done?" she asks.

"Yeah, it's been great," I say, forcing a smile. "Super productive."

"Awesome. Cool." She smiles, but instead of lighting her face up, the smile seems to harden and darken her features. I don't like her.

"You're meeting my mom! I'm so happy you're meeting my mom!" Frankie sings.

I smile and make an awkward exit. Later I tell Javier I met Meredith and he says he knows. He ran into her.

"Oh. What'd she say?"

"She said you were cute. So, what'd you think?"

"Of Meredith?" I ask.

"Yeah," he says.

Before I can figure out how to answer, the phone rings in the other room, and Javier leaps for it. He doesn't return. Ten minutes later, when I go in the kitchen, he's sitting at the side table on the phone, giggling. He sees me and covers the receiver.

"What's up?" he asks.

"Nothing, I just...we were in the middle of a conversation."

"I'm just talking to Meredith. We'll talk when I'm off," he says.

I go upstairs and lie down, suddenly depressed. Meredith is everywhere. Javier is sitting directly under the bed I'm lying on, talking to his ex-wife, and while I can't hear what he's saying, I can hear how he's speaking. Gooey and baby-voiced, the same way he sounds when he's talking to me. When he's off the phone, he comes up.

"What's going on?" he asks.

"Nothing," I say, still lying down. "I just...I'm not sure where I fit in here."

He groans a little bit. "This again?"

I sit up. "Again? When was the first time?"

"Let's talk about this later. I need to stop by my house and pick up some pans. Do you wanna see it?" he asks.

"Sure," I say. Things feel heavy.

I feel inside out in a way I can't quite unravel. When my dad married Sallie, he called us less. When they had kids, I felt like an afterthought. That feeling of being rejected and replaced has followed me all my life, and I feel it now, on this small island in Maine. Only I'm being replaced by someone Javi never seemed to have left, and I don't like how familiar any of this feels.

From the outside, the house is gorgeous and looks like it's holding up well, but the inside is crumbling. The wallpaper is falling off in strips. There are holes large enough for small dogs to fall into. It smells like mold or mildew, and our feet stick to the floor as we walk. "Still needs work, obviously, but we're getting there."

"How long have you had this place?" I ask.

"About twenty years," he says.

That tells me everything I need to know about Javier. Not only is he slow to change, he doesn't want to change. However things were is how they will remain.

We sit on the couch. Our coats are on; it's freezing in here.

"So how was meeting Meredith?" he asks.

"Not that easy," I admit.

"This doesn't work for you," he says.

"No, I didn't say that. It's just a lot to handle."

"This is too much for you to handle," he says. Clearly, he wants it to be too hard for me to handle. "She's part of the deal," he continues. "If you want me, you get Meredith. Until Frankie is eighteen, we'll be talking every day. We're friends. She's a good friend."

Earlier in our relationship, he was "stuck with her" until Frankie was eighteen. Earlier, she wasn't his friend; she was "Frankie's mother." I don't mind if they're friends, I'd actually prefer it. What I mind is that every story he tells changes, and the ground I once assumed was solid softens with each telling; I don't know how long I've been sinking. I push away a thought I don't want to hear—Javi is trying to get me to break up with him.

With Javier, I feel insecure, but with Frankie I've never felt such connection. Everyone always says when you meet the person you want to spend the rest of your life with, you'll know. And they're right: With Frankie, I know. I want to spend the rest of my life being her parent.

I want to stop writing when she comes home, when she pops her head into the writing carrel; I've started calling it F o'clock. I've never been like this before. Until now, I've resented anything that's threatened my writing time, because to me, writing is my family, my security; but with Frankie, I feel no resentment. If anything, I am more efficient, knowing that by the time she's home, I'll be free and clear. She is the family I am choosing, but I know that in order to have her I need to get Javier to choose me.

I'm nearly done with the next book in the Frankly, Frannie series, and I'm taking a nap during a break when Javier accidentally wakes me.

"Sorry," he says, mid-tiptoe to the closet.

"Where are you going?" I ask.

"I already went."

"Where to?"

"Meredith's. We decided about next year," he says. "They're gonna stay here. They'll probably move off the island when Frankie starts sixth grade."

As he's telling me, I realize that I didn't factor into the decision. Despite all the conversations about selling Jersey City and living upstate, he's planning his future without me, because his future is with Meredith and Frankie. I sit up as I realize that all this time I've been living his life, on his terms, and everything I've said I wanted has gone ignored. Yet even though I should take this realization and walk out, I know I won't; I need Frankie in my life. I tell myself I'll find a way to handle the bad stuff. I roll over and don't respond.

As the days on the island draw to a close, I know more clearly than ever that this is the life I want. I can spend half the year on this island and half in New York. I can alternate months; I don't care how we make it work.

Abi and Abu come up during the last night of our stay, followed by Javier's sisters and their partners. The house is chaotic and bustling and I love it. Javier announces that he's off to read the latest revision of my story, but instead of finding a quiet place to read upstairs, he plops down in the center of all the activity.

At dinner that night, his father asks Javi about what he read, and I'm eager to hear Javier's response, remembering how effusive he was about the earlier, less-polished draft. I want him—both of them—to think I'm talented.

"Uh…" Javier stalls. "It needs work. It was better before."

My mouth splits open.

"This was a revision?" Abu asks.

"Yeah. Something got lost, I guess. I don't know. I didn't like it as much."

"Maybe you should give it to Abu," Valentina turns to me and says. "He can help you with it."

I want to say that I don't need help with it. That it's a good story. That Javier loved the story when he read it the first two times, and he'd said as much. I am shocked and hurt by his disloyalty.

We pack that night and then crawl into bed. He can tell I'm upset.

"You know, maybe it was just that I read your story when it was so hectic," he offers. "I think that's why I didn't like it that much."

"Too bad you didn't say that at dinner. Now your family thinks I'm a bad writer."

"Nah," he says. It's an unconvincing sound. "How much time you need in the morning?"

"Probably an hour," I say.

"Okay, I'll wake you at eight."

When Javier wakes me, I putter around a bit before getting dressed. Soon he stomps up the stairs and into our bedroom.

"What are you doing? We're all waiting for you," he says.

"What?" I ask. "For what?"

"For the ferry. We have to leave."

"You said you'd give me an hour!"

"It's nine fifteen; we don't have an hour," he says.

I don't understand why he didn't wake me at eight, and although it's my fault I didn't bother to look at the clock, I'm angry at time for not alerting my body that there's a leaving on the horizon, angry at my body for not counting time to me the way it always has.

I throw everything into my bag, feeling the agonizing pressure of the others' waiting for me, like Melissa and my class when I couldn't tell time.

We rush to the ferry, where Frankie hugs me tight and cries when we leave. On the ferry, we wave and wave until she's not a girl anymore, but air. Javier and I are taking two separate planes home, and he's leaving first thing in the morning for Atlanta for six weeks. When we get to the ferry terminal, we have two hours together before saying good-bye. It's snowing hard, and I go to the bathroom to put on my long johns. When I come out, he's on the phone.

"Probably like half an hour," he says. "Yeah, awesome. Okay, see you in a bit." He hangs up and looks at me. "I'm gonna go meet up with Sam for a while. I'll go to the airport from there."

"Oh," I say. "I thought we were going to spend this time together. We won't see each other for six weeks."

"We've just spent an entire month together," he says.

"Yeah, but we barely spent any time together alone," I say.

"I haven't seen Sam in months. We're not far from his house, and I want to see him."

"So what am I supposed to do?"

"I don't know. Go to the airport," he says. My body crimps like someone kicked the back of my knees. I don't even know where the airport is. We're on his turf, and he's leaving me to fend for myself because he doesn't want to fend for me anymore. I breathe; maybe he just wants to see Sam. Maybe there's nothing more to it. His phone rings and when he picks it up, he turns his back to me, walking away to talk in private. When he returns he looks disappointed and annoyed. "There's a big snowstorm coming. Sam says we should go straight to the airport and I'll see him another time."

We drive to the airport in silence. When we get there, all the planes have been delayed. We check in anyway and walk to our gates together, but we can't seem to ease into each other's company. Soon Javier gets restless.

"I really need to get home and get my gear ready," he says. "I'm thinking I might just drive."

"In the storm? I'm not sure driving is the best idea," I say.

"Got a better one?" he snaps.

I don't say anything, and he leaves to look for a car to rent. I'm sickened by the sense that he's trying to get as far away from me as possible. He returns with car keys.

"Now I just need to find out how to get my luggage back," he says.

"Do you want me to come with you? Or do you want to say good-bye now and I'll just see you when I see you?" I ask, dizzy and confused.

"Whatever you want," he says. "It doesn't matter to me." The inside of me staggers backward.

"You're acting really strange," I say. "I don't understand what's happening."

"I'm fine. Everything's fine. If you want to come, come. If you don't, don't. But whatever you decide, you need to decide now because we have to get our luggage."

"Okay, I'll come," I say, and we hurry to retrieve our bags, and then to the car. I slide into the passenger seat and plug the buckle into its socket for that satisfying click.

"Maybe this is a mistake. Are you sure you don't want to fly while I drive?"

I just had the most expansive, glorious month with him and his family, and now he's acting like he never wants to see me again.

"What the hell is going on?" I ask. "Instead of hanging out with me, you want to see Sam. Instead of driving back to the city with me, you want me to take an airplane. What are you trying to do?"

"Nothing," he says. "I want you here. You're being oversensitive," he says.

I am not.

I'm quiet as we drive. I can see the emotional cliff we're about to plunge over.

"That was really hard," he says, after half an hour of silence. "This past month."

"Seriously?" I ask, turning to him. How could we have had the exact opposite experience?

"Yeah, seriously. It just seemed like there was always something. Things aren't just smooth all the time with you. We couldn't just like exist and coast along. I don't know if I can take all this negativity," he says.

"What negativity?"

"Yours. Every time you were disappointed, your face dropped. Whenever I let you down, I could see it in your expression, and it's like I can't do anything right."

"Javier, when you think out loud and say things like 'I'm not sure I want to get married again,' or 'I'm not sure I want a home base,' or 'Maybe I don't want another child,' you're saying the exact opposite things you've told me you do want. You say one thing and I take it at face value, but you don't mean it, and that's misleading. So yeah, I am fucking disappointed when you take back the safe thing you said earlier to say the unsafe thing you say now."

"See? Unsafe. Safe! That's so negative!" he says. "I can't take it!"

"That's not negative. That's anxiety."

"Well, then it's anxiety I can't take," he says.

"Yeah, that's coming through, loud and clear."

"This is too much for me. You're too much for me. I can't do this. And I don't want another baby," he says.

"Oh my God, what is wrong with you?" I yell. "Why did you invite me to spend the month with you?"

"I wanted you to come," he says.

"But the reason I was coming was to see if we could be a family, and also because you said you were open to having another kid."

"I never said that. You asked me if I was morally opposed to having another child. And no, I'm not morally opposed to it. I just don't want one."

"Javier, you knew what I was asking you. Why didn't you just tell me that then?"

"Because that's not what you asked me!"

"Holy shit! Are you fucking out of your mind? You knew exactly what I was asking, and you led me to believe something that isn't true. I came to Maine and fell totally in love with your kid and had a completely revelatory experience, and all the while you knew we didn't want the same things. Why would you do that to someone?"

"I don't know. I didn't mean to."

I don't speak. I have nothing left to say to him. Everything I've ever wanted I just had, and now it's gone. I'm falling through a bottomless pipe down to the end of the world. I will not survive this.

"I don't know what I'm saying," he says a few hours later. "I spoke too soon. I don't want this to end. It's just too hard. I need it to be easier. I should have waited to say something. I'm sorry. Let's just forget I said anything. Can we sit on this for a bit?"

I don't answer. I just stare out of the window. I'm breathing in and out, counting to five on the inhale, counting to ten on the exhale. I am mute. I am spinning. I am dead.

Hunky Dory

HOW DOES A PERSON stop themselves from being swapped out?
How do you get back something you never asked to lose? Can you force
a person to feel what they used to feel? Make them go back to when
things were good, undo whatever changed somehow? There must be a
way, I just don't know it. As more and more of our friends and classmates report seeing Madison and Tatum together without Amelia and
me, I am taken over by a heavy jealous rage.

Why am I not good enough for Madison anymore? Is it because I'm
always in section C and D classes? Is she embarrassed that I've been
lumped in with the dumb kids? It doesn't matter that she's not my type
of person, that under other circumstances I'd never choose her as a
friend. I can't shake the sense that I'm the problem, that they are able
to see my interior self and that's why they're rejecting me. I wish I were
simply furious, the way Amelia is, but instead I'm something else, something worse. I just keep thinking: Is there a way to turn this around,
change their minds, and prove to them that I'm too special or important
to replace?

The air I sit in, sleep in, eat in, and walk through is filled with jealousy
and anxiety that do not lift. Every empty expanse of time is filled with
images of my friends without me, laughing, bonding, merging into one
another to become one person. I feel myself sliding out of their fast-
forwarding lives, and I can't catch up. I'm consumed by attempts to find
out what I'm missing, but in conversations I'm unsubtle and I come off

sounding both bizarre and possessed. I can't stop thinking that if I were as cool as my brother, or as rich as Madison, no one would ever want to separate from me, and I'd never be alone. It is all-encompassing. I feel it even in my sleep. I'm caught inside a Shallow Countdown that will not subside. People are slipping away from me, and I need to get them back before they die or disappear forever.

On Thursday, the first day of Hanukkah, school is optional for anyone observing the holiday. Amelia and I are the only two Jews in the class, but we both go in anyway, as if we could stop the worst from happening by keeping an eye on Madison and Tatum. But then we discover they're both absent.

"Maybe they're both sick," I offer.

"Maybe," Amelia says. "Or maybe one is sick and the other had to go to the doctor or something." We nod, but I think we both know better.

It infuriates me that they've taken the day off on *our* Jewish holiday. They're capitalizing on our religion! Without us! Madison's family doesn't even *like* Jews!

"I brought you a Hanukkah present," Amelia tells me, pulling out a badly wrapped cassette tape.

"I left yours at home," I lie. "I'm sorry. I'll bring it tomorrow." I burn a note in my skull to buy her something after school.

She waves it off. "Come on, open, open!"

Inside is *Hunky Dory*, my absolutely favorite David Bowie album.

"Oh my God! I love it!" I say. "Thank you so much. Eddie is going to be so jealous!" I give her a big hug. We don't talk about Tatum or Madison for the rest of the day, and I realize how much better school is without them. I know Amelia feels it, too. The pressure of keeping tabs on them has lifted, and with it Shallow Countdown has lifted. My body feels like itself. We're making memories without them, strengthening our friendship. Plus, she had a present for me and not for them. That means she likes me more than she likes them, and that feels amazing.

But they return, and the next day in homeroom, someone slips me a note from Amelia: "They played hooky and went to the movies together. This. Is. WAR."

My chest seizes instantly. No. I don't want to go to war. But if there is only fighting or losing, I can't be a loser. So, despite my strong desire to not fight or to engage even in minor confrontation, I decide I will stand behind Amelia no matter what. I tell myself that I'll nod, stamp my foot, and pout, and I'll call it fighting. But I recognize that whatever fight we have will change everything forever. What I really want is just to let it go and pretend nothing happened, even as I worry about what they're doing now, and now, and now. I have faith that Amelia can conjure the magic to fix this.

But that doesn't happen. Days pass and the war heats up. Madison and Tatum start saying mean things when they pass us, like "Get a life," and "Get a new face." During gym, Magda comes up to Amelia and me to pass along some urgent information.

"Just so you know, Tatum is trying to turn the entire class against you two," Magda says helpfully.

"It's not going to work," Amelia says. "Plus, just because we're in a fight with them doesn't mean we're not still popular."

"You're not still popular!" Tatum, with her bionic hearing, shouts over to us.

"Oh, yes we are!" I yell and storm over.

"You're a couple of losers!" Tatum yells so everyone can hear.

I am taken over by a rage I've never experienced. Tatum has already taken Madison away from me, and I need to protect what I have left.

"Everyone knows why you won't let Clement even feel you up!"

"Why's that, if you know so much?" she yells.

"Because you're a cocksucking dyke!" I yell, not entirely clear what any of that means. The crowd gasps. Victorious as a slanderer, I swell from my awed classmates; but then something hard smacks me across the face. Everyone gasps again as Tatum shakes out her hand.

Horrified by the sudden reversal, I run out of the gym and to the fourth floor to find Kara. I cry and tell her what happened, and she calms me down and helps me breathe. I am shaken and shaking. I'm still out-of-body in my next class, and when I sit down next to Lizzie she immediately gets up and moves away. No one will sit next to me. When I ask Claudine what's going on, she doesn't answer. I force myself not to cry in class. I never should have left the gym to find Kara. When I left, that's when Tatum told everyone to cut me out of their lives. They've made me disappear, and I feel gone. How did they know this was the worst way to hurt me? When the bell rings, I'm the first one out the door, looking for Amelia, whom I feel badly for leaving behind in the gym.

"Is anyone talking to you?" I ask.

Amelia looks like she's been crying, and she shakes her head.

"Me neither," I say.

"You still have me; don't worry," Amelia says.

"Thanks, Am. You have me, too."

"No matter what, we're in this together," she says as we hug.

*   *   *

In the mornings on the way uptown, even the new girl Libby who started in the middle of the year won't talk to me, and we're the only two people on the school bus. At home I throw myself on my bed and sob. When I'm cried out, I find my mom coming in from the garden, a scarf around her head—which always reminds me of Melissa—and I tell her what happened.

"They're just jealous," she says. She begins tidying the already neat living room. Straightening the already straight paintings, and positioning the pitchers and vases in the open armoire.

I tag along behind her. "They're not jealous. There's nothing here to be jealous about!" I am annoyed that she's still using this dumb argument. "I just want them to start talking to me again. I want Tatum to forgive me, and I don't know how to make her."

"Why don't you call and tell her that your uncle died and you're very upset and it's not the right time for her to be mad at you," my mom says. She pulls dead petals off some flowers.

"Is that a good idea?" I ask.

"Of course it's a good idea. She'll feel sorry for you because your uncle died, which means she'll stop being mad at you; it's the right thing to do," she says.

"Is that true?" I ask.

"Would I tell you something that wasn't true?" she says, punching the pillows and cushions until they're fluffy.

My uncle died over a month ago, and while I'm still upset by it, I'm finally feeling better. Tatum doesn't know that, though. I fly upstairs to my bedroom to make the call. My fingers have a hard time finding the right numbers to dial, they're so nervous. Her brother picks up.

"Hi, Tanner; it's Amanda. Is Tatum there?"

"Sure. Hang on." I hear the phone drop on the floor, and then… nothing. No one comes. I wait, and I wait some more. Still, no one comes. I am freaking out. Trying to swallow, but my saliva seems like it's hardened and I need to push it down my aching esophagus. Then, a smothering sound.

"What?" Tatum says.

"Hi, Tatum. It's Amanda."

"What?"

"Well, I just wanted to say that I'm very upset because I just found out my uncle died and I was hoping you could stop being mad at me right now."

"Nope," she says and hangs up the phone.

I stare at the receiver, stunned that it didn't work, and furious at my mom that Tatum said no. I burst into tears and rage down the stairs to yell at my mom.

"It didn't work!" I scream at her.

She's in the living room, fixing the coffee table books so they all line up perfectly. "What didn't work?"

"Tatum doesn't care that Stanley died and she's still not talking to me!" I yell.

"Well, it's not my fault!"

"Yes it *is*. It IS your fault! You said that's what I should do to fix it, but it didn't fix it!"

My mom fixes everything, and the one time it really matters, she fails. I can barely handle when Eddie and Kara leave me out from a two-second whisper at the dinner table; how am I going to tolerate getting through the rest of this year, six whole months, as a pariah?

"I'm sorry. I thought it would help," she says, standing back to look at the coffee table. Satisfied, she once again straightens the painting above the couch.

"Well, you were wrong!" I yell, and throw myself onto the couch.

"No, not the couch!" my mom shouts.

I jump off the couch. It terrifies me when my mom snaps or yells at me. There's no greater threat. All the terrible minutes that I'm separated from her when she's mad at me feel like death. Now I have no mother and no friends; I have nothing and no one. I am alone in the world and I will die. I don't know how to get her back. Fear glances across the surface of my belly, rippling it with impending doom. The dying is starting.

"People will be here in two hours, Amanda. I just fluffed that pillow," she says, aggrieved.

"Sorry," I say. The anger slides out of her eyes. "What people?"

"It's the Christmas party," she says. "I laid your outfit on your bed."

I'd forgotten. Shit. Amelia is coming to the party with her mom, step-dad, and sister, Sara. My mom has this party every year, and normally I love it because we're allowed to invite our friends. Tatum and Madison were invited, like last year, and I hold out hope that they'll show up, that their parents will make them because it's the right thing to do. In my room I see the stupid dress with the dumb Peter Pan collar I have to wear, and I lie down on top of it and cry again until I fall asleep, only to be woken by sounds of the doorbell ringing every five minutes. I quickly change and hurry downstairs, excited to see my mom's friends, who think I'm adorable. I'm glad they haven't figured out how ugly I really am. I can't help but stare at Kara, who looks so pretty with her frizzy red hair in two side barrettes and her braces—they look so much better on her than on me—and Eddie is always handsome, even when he's angry about having to wear his uptown clothes. Waiters walk around with hors d'oeuvres and trays of alcohol. Eddie skulks behind them, trying to filch a glass of wine.

Eventually, Amelia arrives and we all convene in the TV room, which, for the party's purposes, is the kids' room. Classical music is playing and adult conversation is growing louder, and the doorbell keeps ringing, and I feel, for the first time in a long time, like everything might be all right. I look over at Amelia, who smiles her dimples at me. Eddie's bad-influence friend, The Worm, is here. He's two years older than me, fifteen like Eddie, but acts much older, like sixteen and a half or something. The whole night he's been drinking backwash from everyone's discarded wineglasses. He's drunk, but he spies a nearly full glass and stumbles off after it. Amelia slides into his seat. She'll do anything to be near Eddie. Even after he fractured his chin on his friend's head playing football and had to wear a mouth guard, she liked him. Now he's wearing a bandage because his Swiss army knife closed on his finger while he was carving his name into a tree.

Jimmy comes in to fix the blinds that aren't broken until Mom comes and pulls him out. I wander off to fill a plate with appetizers for Amelia and me, and I say hi to some of my mom's friends, and the garden people. On my way back, I spy Jimmy in a corner, his back turned to the party, shoveling pigs-in-a-blanket into his mouth. He sees me and winks—our secret. When I get back to the kids' room, it seems I've missed all the fun because the only person left is Amelia.

"Where'd everyone go?" I ask her.

"Kara's room."

"Oh," I say, knowing that means Amelia wasn't invited. I sit next to her. "So, what do you want to do now?"

"Nothing," she says.

Something's off.

"I didn't know it was just Eddie's birthday." Two cold hands land on my stomach and flip it, like tongs on a raw steak. I know what she's about to say. "I asked him what you got him for his birthday," she continues. I nod casually, playing dumb. "Seems like a weird coincidence that you gave him *Hunky Dory* just a day after I gave *Hunky Dory* to *you*," she says.

"I know, right?" I say, my heart hammering. "So weird. I bought it before you gave me mine. I didn't say anything because I didn't want you to feel bad."

"Why would I feel bad?" she asks.

I shrug. "I don't know."

"You gave him my present," she says.

"No, I didn't. I bought that for him," I say, hoping I don't sound as desperate as I feel.

"Yes, you did."

"I didn't. Really! It's a coincidence."

"I don't believe you. I think you're lying to me."

"I'm not lying to you." Of course I'm lying. I should just come clean. I didn't have a present for him, I knew he'd love it, think I was cool; and plus, I never in a million years thought Amelia would find out. But the horror of admitting that weakness is blinding me to any reason.

"Okay, then let's go to your room and you can show me the copy of *Hunky Dory* I gave you," she says.

I'm panicking. "I'll bring it to you tomorrow," I say.

"That won't prove anything. If you can't take me with you and show it to me right now, then I'll know you're lying."

"I'm not lying."

"You know, if you can admit that you're lying I can forgive you, but if you keep saying that you're not lying, I don't know . . ." She trails off.

I can't go from lying so hard to admitting I've been lying—it's just too mortifying. That would mean admitting I am a failure. "I'm not lying," I say.

"I thought we were best friends," she says. "But best friends do not lie to each other, and they do not give away special presents!"

"I swear—" I say, desperately trying to make myself admit it. But I can't.

"I'm leaving," she says.

"I am telling you the truth! I really did buy that tape for him myself. I did. It's a coincidence."

"Funny, because when I gave it to you, do you know what you said?" I can't remember. "You said, 'Eddie is going to be so jealous'!"

"I . . . I was being polite. I didn't want to hurt your feelings." I'm desperately scheming how to sprint over to Bleecker Bob's and buy another copy of the album so I can show her both together, but I understand that it's already too late.

"I'm going home," Amelia says, and she walks out.

I think I'm hyperventilating. The room rushes in on me. I feel like I'm going to be crushed to death in my own house. In my bedroom I sob and sob, hoping to cry out the body butterflies. Eventually, I wake up to a quiet house. Still in my dress and shoes, I grab my pillow and blanket and drag myself down the dark stairwell to my mom's room, where I curl up on her couch. I know that at thirteen I'm too old to still be doing this, but this is the only place left for me in the world.

*　　　*　　　*

There is only one more day of school until Christmas vacation, and it's gruesome. My fear is happening: Everyone I love is leaving me, the nightmare unfolding loud and clear in real life.

By the time I get my books from my locker in the morning, Amelia is laughing at the end of the hall with Madison and Tatum, and I can't stand the sight of them all together without me. When I turn away, something knocks my shoulder and I trip off to the side. I've been pushed by Madison, who's hooked arms with Tatum, who's hooked arms with Amelia. They are a white picket fence of girls pulling their stakes up away from me, moving to a new, secret location. They unchose me when I'd already been chosen. Just a week ago, I knew where I stood, but now I'm disposable. The world is always changing its mind on me. Once I had a family at school, but now they don't need me anymore. Maybe they never did.

A burning clot of dread develops under my rib cage. One hundred radios are trapped in my head, all playing different stations at once. Not even Magda is speaking to me anymore. I am invisible because no one will look at me, no one will listen to me, and no one will answer me. I want to yell and scream I TOLD YOU SO at my mom—people *do* disappear! People go away and they don't return, just the way I'm still afraid I'll never return from a weekend away at my dad's. My friends disappeared into thin air. Just like Melissa and Baba. I don't exist because I don't matter. I am a terrible person. I called Tatum a horrible name and I lied to Amelia and I gave my brother the present she gave me and I was caught, and I lied about it, and I deserve to be invisible because someone like me should not count.

1983

Dr. Joan Azam

<u>Summary of Test Impressions</u>

Amanda is a 13-year-old girl having trouble taking tests. There are two factors contributing to Amanda's poor performance on Standardized Testing: extreme anxiety and difficulty extracting meaning from silent reading.

Amanda's anxiety around test taking and her fear of failure is so extreme, no test will adequately assess her true ability, aptitude, or level of achievement. Her scores should be interpreted with great caution. At the same time, she does have some obvious learning disabilities. Recommendations are to see a child psychiatrist to treat the anxiety and tutoring to help with learning.

I enjoyed testing Amanda. She was fun to be with and was most cooperative in doing the wide variety of tasks I presented to her. She definitely has many many strengths, along with the areas that need some help and support. I hope that she realizes that the difficulty she has taking Standardized Tests is a specific problem which many people have and does not mean she's not intelligent. I will happily talk with her if you think that it would help her to understand the wide differences among people.

My Life Stained the World

AFTER CHRISTMAS BREAK, I figure everyone will have forgotten they hate me and will talk to me again, but that's not what happens. I spend January without friends, faking sickness so I can stay home and try to come up with schemes to get myself back in everyone's good graces. I'm not certain I can live with this feeling much longer. I try to separate myself from the Shallow Countdown sensation that has permanently taken over my body, but I already know the only way is to be relieved from the worry, and I don't know how to solve this problem. I obsess over possibilities, unable to concentrate on anything else: not homework, or boys, or what Amelia is doing right now. Even though I'm not missing like Etan, my friends have made me disappear. Even though I can see my own body, I can't seem to feel myself. My mom is no help. She continues to insist that everyone is jealous of me, and it's starting to enrage me. It's like she's not even listening, just playing back the same old recording.

Eddie's been growing out his hair, wearing combat boots, and dressing more like a punk. At school, he's been part of the bad crowd for a while, with The Worm and Tony the Terror, but now he's in the biggest trouble of his life. They all played hooky to get David Bowie concert tickets, but they got caught by a police officer and now he's suspended from school. He is so lucky. Suspension means missing school, and that would solve all my problems. But how does a person who isn't Eddie go about getting suspended?

On the days I do go to school, I'm saved by Kara, who lets me into her circle. I make her friends laugh, and they adopt me. I get closer to the kids in the art room, too, and I feel a separate space being carved out for me, one my ex-friends can't touch. Despite all this, though, I stay angry. Angry for being the one who got rejected, mad that I can't make it go away, mad that neither my mom nor Kara can protect me from such abandonment and betrayal.

At the end of this year Kara is graduating, and we won't be in the same place ever again. She won't be with me at Dad's house, and she won't be with me at school. To my body, this feels like a terminal diagnosis, and it begins preparing for her death. Who will protect me if she's not there? Not Eddie. Why do Eddie and Kara know how to protect themselves when I don't?

Eddie spends his suspension playing guitar, hanging out in the East Village with his hoodlum friends, and listening to punk music that leaks out from under his closed door, filling the house with its intensity. Something inside me I can't access is being expressed by the music I'm hearing, as if, in life's great Memory game, I've finally turned over a card that matches me.

He agrees to lend me a couple of albums that I listen to over and over. The music makes me feel invincible and fills me with a sense of confidence that disappears the second the song ends. Eddie's new look matches this music. He looks tough. When you look tough, people are afraid of you and will not slap you and make the entire grade stop talking to you forever. When you are tough, your worries and fears leave and never ever return.

One night, after distracting my relentlessly nervous body from itself by listening to Eddie's music, I discover he's dyed his hair, and the bathroom, maroon. Mom is livid. She does not want him going to school looking like that. It's not just his hair she can't stand, it's also his combat boots and ripped jeans and holey T-shirts. Night after night, Eddie sits calmly on the end of her flowery bed, his combat boots dirtying up the frilly bed skirt while she yells at him, but he won't change. Jimmy stays out of it. He built himself a workbench in the basement, and now he spends time puttering around with Norman Bates.

Outside, on the street side of life, strangers call his name, and when I'm not with him, they stop me and ask if I'm Eddie Stern's sister. The transformation that's undoing my mom in the house is raising Eddie's profile in the world. Maybe I can transform myself.

I know my timing is good. Mom wants Eddie to fit in and he wants to stand out, and I am standing out but I want to fit in—which is what my mom wants for all her children. Appearances matter to her. She wants us to be normal, and we're not. She and Dad both are like this— there's a type of kid they want us to be; it's obvious by the clothes they make us wear, and the schools we go to, and how we have to dress up when we go on an airplane. They want the world to look at us and be impressed. To be envious of us, and of our parents. The kids they want do well in school and don't have tutors or stay behind a grade or dye their hair maroon. They want us to match the pictures in their heads, but we don't. I wait until Eddie leaves and then swap places with him at the end of her bed.

"How do I look more like my friends?" I ask.

"I don't know. How do your friends look?"

"They all have straight hair," I say without hesitation.

"So let's get your hair straightened."

I feel my octaves grow higher. "You can do that?" I ask. "That exists?"

"Of course," she says. "People chemically straighten their hair all the time. I'll make an appointment."

And just like that, my world opens up again. In one week, I'll have straight hair and my friends will take me back. But even as this thought makes me deliriously happy, a prickling dread appears.

I tear out images from magazines: Christie Brinkley and Cindy Craw-ford, along with other beautiful blond models with silky waterfalls of sleekness. When I hand the hairdresser the small pile, he laughs and ex-plains that he can't "perform miracles" or give birth to a brand-new me. He says he has to work with "the mess that exists," and then he gets busy burning my eyes with the chemical fumes and wrapping hundreds of pieces of tinfoil in my hair. When he's finished, my hair is a glossy chestnut brown, and longer than it's ever been. All the way to my collarbone. He promises me that even after I wash it, it will dry just like this. I'm at once thrilled that my mother suggested this and furious at her for keeping this information from me for so long.

I don't wash my hair all weekend. On Monday, the teachers all compliment me and other students do double takes. I feel like I'm in an issue of *Seventeen* magazine. I see Madison, Amelia, and Tatum down the hall. They're staring at me, I can tell, but I don't look back. Suddenly, I'm nervous and worried I've made a mistake. To prevent myself from walking in their direction, I open my locker and stick my head inside until my breathing slows. It's not until second period that I come face-to-face with Amelia, when she's assigned as my lab partner.

"I like your hair," she says, staring at a test tube.

I can't believe this. My hair made her speak to me! A long Torah scroll of things I want to change and improve about myself unfolds in my brain. "Thank you," I say. My mom is a genius.

"How have you been?" she asks with pity.

I know I'm supposed to satisfy this pity. Otherwise, she won't take me back. "Not very good," I say, throwing her the same martyred expression my mom uses when she feels she's been wronged. I hope it works.

"That's too bad."

We follow the lab directions and pour some solution into the left test tube and watch it bubble over.

"I'm sorry for what happened," I say, admitting to nothing.

"Me too," she says.

We turn the right test tube into a bubbling soda.

"Do you want to sit with us at lunch today?" she asks.

I look at her. "Are you sure?"

"Yeah, I'll tell the other girls we're being nice to you again," she says.

"Great!" I say. "Thanks!"

I can't believe this has been the answer all along. My parents are right. If you look and act like everyone else, you'll be accepted, and all your bad fortune will reverse. If only I'd straightened my hair when I was a baby. I guess it's time to dye it blond.

It's not until we're all at lunch together, pretending like nothing happened, that I feel something stuck inside me, a residue of despair. As happy as I am to be past this awful experience, I don't feel as good about myself as I thought I would. I still feel like a bad person, a stupid, ugly person, even with my new hair—which, while it says I must be accepted because I match everyone else, also reminds me that the way I used to be, the way I was born, wasn't good enough. Even my mom thinks so.

When I hear the other girls making jokes about reversing the decision to take me back, jokes just like my dad would make, I realize I don't trust them, or anyone else in my grade. I sift each word carefully before saying anything, and even when I say it, I float away from myself just in case it's wrong. I am constantly floating away.

Turns out, they were wrong about my hair because when I wash it, it doesn't dry straight, it dries frizzy. Kara tries straightening it for me, but it just turns into straight frizz. It's not just mortifying—it's an actual threat to my social life, and therefore my life overall. If I don't look like them, my friends will bump me out again. Kara suggests a french braid. Lots of girls wear their hair like that. In the morning she gets to work, furiously braiding to disguise the monstrosity. I stare at her in the mirror, trying not to think about the unbearable: What happens next year when she's gone? Even when I'm not thinking about it, my body holds the information for me, always knocking and trying to get me to look. Kara is thrilled, but I dread her graduation. What's to celebrate? I'm losing my sister, my second mother. She keeps reminding me that she'll be home for holidays, but holidays happen only twice a year. I've been sobbing every night, going through all the color stages of countdown. Always ending up in Empty Countdown. I need Kara here. I don't want to be left behind with just Eddie and Holly; Eddie is always in the East Village and never around enough, and even though Holly is less scary than she used to be, I still keep a safe distance, even at school. Everyone likes the french braid, though, so that's one good thing I can hang my hat on.

Holly is getting in trouble at school, too, and so there are fights now about that. Daniel keeps to himself, and David is at college. Kara never gets into trouble or does anything wrong. She's so good, in fact, that she's our mom's favorite and gets special treatment. Mom even bought tickets for Kara and her friends to see a play on Broadway. I never got that. When Kara is sick in the middle of the night, if she has asthma or is throwing up, my mom gets up and sits with her, but when I'm sick in the middle of the night, she doesn't do that with me, or with anyone else. She has more in common with Kara than with me. It's a realization I don't like, but I know it's true.

My mom and I get in fights now, too. When she tells me I have to do something I don't want to do—like call a friend of hers to say sorry about their husband getting sick, or go to a funeral, or some other "right thing," something that feels terrifying instead of "right"—I say I don't want to, and this makes her lose her patience with me. She says I'm selfish or a brat and that I never think of anyone but myself. Then I cry on my bed and she comes in and apologizes and takes it all back, but all those words stick inside and never go away.

I can't get anything right. Everything I do is wrong, and it's always being pointed out. When it's not my grades, or my inability to understand how to read a map or take tests, it's my hair, or my clothes, or my attitude. Why can't my mom see the things about me that *do* work, like she does with Kara? I want her to fix me, but she keeps trying to change the parts of me that make me who I am, and not the parts of me that are broken.

*   *   *

CBGB, Scrap Bar, Mudd Club—these are just a few of Eddie's favorite places. He hangs out primarily in the East Village now, where purse snatchers toss stolen bags onto tar rooftops. Small piles create a new hilly landscape. Something about his new persona both frightens me and appeals to me. I wouldn't want to come across him in a dark alley, but I also know he would never hurt anyone. Deep down he's very gentle, but you'd never guess that by looking at him, and I like that a person can keep themselves a secret in this way. I thought my blazer and uniform would do that for me, but they didn't. It wasn't the right disguise. I'd hoped that external aids would express to the world what was broken in me that needed fixing, but I didn't do it right because what they're trying to fix is different from the thing that's broken. Like I've gone to get a tonsillectomy, but they gave me a neck brace. Now I feel like I need to protect the part of me I've always wanted fixed because it's getting injured every time it's neglected. Although I do feel pulled toward being like everyone else, to look and act and get good grades like my friends, I know that deep down I couldn't, even if I tried, because I'm not smart. It might be time to resign myself to that fact.

One day Eddie comes home with a Mohawk and a nose ring, and Mom is furious. A skid mark of long red spikes tracks down his otherwise bald head. I run my hand down my french braid. I'm growing my hair out. Maybe if it's longer it will get straighter.

"You cannot go to school looking like that," she yells at him. "What will people think of you? What will people think of me?" she asks, getting more and more agitated.

"Great," Eddie says. "No school."

Eddie doesn't care what people think of him, or if he does, he's good at hiding it. I care what people think of me too much, which is why I give people what they want, even if it's not true, which gets me in over my head—like telling Amelia I bought Eddie *Hunky Dory* when I didn't—and then I become a bad person.

Some days my brother compromises and goes to school wearing the Mohawk down so his hair is long, but other days he sprays it straight up, molding sections into spikes. He wears army green sweaters and black skinny jeans with holes and safety pins all over them. Someone gave him a job working as a bouncer at a bar called Beulahland on Avenue A be-

tween Tenth and Eleventh. No one cares that he's not eighteen. Eddie
is the coolest person I've ever met. He's a real, live punk living in my
own house. I've seen some of his friends from the East Village and they
all look generally the same, although one guy has a tattoo on his face of
stripes, like a zebra. They all grabbed at something from the world and
made it their very own thing. I don't know how to do that, but I want
to. Part of me feels ready to branch out and away from my mom, to be
separate and independent, but part of me is panicked by the very idea.
Worse, I sense that she doesn't even want me to be separate and independent, as if I'm not allowed.

Eddie is moody and sullen and he barely talks to anyone anymore. It
feels like a privilege when he pays attention to you now, like when the
Italian women call down for Loosies.

One night I'm playing Nerf basketball in my room when Eddie
knocks on my door.

"You wanna help me dye my hair green?" he asks.

"Sure!" I say, dropping the ball and following him into the bathroom.
He shows me what to do. The whole time, though, I can't help checking
if he's sure. Green is not the most flattering color for my pale, redheaded
brother. But he's sure. When we're done, and he looks in the mirror, he
looks so ugly I'm scared he's going to murder my face off, or worse, dye
my hair green.

"It's fucking awesome," he says.

"But...it's sort of...ugly," I tell him, nervous.

"That's the point, dumbass," he says and walks out of the bathroom.

I'm confused. Doesn't he want to be good-looking? Doesn't everyone?

When I hear my mom screaming at him later, I know she thinks it's
ugly, too. I know she doesn't get it either. I worry Eddie might be the
only one who does. But what if he's right? If ugly is the point, then pretty
isn't the point, and if being pretty isn't the point, then maybe I actually
have a chance. No matter how many things I try to do to make myself
look better, I'll never actually be pretty, but maybe there is another avenue to reach for. Maybe Eddie is showing me the way. Changing how

you look might be the answer after all, just not the way I thought. My mom probably never imagined we'd grow up to look and act the way we do. Sometimes I think about Etan's parents, and his siblings, and I feel stabs of sadness that they don't get to see him change the way they're changing. It makes me feel guilty for wanting to be different from how I was, because he'll never get that chance, and because it means we're all moving farther and farther away from him.

*   *   *

Spring sprints toward us, and soon it's June. Everyone else in my family is sitting together in the church, but I'm with my class. I know I'm going to cry hysterically when I hear the first notes of Pachelbel's "Canon" and see my sister walking down the aisle, like we're giving her away. Mrs. Baldwin gives me permission to stand behind the column, where I can see my sister better. How will I survive this? I'm so homesick for my sister. At home it's all I've been able to talk and think about for weeks. Kara says she'll come home in a few months and I'll see her then, but that's too far in the future to feel real. Jimmy says we can visit her, but I know we won't. Eddie says I'm a fucking idiot, and my mom says she wishes Kara didn't have to go either. I am too old to feel the way I do, I know. But somehow, while I'm no longer in grade school, I've yet to outgrow my fears. Maybe I got stuck, like a clock that broke at noon; I can't move forward until someone restores me, takes me apart and rewires my interior, which I know they won't do and never will because all anyone's done is focus on my exterior: resanding and repainting the outside, never going farther than my stuckness, never finding out the why of me.

My sister is the smartest person I know, and of course she wins a lot of awards at the graduation ceremony, which makes me feel proud, but also inferior. When her name is called for her diploma, I'm practically hyperventilating, but I clap because I know people will notice if I don't, and then they'll see for themselves that I'm a fucking idiot. Everyone is happy except me.

Although she's not leaving for two more months, the air already feels buckled and warped. Who will I be without Kara? When Mom is mad at me, Kara talks to her and makes things better. I don't want Kara to leave me. I don't know why she even wants to go to college. The invisible wrongs inside my body feel embossed onto the atmosphere. Maybe every error or mistake I've made in my life stained the world, and each dent and divot I try not to fall into is a piece of old me, a pockmarked reminder of my difference and abnormality. Is this how I'll leave my mark?

*   *   *

Even as I'm trying to wrestle down my future, the past and I can't let each other go. A photo of Etan is found in Massachusetts, and a New York City cabdriver comes forward to say he'd picked up an older man and Etan the day he disappeared. The photo appeared in a calendar and led the police to NAMBLA, the North American Man/Boy Love Association. The cabdriver's story doesn't pan out, but now the police think Etan was pulled into a sex ring. I don't want to think about whatever that might mean. It's May 25, 1984, five years to the day since Etan went missing, and the second year of National Missing Children's Day, created in Etan's honor. Enough kids disappear for there to be a commemoration day. Why do people lie about what happens when reality always knows where to find you and tell you the truth? He's eleven now, and he wouldn't look like his picture. We might pass by him all the time, never even knowing. Just like us teenagers, we're unrecognizable. I don't know what he'd look like anymore; no one does.

As the summer arrives, my countdowns get worse in preparation for Kara's departure. I'm desperate to stop this all-encompassing dread. I have to toughen myself up somehow, but how? I see Madison over the summer and we practice smoking, which is awful and doesn't work at all. Then I try drinking, which is even more revolting and makes me throw up. And then Eddie puts a bunch of his clothes in a box to toss out, and I go through it and take every last piece. As I'm trying on his army green sweater and rolling up the too-long holey black jeans, I look in the mirror and see a different me. A cooler, tougher, jaded-looking me. For the first time in my life, I see something I haven't before—the outside of me is telling a story about the inside of me, and even though the stories don't entirely match, I like what the outside story suggests better than the truth, much better than any dumb blazer.

Then I spot the buzzer that Eddie used for his Mohawk, and I clip one side of my hair short, keeping the other asymmetrically long. When I stand back and look at my uneven, crazy haircut, I see myself out of someone else's eyes. WOW! Look at that girl! She's tough and scary, not at all fragile and scared or feeling like she's dying because her sister is going to college and she still can't leave her mommy. My new look tells the world to *back the fuck up* and not hurt me because *I'll hurt you first*.

1984

Dr. Parker Prentice

Amanda's mother brought her in for a language and learning evaluation because of school troubles and low scores on Standardized Tests. After doing poorly on an ERB Intelligence Test in 1981, she was twice more evaluated for learning and language problems. Previous testing identified weaknesses in sound discrimination, auditory memory, and integration difficulties. However, it was evident that emotionally based factors contributed to her vast unevenness of functioning during testing, and it was recommended that her overall scores be interpreted with caution.

Mrs. Stern did not find that evaluation helpful. After repeating sixth grade, Amanda's scores did not improve, nor did her grades, and further testing was administered in 1983, with similar results. Using my own methodology, I aim to interpret Amanda's accumulated test results in order to build a portrait of her as both a learner and a person. This assessment aims to uncover academic weaknesses that may have been overlooked, as well as personality traits of the child, in order to better understand Amanda as an individual and as a student.

I'm the Test to Solve

MAYBE IT WAS THE summer break; maybe it's my new look. Whatever the case, when I show up in Eddie's clothes for the first week of eighth grade, I'm popular again. People start buying the same clothes as me. Soon Madison, Tatum, and Amelia all have asymmetrical haircuts, a double pierce, and spiked jean jackets. It's so annoying that when I'm finally trying to be different from everyone that everyone wants to be like me. Except Libby. She still dresses like Madonna, and I respect her for that.

I feel like I'm in some sort of powerful disguise. I try to act the way I look: invulnerable. It's easier than I'd expected. Pretending I'm unafraid of the world actually does make me feel safe and in control. I have never felt in control. It helps me deal with the loss of Kara. The more I play up this new persona, the further away I, and everyone else, get from the fucking idiot who is the real me. This works out well because I loathe that me.

Friends again, Tatum and I have decided we want to be famous actresses. We're not sure how to make that happen, until the school drags us into a special assembly about available after-school programs. Onstage a collection of grown-ups perch awkwardly on chairs, facing us. One by one, in their suits and pearls, they stand and sell us their wares: cross-country skiing, croquet, horseback riding, golf, sailing, art collecting for children, and then, finally, an acting school for teens. The presenters are Taylor and Gwen, a cool, casually dressed, artistic couple in their late twenties or maybe early thirties, and I'm instantly mesmerized; even their names sound elite. Two expensive-looking stalks, synchronized down to their split ends. Gwen is the color palette of my dreams, the living, breathing incarnation of how I wish I looked, but know I never will. Their school meets three times a week for acting and playwriting classes. At the end of each semester, they perform their plays in front of an audience, on an actual stage that is not a school auditorium. Also, it's coed.

Tatum and I exchange knowing glances. After school, we take the crosstown bus to the acting school on the Upper West Side, where a line of teenagers runs halfway down the block. The line moves oddly fast, and when we near the front we discover they're taking in eight kids at a time. We're led into the basement of a town house. A blackboard is on the wall and a long conference table has been pushed off to the side. Fold-up chairs pile on top of each other, frozen-looking, like teens trying not to get caught by their parents. No longer sandwiched between lady-suits and matching pearl sets, Gwen doesn't look different from any other young, rich woman whose parents bought them a classic six as a wedding present. Gwen moves with the confidence of an Upper East Side girl, the swagger of knowing she can have anything she wants and, worse, the belief she deserves it. She reminds me of Madison and I get a twinge in my gut. Tatum loves Madison, and I am getting closer to Tatum, and also Libby, but despite how hard I fight to get back into her good graces, outside of school Madison is becoming less and less appealing to me. I feel like we're growing apart, even though I don't feel like I'm growing in any direction at all. Taylor looks like a poor boy dressed up in rich person's clothes. Tattoos wrap around both his arms like sleeves. I wonder whose house we're in.

Four kids are already sitting on the ground. They look too comfortable to be auditioning. Aren't we supposed to be reading monologues or something? The eight newcomers are told to join them and sit, and Tatum and I lower ourselves into a clinging halo of cigarette smoke. These, it turns out, are the kids already in the acting school. One boy has long black curly hair and wears an army jacket, torn black jeans, and combat boots. A small, curly-haired boy, in puka beads and loose Guatemalan pants, twists the bottom of his shirt, then draws it up and over his collar so it hangs down like a ponytail between his nipples. Next to him is a beautiful blond girl with a pushed-out pucker, and another boy—or maybe a girl? It's hard to tell with the pink hair, blue nails, and faint facial stubble. Tatum and I are the only ones in school uniforms. Taylor and Gwen want to know all about us. Who are we? Why do we want to act? Do we have prior experience? How is our home life? Do our parents treat us well? What are our struggles, our troubles, our demons? What pains us and brings us shame? Trouble, they tell us, is the source of acting. Pain is the wellspring from which performances rise. The more we suffer, the better actors we'll be, and we are here to become the best, right? Perhaps sensing some skepticism, Taylor adds: We do want to become actors ... don't we? The acting kids stare, and the eight of us nod in the affirmative.

"So," Gwen says, "that's why you're here today. To tell us your story, to tell us who you are. Convince us, convince me, that you've got what it takes, that you deserve to be one of us."

I have no idea what she's asking, and I look at Tatum, who shrugs, not panicked by the not knowing.

"Paul, why don't you kick things off?" Gwen asks.

"Sure thing. I'm Paul; I go to Dwight, otherwise known as 'Dumb White Idiots Getting High Together.' My brother is gay and I wish he wasn't."

A wash of realization spreads over Paul's face and he quickly looks over to the kid with pink hair. "I didn't mean ... Sorry, Cole, you know what I mean, right?"

Cole stares at his lap and nods. Okay, he's a boy, and I guess he's also gay.

"Anyway ... I wish my brother wasn't gay because my parents take it out on me. And that sucks." Paul turns to the blonde with the lips, but she stares straight ahead until he pokes her and a confused giggle escapes.

"Oh! My turn!" She talks in a baby voice and leans her head onto Paul's shoulder. "I'm Claire. Paul's my boyfriend, so you bitches better stay away!" She laughs while glaring at the circle. "No, I'm kidding! Of course I'm kidding. Well, not about the fact that he's my boyfriend; he *is* my boyfriend, but about staying away from him. No wait! I do want you to stay away from him...Paul! Help me!" She blushes and shoots an angry look at Paul because he isn't doing a thing to save Claire from herself. Gwen cuts in.

"Graham?"

"Hi. I'm Graham." The boy is all monotone. "I used to live with my dad, but he killed himself so now I live with my mom, who's a drunk. Fun times."

And on it goes, and the nearer it draws to me, the more horrified I become. I have an extended and confusing family, but it's obvious how lucky I am by comparison. Although my parents divorced when I was a baby, and they don't truly seem to see or understand me, and are constantly trying and failing to fix me, I still have them. I may feel rejected by my father in favor of his new, holiday-card-perfect kids whom he takes on separate vacations, has celebratory family dinners with that don't include us, and absentmindedly refers to as "his children," even when telling Kara, Eddie, and me about them—but he's still *alive*. Sure there are screaming and yelling fights at my house, and my mom and stepsiblings are at one another's throats. There are eight people in my house, and though we barricade ourselves in our rooms and barely interact, the house is big enough for eight people to have their own rooms, and there is always food in the refrigerator. My family is every dysfunctional family. I feel alone and desperate for recognition and deep connection, but that's because *I'm* broken, not because my family is broken.

I am scrambling to come up with something I can give to this group, but I'm stuck. I glance at Tatum, who doesn't look frightened, just appalled. Around the circle every confession offers up a perpetrator, maybe a parent who harmed them either physically or emotionally; but no one has anything wrong on the inside of them, like I do. How will I be a good actress if I haven't suffered? I never expected that one day I'd be forced to publicly expose my secret defects.

What am I supposed to say? I was born with a basketball net slung over my top ribs where the world dunks its balls of dread? That since I was small I've had an army of tutors and testers and evaluators assessing my brain because I'm an idiot who can't get anything right? Or that I still think about a boy who went missing more than five years ago and even pretended to find him? My best friend and grandfather died the first time I left home, and even though I'm now fourteen, I still believe I'm a jinx? That I can feel a part of the world no one else seems to, that my body betrays me all the time?

When my body starts freaking out in public, the only way I can control my internal hysteria is to withdraw as much as possible. Fear—and my reaction to fear—governs my life, but no one beats me or locks me in closets; no one burns cigarette holes into my arms or pushes me down uncarpeted stairs, and as the revelations have rolled around the circle, I've felt a twisted envy, awed by the traumas sustained by these kids, jealous that what Taylor and Gwen want, these kids have to deliver. I am envious they have a name for what hurts them. My new look broadcasts toughness, but it doesn't say what's wrong. Imogen's hearing aids did that. So did the hook on Omar James's hand. I can't believe I am still yearning for some visible sign of a problem that can be fixed. My terror grows as soon as it's Tatum's turn—I'm next, and I will never have anything good enough to say.

But Tatum just rolls her eyes. She isn't buying it. I didn't realize not buying it was an option. "Honestly, I feel sorry for all of you. Your lives totally suck," Tatum says. "I'm not sure how this is supposed to make you a better actor. All it's doing is depressing me." Tatum isn't afraid people will leave her if she's true to herself.

"You don't get it," Paul says.

"Well, that's one thing we can agree on." She turns to me with a big smile. "Your turn!"

My brain is inflamed with suffocating white noise. As the group waits for my answer, I hear individual swallows; their nervousness for me activates my concern for them, and in order to alleviate them of their uneasiness, I have to say or do something, even if it isn't what I mean to say or do. When I shake my head, I know they can see my scrambled insides. My expression is revealing every humiliating secret about me. They will never let me into this acting school.

As the next person speaks instead, and sweat leaks off me, Taylor stands, walks around the circle, and crouches behind me. A moment later, I feel his hot breath squatting on my neck. "Hey, can I borrow you a sec?"

Another wave of heat and sweat careens through me as I stand, unsteady amid the wild bucking frenzy inside me. On shaky legs I follow Taylor out of the room and into the main hall, knowing he's about to ask me to leave, worrying because I left my backpack behind, and I'll have to go get it, and everyone will see I've been rejected. My breath is caught in a very narrow gap inside my esophagus. My life feels like it's about to be ruined, and I am just waiting to find out how. Taylor sits on a wooden bench and taps the emptiness beside him. His black hair is shiny and thick, slicked back by a waxy pomade. He cups my shoulder with his inked-up hand and leans in close, like he's going to tell me a secret.

"I just want to let you know that you can tell us anything," Taylor says to me. "All right, kiddo?" A surge of energy, like adrenaline, goes through me. He's looking at me as though he wants to listen. This is like Mr. Indresano's attention, but more intense. "That's what we're here for, to, like, help you."

"Okay," I say, cringing at how inarticulate I sound.

"Whatever it is you feel you can't say, you can say here. We've heard it all." I nod, not wanting to say okay for a second time. "You don't need to hide. You're like me; I'd recognize that anger anywhere."

I'm confused. Is the audition that I'm supposed to say something, and I said nothing, or is the audition that there is something I should have known to say, and I didn't? I'm nervous, waiting for the part where he tells me to leave. Is suffering, and being harmed, really the prerequisite for being talented? Am I supposed to get myself into bad situations so I have something to share every time?

"So, you want to tell me out here, in private, what's going on at home?" he asks. I could run now, and then hope Tatum takes my backpack home for me. I'll have to figure out a way to never cross paths with these people again. I certainly can't come to the Upper West Side for the rest of my life. I shake my head slightly, not too hard, but enough so he can read it. "Okay, I get it. You need time. I respect that. Just don't forget, when you're ready, I'm here, okay?"

I nod again and he says, "Let's go back inside."

As I follow him inside it dawns on me that he thinks I'm hiding something. He read my panicked no as a secret, an enemy war code he wants to break. Another person might reach out, tap him, and tell him the truth, that I'm not hiding family secrets, that I'm scared, and also stupid, that the world and all its rules and directions do something strange to my body and brain, but I can't do that because that's what I'm hiding. Not to mention, no one's ever worried about me the way he just did, and I sort of liked it. It felt good to get the attention of an older, good-looking tattooed man, one who isn't trying to have sex with me but just wants to help.

This is a new feeling, expansive and open, unlike any of my other emotions. It actually feels good, like I'm the test and he wants to solve me. All I've ever wanted, since I was small, was for someone to worry about me, to crack me open and look at the inside of me, to get to the root of my truth and recognize me for my emotions. No one ever has, before now. Maybe with him I won't always have to perform to distract him from seeing the real me, because it's the real me he wants. Even if he was searching for the wrong thing, he probed, and it broke open a new feeling in me.

*   *   *

Over beige cafeteria trays the next day, Tatum reenacts the whole thing for Amelia and Madison.

"That's not acting," she says. "That was like…creepy and weird."

"I didn't mind it," I say.

"And, like, what did he say to you, that guy?"

"Just that I could tell him anything. That I didn't have to hide," I tell her.

"What a moron. Uh, hello! I'm not telling you freaks anything private!"

I make my face laugh along with the others, but I loved acting, or whatever that was called, and I especially like Taylor. I've already decided to join if I get accepted to the group, but Tatum hates those people and refuses to go back.

Each meeting starts with the same group therapy session. Every time I suddenly remember I forgot to get myself into a bad situation and have no suffering to contribute, which sparks my terror and mutes me up, which incites his worry and sends him tapping my shoulder and leading me outside or off into the corner where he tries to get a confession. I look forward to this concern, hoping that this will be the time he breaks the enemy code inside me, the one I don't have a name for. After a few sessions I realize he's still on the wrong track, but I'm not sure how to redirect him, to let him know my suffering is different from what he thinks.

I like the acting kids a lot. More than I like my own friends at school. These guys are creative—they're misfits, weirdos, and, most important, they've created a little nook in the world where I start to feel at home. The other kids meet on the stoop of the town house I learn belongs to Gwen's parents to hang out and smoke before we have to go in, and soon I'm racing out of school to go meet them, not really caring what Tatum, Madison, or Amelia is doing, feeling superior somehow, hanging out with older kids, and boys. I start smoking, too, practicing until I can inhale, and I'm amazed at how much it comforts me. It's like a replacement for my two sucking-fingers, which I miss. After the late-afternoon teen confessional, the clichéd acting games and writing exercises, Taylor and Gwen take a cab downtown. Since I'm the only kid member who lives downtown, they start offering me rides. I turn them down until finally I don't. I try not to listen to their conversation, but they make it hard to ignore. "I know it's only 6 p.m., but I'm already hungry for dessert," Taylor says.

"Yeah, what are you hungry for?" Gwen asks him.

He leans over and puts a hand near her crotch. "Boston cream pie."

Gwen giggles and smacks him, and he winks at me like he's entirely positive I understand. They treat me like someone who's had life experience. On the other hand, they also seem eager to *be* my life experience, especially Taylor, who never fails to remind me that I can call him any time, day or night. If I need them, if anything bad is happening to me, if I'm in trouble, if my parents are hurting me, he and Gwen are the people to call. He treats life like an after-school special.

Maybe it is. What do I know about life?

When I don't call, their concern for me grows, and eventually their attention on me is so concentrated the other kids in the acting school start complaining that I'm getting special treatment. Some days, Madison, Amelia, and Tatum will walk with me to the town house to catch a glimpse of Taylor, whom they call "weird but hot," and to watch the cool kids smoke and skateboard down the stoop. There's a comfort and a strange sense of control in watching my snobbish friends feel out of their element, since that's how I feel in the world all the time. Occasionally I'll catch Taylor taking one of the kids aside, to a corner, where he seems to be confiding in them, and maybe it's paranoia, but I feel like it's about me, because sometimes they look over, and, afterward, whichever kid Taylor was talking to starts being extra nice to me.

"Taylor said you're filled with rage and anger," Cole says to me one day after a chat with Taylor. He looks both impressed and frightened.

"He did?" I ask, surprised and curious about this enraged and angry person he sees. Do I really look that tough?

I'm starting to feel obligated to give him what he wants, but I don't know how. It's becoming clear to me that adults are most attentive when something is wrong. For instance, my stepsister, Holly, is constantly stealing things from school and from our bedrooms; and now, instead of Eddie, she's the center of attention. Kara, Daniel, and David are all in college and never around. I am tired and embarrassed of having so many tutors and fed up that I'm still getting tested without having a name for what's wrong with me. I desperately want it all to end, and I beg and plead with my mom to make it stop, but she tells me I'm being difficult and we're not having this discussion anymore "because I said so, that's why." It's infuriating. I need something from her she can't give me, but I don't know what that is.

A few months into the semester, Taylor calls me at home. He wants to see how I'm doing. He's never called me before and I'm surprised. It feels weirdly invasive, like I found him hiding in my bedroom. Does he call all the acting kids at home?

"How's it going over there?" he asks.

"Good," I say. "Just about to eat dinner."

"Aww, all by yourself? Do you want me to come over?"

Now I'm really confused. "I'm not all by myself," I tell him.

"The TV doesn't count."

"I know," I say. Suddenly, I feel mute. No matter what I say, he answers like I've said something else.

"Whatever's happening to you, I can help you," he says. "I've been there before. My parents, they neglected me, too. You're not alone, runt," he says.

I'm hurt by the term "runt" but try to ignore it.

"I'm really okay," I admit, unclear what I'm supposed to be saying.

He sighs. "I know your pain. You don't have to protect them. I see your anger."

His calls become frequent and so do his questions. When no one is home, I even let him come over. I don't tell my friends at school, and by instinct I know to keep him away from my family. I like his attention, and even if his questions are too personal and off the mark, he's still asking. If only I could get him to see that the badness isn't around me, it's in me. I've tried telling him that there's nothing wrong with the people around me, it's that there's something wrong with the person I am, but instead he says I wouldn't think that about myself if the people around me were good. If I do get him to believe there's something wrong inside me, he might run away and leave me alone, and I can't risk being left. Someone else needs to say what's wrong with me first. And I'm hopeful Taylor will.

Whenever I mention a guy I have a crush on, he asks me if I've slept with him. "Howard Jones?" I ask, incredulous. "I wish."

No matter how many times I say that no, I haven't slept with this him or that him or any him for that matter, he keeps asking me. It's like he wouldn't be able to hear me even if I screamed in his ear, "I'm a VIRGIN!" Taylor wants something from me that feels different from what I want from him. Out of all the acting kids, it's me he's always watching.

"Maybe I've been reading this all wrong, and you don't need my help," he says. "You know how many girls would kill for this attention?"

He is threatening to take himself away and disappear. The sand timer is running out, and I have to pick an answer. What if this is my only chance to ever get someone to see me? I feel pressure to be the version of me he sees—that's going to be the only right answer. And suddenly I realize it's happening again: All the tests, all this time, have been meant to change me and make me better, and now Taylor is telling me in no uncertain terms that who and how I am isn't good enough for him either. He wants me to be the person he knows how to fix. Right now, I am a question whose answer he knows and all I have to do is match it, and I'll be right. Will I never get help if I don't start acting like the person he wants to help? Is this what real life is then? An endless effort to match the story of yourself someone else tells?

I have no choice. I start moving toward that angry, brooding version of me, and each time a dizzy hot spray sweeps over me. All these assumptions he makes about me push me into playing the part, and it all feels like a big game, one immersive acting exercise. I don't stop him when he starts answering for me, with answers that aren't even remotely true.

If I'm invited to join another actor's family for dinner, he'll say, "Amanda doesn't need to ask her parents. No one will notice she's missing." When Paul is telling me the proper way to roll a joint for a scene we're doing: "I don't think you need to explain drugs to Amanda. She knows plenty." I feel buried a bit deeper with every answer, but I don't know how to contradict him any more than I already have, or how to extract myself. I know the person he's inventing on my behalf isn't me, but I'm not sure I can identify the person who is me. I just know there's something I aspire to about the girl he's invented, a girl who isn't afraid of the world, just mad at it. The girl he's invented not only understands her emotions, she knows how to manage them. The girl he's invented has problems, but they're not my problems. Taylor has created a new me, a me who is cool and tough and doesn't need saving, and I love that version of me so much. It's way better than the me my mother has invented, the me that never understands, is incapable of doing anything for herself, and gets everything wrong.

I eagerly become the fucked-up mess Taylor desperately wants to save. The truth is, I am fucked up, and troubled, but I don't really have a reason. My parents don't abuse me, and yet I feel abused. I'm not adopted, and yet I feel adopted. I know I exist, and yet I don't feel seen; and now someone not only sees me but wants to be my hero, and I've always wanted a hero.

When we get to Mercer Street, they invite me upstairs to their apartment. It smells like Irish Spring and vacuum fumes, but suddenly something doesn't feel right. I'm instantly nervous when Taylor closes the apartment door. I watch his hand as he locks it. The final click starts the ignition on my heart. We're on the sixth floor. I can't jump out the window. They offer me a beer, tell me to relax on the couch, and then Taylor pulls out a bag of pot and hands it to Gwen, who begins rolling a joint. My coat feels too heavy on my chest. I'm probably the only fourteen-year-old in this city who's never smoked pot. I look at the clock.

"Aw, man. I really have to go. I'm gonna be late," I say.

"Like anyone will even notice you're not there," Taylor says.

Right. Right. That. I'm trapped. I have to unzip my coat because it's weighing too hard on my chest. Too much pressure and my heart might stop altogether, but the unzipping makes them think I'm staying. I feel like Irene Cara in *Fame* when she's pressured to take off her shirt during a screen test. Gwen lights the joint and passes it to Taylor, then he passes it to me. Are they going to make me take off my shirt? I take the joint and the requisite drag, but I cough hard on the inhale. They ripple with laughter and my mind is screaming, These people are not safe! and I fucked everything up! at the same time. I hand the joint back to Gwen and then motion to the clock and the door again.

"Really," I say. "I have to go."

"Oh please, you can smoke a little more," Taylor says, handing the joint back to me, although I've just had it. After the second hit, a sweat-inducing nausea begins to rise and then I feel it, a tickle in my throat. Nothing is more embarrassing than allowing my actual truth to escape in front of these people. Any bodily function that reveals I'm human, and not the character they've invented, must be blocked at the pass. My own human self is fragile and sensitive; I can control my performance but not my bodily functions, which threaten to topple the entire empire. The only way to get beyond the moment is to move past the cough and the only way to move past the cough is to cough.

Instead of scratching the tickle and sending it away, however, the cough seems to thicken it, morph the tickle into an object, something lodged there, not sliding down. My fear escalates that I will never catch my breath, or I'll vomit or choke on my vomit and die. Am I allergic to pot? Can you die from pot allergies? Are they on to me now because I am unwittingly giving myself away? I cannot stop coughing. I am dying, which is the most embarrassing thing a human can do. Once you're dead, you have no control. People can do anything to you; they can move your limbs and contort your body into mortifying positions, mocking you in death, changing the world's impression of you.

Gwen hands me a glass of water, which does not help, and I know I have to leave, to get out before the unseemly and weak process of dying begins right here on their freshly waxed and polished hardwood floor.

I feel the familiar loop begin: sweaty palms, tightening chest, the walls closing in, and the dizzy start of floating away. I manage to squeak out, "Bathroom." I turn on the faucet and throw up in the toilet. I stumble out and murmur something about my watch, something about a reason, something about getting in trouble. At the word "trouble," they let me go.

On the street I can breathe again, and I feel I've escaped death, but a block or so later I find myself leaning over pissed-on piles of paper and Styrofoam cups, throwing up my entire day. When I'm finished, I turn and look up to their building, worried they are watching me, laughing and pointing. I worry that they'll pass this garbage can and recognize my vomit.

I walk home, but I must be really stoned because the blocks look less and less familiar and I worry that I've entered a part of the world that doesn't exist. I stop, and I feel the out-of-body experience begin. These streets seem to tangle whenever I walk down them. My gut wraps its familiar fist around itself, squeezing out the same sensations I had when I was lost on these streets that first day of sixth grade, only this time I'm stoned and can't call my mom and have her save me. I don't know how to rescue myself; I'm never getting home. It occurs to me finally to look up at a street sign, and that's when I see I'm on Lafayette Street and walking the wrong way. I can't manage to get anything right, not getting stoned, not walking home stoned.

I don't know where anyone is when I get home, but I run straight to my bathroom and throw up several more times. The intercom goes off in my room. It's my mom: "Are you home?" she asks.

"Yes, sick," I manage.

"Did you take anything?"

"No, I'm fine. Need to sleep."

"Okay, I'll leave some Tylenol outside your door."

I spin in bed until the morning, where I wake into a hot cloud of shame. I'm starting to realize that once you start lying, you can't actually ever stop unless you come clean, and I can absolutely never come clean—about the pot, about any of it. I like this fake person they've invented on my behalf, and besides, isn't it my job as an actor to embody other people? Plus, no one has ever wanted to access my deepest self, and I like how it feels. Paul smokes pot. I can practice with him.

Turns out, he's totally game to deliver drugs and smoke them with me. When he comes downtown with the pot, which he doesn't know is practice pot, I feel confident in my ability to overcome my first-time reaction. We go to the roof and I watch as he rolls the joint, determined to master that next. He lights up, takes a drag, and hands it to me before lying down to stare at the stars. We pass it back and forth until a creeping horror begins to spread inside me. It's happening again; this time it's worse. I'm in a dream I can't escape, a dream not happening in my sleep, but in my waking life. I'm being squeezed from the outside by the atmosphere, and no matter where I stand the air won't let me breathe all the way in. The roof is untrustworthy. I feel something tugging on me; an energy wants to drag me toward the edge and fling me over the side. I feel like I am watching it happen. That's how I know to climb down from the roof and get back inside my house. In the bathroom I vomit and cry. I do not like smoking pot.

How am I going to fake this? I live in fear of going back to Taylor and Gwen's place, but I can stay away for only so long without having to provide some sort of believable excuse. I come up with one-liners for when he pulls out a bag of weed. None have traction. I can't "already be high," not when we've been together all afternoon. I can't be "trying to quit," because no normal teenager in the prime of their pot-smoking years makes a measured decision to scale back their drug use. Maybe I could start smoking cigarettes instead, and that will be my thing.

When I do return to their apartment it's for a party. I'm surprised to find out that Paul and I are the only kids invited. I'm overwhelmed by the adults, but Paul seems to know them. He even knows what Taylor wants when he asks to "borrow" him. When they return, Taylor brings me down the hall to the bathroom, and presses something small and hard into my palm. "Have fun," he says and kicks open the bathroom door for me.

In the bathroom, I look at the object in my hand, which I recognize as one of the discarded drug vials I step over on the street, but I have no idea what it is, or what I'm supposed to do with it. Is this crack? Or maybe it's heroin. Even cocaine. How much is normal for a person to do of whatever drug I'm holding? I open the vial, shake a little out, turn on the faucet, and rinse it down the drain. To be safe, I empty a little more and when I clear the sink basin of the granulated remnants I return to Taylor and Paul and hand it back. Taylor investigates.

"Wow. You're a fiend," he says. "Nicely done."

"Thanks." I accept a beer.

Gwen and Taylor introduce me around, looking proud. They always have their eye on me, watching to make sure I'm okay, like I'm their kid or something, and I love how attentive they are to me, love how protected and safe it makes me feel when they check in on me and ask if everything's okay and how am I doing, and do I need to talk about anything? I feel weirdly safe, even if a part of me doesn't entirely trust them as people.

I still do things with Madison, Tatum, and Amelia, but they're offset by how often I hang out with the acting school kids, and Taylor. They think it's cool that I have a separate life outside of school, and they like hearing about it, just not so much about Taylor, who seems to scare them, despite the fact they think he's hot.

The next time I go over to their apartment, it's with Taylor alone, who has a "surprise" for me. I am afraid. The last time a man had a "surprise" for me, he made me sit on his lap and put his hand down my pants. But each time I step into the persona side of myself, the more in control I feel. The more time I spend playing this angry teenager, the farther down I can press the real me. I much prefer this other me, the tough, punk, no-bullshit, nothing-can-hurt-me, my-family-is-more-fucked-up-than-your-family version, over the scared girl who is, quite frankly, a fucking baby.

Taylor was so impressed with my aptitude for doing coke—I am relieved to hear it wasn't crack—and he holds up a bag now, not of buds, but powder. He wants to do two things with me, he says; the first is "do blow," something I've done a million times, obviously, as evidenced by last week's party. There is no getting out of this. I watch everything he does. The way he cuts the block of hardened powder into loose mounds, and separates them into fire drill lines. He has a cut straw he places under his nostril and vacuums up each tidy spill. My turn.

Coke, it turns out, does not make me feel scared. It knows me better than I know myself. It makes me more hyper, more vigilant, more masterfully in control of my body and self. There is no impending death, no fear, no conviction of my weakness and failings. But more importantly, it forces me to be somewhere I never am: in the present moment. Off the drug, I am always in the future, anticipating the horrible next thing that will trigger the dying. In fact, for the first time in my life I feel the way I've been pretending to be all along: invincible, in control and unafraid. Even my lies feel true.

"Don't you want to know the second thing?" he asks.

"Oh. What?" I ask, suddenly feeling clammy and vaguely nauseated.

"It'll have to wait until you're eighteen," he says. I think he means he can't tell me until I'm eighteen, until he continues, "Because then it'll be legal to fuck you."

I have to respond quickly, to deflect from what's happening inside me, to throw off the scent of my abrupt fear and sense of betrayal.

"Ha-ha, good one," I say, standing up.

"Man, I can't wait to get you into a bathing suit," he says, eyeing my body.

"Good thing I don't own one," I lie. I am officially in over my head, I don't know what to do, and I am sickened by disappointment. I want the Taylor who didn't say these things to me, who doesn't talk about having sex with me, even if it's not now. Doing drugs is tough and cool, but having sex is intimate, too intimate. I've never had it, and I don't want to have it with Taylor, not now, not later. My body, my personal bits, that's the real, true me. It's feminine and girly, and right now I am not feminine and girly. How can he even see my body when I'm always in baggy clothes?

"Well, you better buy one for the summer party Gwen and I are throwing," he says.

"What summer party?"

"We do it every year. It's an acting school thing, and it's mandatory," he says.

I don't know if Eddie's ever scared or not, but he never, ever looks it. In fact, people are probably scared of him, too afraid to say things like "Man, I can't wait to get you into a bathing suit." And while I'm pretty sure he does drugs, no one would try to pressure him into doing them.

"'Kay, I gotta bolt. See you tomorrow," I say as cool as possible, trying not to look like I'm racing away, back home to the house I know will protect me.

1984

Dr. Parker Prentice

Amanda likes people, which might be a little bit of a downfall. She might want to belong too much. She is sensitive to people and their needs, but has down periods. She's not as sure of herself as she deserves to be. She needs a better understanding of herself. She's beginning to tell herself she can't do some of the things being asked of her and is starting to pull away.

Everywhere I Look, Families

JAVIER AND I STOP at a hotel and get a room. The storm is too rough and we can't see. He wants to break up, and I am spinning through the universe, unable to stop. I am catatonic. I am sitting in an armchair staring. I have not removed my shoes, winter coat, scarf, or hat. Javier is sitting on the bed. He doesn't know what to do and I don't care that he's in over his head, that I'm scaring him and he's terrified to speak in case I break.

I am so old. I am forty-one and have nothing. I am forty-one and losing the only something I've ever wanted. Without Javier there is no Frankie. For four weeks I had a family, and now it's being taken from me, although it has never been mine to keep. He's not losing anything. He has a family; he's had one all along. He's safe and I am out.

Why can't I get a family? How is it that I keep getting closer and closer but never achieve the goal? There seems to be some trick that I don't know, a code I can't crack. Who can teach me?

"I don't know what I'm saying," he says. "Can we not make any decisions right now?"

I don't know if I've even blinked. Javier thinks he's broken me, but I broke a long time ago.

✳   ✳   ✳

I once admitted to him that if we broke up I'd be devastated.

"You won't be devastated," he said. "I don't have that much power."

"You do, just not in the way that you think. I have more at stake than you do," I said.

"Let's not dwell in the negative. Let's look at the light," he said.

I was glad we were on the phone so I could roll my eyes.

*   *   *

Ever since I met Frankie, when I have imagined the future, all the places I once occupied alone are now filled with thoughts of her. She is my motivation, my real-life Frankie Bird. Every store I go into, I look for things she might like. Silly things I see or hear, I tuck into the Frankie part of my brain, eager to watch her buckle with laughter, tears licking her cheeks. Sure, I imagined Javier in my future, but it was all about Frankie.

Frankie could have been my daughter. I felt that; I know she felt it, too. She might be the only child I'll ever have. What if she needs me? What if I let him leave me, and Frankie has no one to turn to when she's in pain? I can't let this happen. We cannot break up. We have to make this work.

I know that Javier embodies my last chance at having a biological baby, and I also realize that the anxiety I feel about losing that chance is, paradoxically, what is ruining it. But I can't stop. Even though I know I would be fulfilled and satisfied with just Frankie, the fear of never having a biological child becomes a worry stone I cannot stop rubbing. I cannot stop pressuring him about having a baby, about getting married, about creating a family, even as I'm unconvinced he is the right partner for me. Even though I know, if I had to, I could just have a baby on my own.

My therapist tells me to take the baby thing off the table and see if that changes things. When I tell Javier I'm going to do that, he is instantly relieved. I am surprised at how quickly my anxiety recedes the second I let go of something. Maybe it's knowing that I'm not losing everything—I still have Javi and Frankie.

A few days later, alone at the farmers' market, I run into Max and Jane. Jane is pregnant. I'm happy for them, but still, sadness flakes off my body, and I hope they don't see it.

"We need your naming input," Max says. "Come over for dinner and we'll begin the proceedings." I look forward to dinner, yet the whole exchange makes me feel outside of time, in a place the world can't reach. Everyone advances, and I stand still watching them pass me by. Down at the bread stand, partners are discussing what to buy for dinner; mothers are strapped to their babies; fathers are pushing strollers. People hand their money over to the vendors with gleaming, wedding-banded hands. Everyone has someone; no one is mine. Later I run into Franklin and Iris, who is about to pop. I offer my help to them, too, but they're all set.

"Can you tell me?" I ask.

They look at each other and smile. Iris leans in and whispers, "Frances Wren. Either Frankie or Bird for short."

At first I think it's a joke, that I must have told them; but no, I never told them. My entire future slips out of me, like my own water broke, and I swallow my urge to yell, "No! That's my name and you can't have it!" Instead I force a smile and say, "That's the name I was going to give to my daughter." Then, head down, I hurry home.

Upstairs, I leave my produce on the floor, climb into bed, and cry. I feel forgotten, somehow, like I don't exist on the same linear plane as everyone else, as if I am nothing but a witness to their realities. I've named so many babies, given so much advice, saved so many relationships, set so many people up; the couples I introduced got married and created families, and now I feel like I barely exist anymore.

To clear my mind, I go with some friends to a Saturday-afternoon African dance class at Mark Morris, my third time trying the class. For a while I am happy: the rhythm of the drums, the vibrations of our bare feet on the wood floor; this is what I need to get my mind off everything. But as we dance across the room in sections and I lag behind, still unsure of the steps, I suddenly feel quite singularly alone. The next group can't begin until I've crossed to the other side, and no matter how fast I go, it's not fast enough. It's clear to everyone ahead of me that I'm not one of them, and I'm even ruining things for the people behind. There's never been a place for me. Once I thought there was, but I was wrong.

Javier and I have been together nearly a year, and as I hurry to catch up with my group of dancers, I'm struck by how little of that time we've spent together. He's hardly ever in New York. If I want to see Frankie, I'll have to go to Maine and face my jealousy about Meredith. I'll have to wait a year till they leave the island. But can I really trust what will happen next? Can I drag myself through another year of this uncertainty? My body tells me no.

Not even for Frankie? I ask it.

No.

My body always knows, even when my brain tries to override it. But what even my brain has to agree is this: To Javier, I am not a priority. I'm cut out of his decisions because I'm not part of his family. I'm sideswiped by an epiphany. To Javier, Meredith is still his wife. They're still enmeshed, although she has a boyfriend and he has a girlfriend. Javier, I'm nauseated to realize, already has a family. To make one with me would be redundant.

I stop dancing. I stand off to the side, struck and encased by this discovery. Profound dread forces me out of the classroom and outside. He has no incentive to move toward me. I'm in this relationship alone.

I have to break up with Javier.

I try to talk myself out of it on the way home. On a whim, I pull out my calendar and count up the days that we have spent together in the last ten months. Sixty-three. I have a choice. I can continue on, feeling like I'm chasing a family who doesn't want me, or I can cut myself free. I can take that pain out of my life.

I sit on the edge of my bed, trying to breathe. Breakups undo me, and I don't want to come undone. For once, I just want to break up with someone without worrying I'm going to die. When I try to imagine the worst that can happen, I can't seem to see or feel anything. My feelings go dark. The worst that can happen is that I will stop existing. I know I faced this same sense of extinction onstage, but it's never felt like an option in my personal life. Maybe the only way to get through this is to pretend I'm onstage.

I call Javier, trying to keep the image of my bombing but not dying onstage in my head, but when he picks up, I fight back the urge to throw up. I breathe, and I tell him, as calmly as I'm able, that I can't do it anymore. He doesn't seem upset. He may even be relieved; I can't bear to think about that. I will write Frankie a letter and send her a package. I'll call her. I just need a few days. As I put the phone down, I wait for the devastation to set in, wait to spiral off into an endless world without a bottom. But the anguish doesn't come.

I wait. I am sad and empty, but for the moment, that's all. When the welling in my chest begins to take shape, and the world expands before me, vast and frightening, I move toward the panic—although I don't want to. Wait! Wait! I say to the world, or maybe to myself—wait! I am being pulled toward my new stark reality of being without a family, of never getting what I want, when I remind myself how my body felt when I took the baby thing off the table. It was just a decision, a simple choice, but it shifted my feelings. I realize that I have a choice right now. I'm the one who makes the feelings; the emotions don't already exist in the world, waiting to trap me. Usually, I let the emotion happen to me, following it until I lose control and need someone else to care for me; but what if I just decide I can care for myself, that I know how? That I am not going to die because I'm without Javi. I can believe my feelings are not facts, just as I told Frankie.

The groove I've worn into my life is there, I suddenly see, because I've followed it. After every breakup, I have always followed the helpless groove it led me into. But if I made that groove myself, that means I can make another, different groove; and if I keep following that one, maybe I can get myself out of this cycle. The degree to which I fall apart is a choice.

I breathe deeply, and I make the choice. I was fine before Javier, and I'll be fine without him. I can want a family and feel sad I lost this one; but, I remind myself, I want a family who wants to be my family in return. I'm saddest about Frankie. She's the person I really need to mourn, and that loss is different. I know I've lost the island, too, that I'll never be able to return because the island is Javier's, just like Frankie is his, and I am still looking for something to call mine. But at least I had it. For four incredible weeks, I had a family.

1985

Dr. Nancy Weinreb

A highly verbal youngster, she is quite comfortable expressing her ideas. Her interests are varied: art, music, the theater, philosophy—almost everything except traditional academics. She is, however, interested in learning—the kind "that pushes your mind" and "forces you to think." She clearly has some insight into her own functioning and is aware that she is a visual learner ("I memorize easier if I can see things. I have to write everything down; if I can see it, I can know it"). On the other hand, she does not feel she needs tutoring because she feels her major problem is lack of effort. In fact, she doesn't think she has a learning disability at all.

Anarchy

WHEN EDDIE GETS KICKED out of high school and the attention gets shifted back to him from Holly, something occurs to me. If I got in trouble at school, then I'd have stuff to tell Taylor. If I got suspended or kicked out, I'd be a real troublemaker who couldn't be tamed, and he'd love that. He'd stop trying to get me to admit to things about my family that aren't true, and he'd focus on my own brokenness. So I stop wearing my uniform to school, and I start using the elevator even though I'm not a teacher or a senior. The first time I showed up in combat boots, black jeans, and Eddie's Bauhaus T-shirt, I got sent home to change, but when I didn't return, they just let me get away with it, kind of the same way they let me get away with dropping History class (which was way too hard for me) and put me in AP Art.

I spend most of my time in the art room now.

"Wow, you like Bauhaus?" Basi asks when she sees me in the shirt.

"Yeah, I love Bauhaus," I say, surprised she's heard of the band.

"I have some Paul Klee over here. Come look," she says, pulling out a big art book. "Let me find my favorite."

She turns the pages, stopping on a light blue and pink painting with drawings of stick figures. "He used such innovative techniques, very ahead of his time."

"Wow," I say. "Cool." I don't understand what this has to do with the band Bauhaus, but I want to pretend I am the person she thinks I am. After all, I have the weird ability to identify the work I've never seen before of artists working in expressionism and cubism. She keeps turning the pages and describing the techniques of terribly named artists I've never heard of before, like Gropius and Muche. Basi calls me all the names I'm not: precocious, ahead of my time, a wunderkind. I would give anything for just one of those words to be true. When her class comes in, I linger with Mr. Indresano, who also compliments me on my outfit.

"How have you not been sent home yet?" he asks.

"Voehl sent me home the other day, and I didn't come back, so now they're making an exception."

He laughs. "Only you could get away with something like this."

He looks around me toward Basi in the back and then motions to my shirt. "Don't tell her it's a band. She'll be destroyed," he says.

"Scout's honor," I say.

"So, uh...I've been seeing a lot of graffiti around the Village lately," he says, glazing a vase before tossing it into the kiln. "One of them is a big circle with a large *A* spray-painted in the middle. Yours?"

I flush with pride that he thinks I'm tough enough, and brave enough, to be a graffiti artist in the East Village. "Yeah, that one's mine," I say. "It's an *A* for Amanda."

He laughs. "You're such a funny kid," he says.

I laugh, too, even though I don't understand why it's funny. When the bell rings, I go back downstairs and immediately head to the library, where I discover Bauhaus is also an artistic movement. Now, whenever any of the other students ask me what Bauhaus is, I scoff. It's a punk band, and also an artistic movement. They've never heard of Paul Klee or Grobus or Mush? Wow, where've they been?

On my way to Mr. Zunkel's I run onto Emily S., the smartest girl in the class, and I ask her if an *A* with a circle around it means something.

"Does it look like this?" She takes my notebook and draws a capital letter *A* and then a circle around it.

It looks familiar, so I say yes.

"It stands for 'anarchy,'" she says. "The circle is an *O*, and it stands for 'order.'"

"Oh, anarchy. Order. I didn't know that."

"Yep. Now you do."

I scurry to the library to look up "anarchy."

-noun

    1. A state or society without government or law.

    2. Political and social disorder due to the absence of governmental control.

Whatever that means, it definitely does not mean Amanda. I'm pulsed by shots of mortification, but then the bell rings and I sprint to class, where Amelia leans over and says, "Let's do something crazy."

"Crazy how?" I ask.

"Like, this class is so fucking boring. Let's take off our socks and pass them around, and try not to get caught—something, anything."

"Anarchy," I say.

"I guess so," Amelia says, not knowing the word. This is my moment to get in trouble, I realize. Out of nowhere, an image appears in my head of bras flying from person to person during class.

"I got it! Take your bra off during class and pass it to me, okay?" She smiles and nods. We write Emily S. a note with the directive and pass it to her.

Class begins, boring as usual, until Amelia starts fumbling under her shirt, dropping her hands each time Mr. Zunkel turns to face us. When she frees the bra, she pulls it through one sleeve, handing it to Sofia. Emily S. is taking longer, but soon I have two bras in my possession, and I tie them together. My plan is to play catch with the bras during class. Each time Mr. Zunkel turns around, someone will throw the knotted bras to someone else, like the game of Hot Potato. I start the game off by throwing the bras to Amelia, who catches them. There are a few gasps and a couple of titters. Mr. Zunkel turns around.

"May I help you?" he asks.

We blink at him innocently; we're good, thanks. He looks over his shoulder at his backside to see if perhaps there's something clinging. As soon as he begins writing, Amelia throws the bras to Emily S., who throws them to Natasha up front, but Emily S. is too exuberant, and the bra-ball sails past Natasha and lands on Mr. Zunkel's shoulder. His head cocked, he side-eyes the dangling bras.

"Whose, may I ask, are these?" He holds up the tangle of bras, and everyone goes absurdly silent, except for me. I can't control myself. I fall off my stool and onto the floor in a puddle of hysteria. I'm laughing so hard, I don't even see Mrs. Toro, the school's "benevolent dictator," before she grabs the side of my head and leads me out of class, ear first. It is surprisingly painful.

I'm told to wait in Mrs. Voehl's office. A few minutes later, Amelia and Emily S. join me. While Mrs. Toro goes to find Mrs. Voehl, the three of us giggle out our nerves, uncertain of our punishment. Amelia looks sheepish, whereas Emily is trying to project confidence. I know they don't want to get kicked out, but I do. Although now it's just occurring to me that if I get kicked out, no other school might accept me. I hadn't thought of that. Knowing my mom, she'll pull some strings and get me in somewhere decent, but still, nerves begin to lower themselves toward me from the ceiling. Why am I so stupid? I consider the consequences only after I've done the action. If I get expelled, I'll have to tell my dad, and after Eddie I'm not sure he will actually let me live.

"A bra? A *bra*?" We hear Mrs. Voehl's voice down the hall. She walks into her office. She sits across from us.

"Two bras," I say, correcting her. Then, instantly scared: "Sorry."

"Let me guess whose idea this was," she says, her eyes locked on mine. I shrug, but I am filled with pride. The more attention I get for being a troublemaker, the less anxious I feel, and there is nothing I want more than to feel less anxious. I start confessing.

"They didn't have anything to do with it. I made them. But it was an accident that it landed on Mr. Zunkel."

"Is that true, girls?" Emily and Amelia nod. "So you were the mastermind?" Mrs. Voehl asks me.

I like being associated with that term. "Yes. I was the mastermind."

"All right then. Here's what we're going to do. Emily S. and Amelia, you are suspended for the rest of the day. You may return tomorrow. I will call both your mothers and tell them."

Amelia starts crying.

"But you, Amanda, are suspended starting now through Friday," Mrs. Voehl continues.

"But final exams are next week. I'll miss review week." This has just occurred to me—if I'm only suspended but not expelled, I still have exams, and I can't fail those. Now I'm worried.

"Not my problem," she says. "In addition, you're in charge of informing your parents of your suspension," she says.

"What? Why? That's so not fair!" I say. "I can't do that."

"You will come to school for the remainder of this week, but you'll spend it in the basement, doing in-school suspension. You may not take any of your textbooks. You must sit there by yourself alone for the next four days. Am I clear?"

I am furious and miserable, but I nod.

"Okay, please collect your stuff and leave the building immediately. I'll see the two of you tomorrow; and Amanda, see to it that you sign in tomorrow morning by 8:40 a.m."

Emily and Amelia feel really bad for me. Emily especially, since she's the one who overshot the throw.

"It's okay." It isn't, though. The only thing I didn't want to happen— getting expelled for being an idiot—is what's going to happen now that I can't review for exams. I'm terrified. I'm also terrified to be trapped in a basement by myself. The two sides of myself keep crashing into each other and I don't know what to do. Just when I feel practiced at being confident and tough, which keeps my fear at bay, something happens to override the fake me and pull the real me to the surface. How do I get rid of that me? How do I get rid of this fear?

When I get home and tell my mom, I'm expecting a full-out war, but she laughs and thinks it's funny. When I explain that it's in-school suspension and I'll be stuck in a basement, she calls the school and tries to fix it, but even she can't do that. The best she can offer is securing me a tutor to make up for missing review week. I reverberate all night, unable to sleep, terrified of the basement I'm going to have to sit in all week. Will it be like a dungeon, the place I used to imagine Etan Patz shivering in? Will they lock me in there and forget about me? What if I never see my mom again, or the rest of my family? How will anyone know where I am?

As I make my way toward the basement, I feel like I'm walking to my last execution, but I am surprised to discover the basement has offices in it, with people working. It's carpeted, lights are on, and it's not an industrial warehouse with racks of bloody meat. Still, as soon as the door closes on the room I'm in, I feel isolated and afraid. There's a small vent in the wall but no window. I sit at the desk and begin to worry about final exams, none of which I can study for, and all of which I'll fail, even with a tutor.

Some days Mr. Indresano sneaks me lunch, but he's not allowed to open the door. He can only talk to me from the other side, and I can collect the tray only once he's gone. If anyone is caught talking to me or looking at me, they'll get suspended, too. I don't know what they'd do to a teacher. Just like last year, I'm ignored. Except my only consolation is that this time it's for being a rebel, not an outcast.

Emily S. calls me the first night and tells me they had an assembly about the bra incident, and Mrs. Toro held up the tied-together bras to show the students. It didn't go over as planned because everyone laughed. I'm not supposed to know this, but Mr. Indresano told me I'm a celebrity. I can't wait to tell Eddie. And I can't wait to tell Taylor that I'm officially bad news.

*   *   *

I never get expelled, and I get through eighth grade by the skin of my teeth. Despite the tutors, after-school labs, and study help, my highest grade is a D+. It doesn't matter who tries to help me, or how many tests doctors give me, even my very best isn't enough. Even when I study twice as long as everyone else, I still don't understand, and I still fail the tests. In order to really learn something, I need to experience it, to live through it, but all we do is study textbooks. My tutors don't help much because they're distractible, and I keep them talking about things other than school, like movies and actors and plays we like. That's why I've stopped studying. I'm just not the kind of smart that counts.

"I hate Whittaker. It's too hard! Why did you make me go here?" I write to my mom.

"You wanted to go! You wanted to wear a uniform."

"That's not a very good reason," I write back.

"You wanted to go there."

"I was twelve, I didn't know anything! Why did you let me go here when it's too hard for me???"

"You wanted to be with Kara. You said that's what you wanted."

"Well, she's not even here anymore!"

"Do you want to switch schools?"

"YES!"

Everyone keeps using the same words as my school textbooks to describe the things I don't understand, as though the solution is to have different people try saying the same things to me. Why can't anyone just use their own words and speak in my language instead of theirs? Why does sitting in a chair all day listening and taking notes work for everyone except me? Why can't anyone explain things using stories, or take me out into the world where there are objects I can see and feel? I'm the slowest out of everyone, and I'm the oldest. I'm older and dumber, older and littler. Day after day, everyone around me gets smarter. How will I get through life? I worry about what happens when my friends start catching on.

There are other things pushing at me from inside, trying to get me to think about them, but I don't want to. I don't want to think about how

I'm going into ninth grade, and even though I've perfected my tough exterior, I still get homesick, still sometimes sleep on the couch in my mom's room, still get countdowns; and even though I now occasionally sleep away from home, it's torturous. Even though my mom and I fight, and communicate best through notes, I still can't be away from her without short-circuiting. I am one person in the world and another at home; but inside my body, between those two selves, is a crack in the floorboards, and that's where my I is stuck. If only someone could take a knife and flick me out.

The day after eighth grade ends is Taylor and Gwen's summer party at Gwen's family's house in Connecticut. In the morning, I put my bathing suit on under Eddie's Bauhaus T-shirt and his army green cut-offs, so I don't have to reveal myself to the other girls when we're changing. I'm wearing a one-piece from Capezio; it's dark gray and ribbed, with a high neckline. It's the most Amish bathing suit I could find, and because I'm terrified it's still too revealing, I plan on swimming with a T-shirt on. I don't want to show Taylor my private body—I don't want to show anyone—and I don't want him to think I'm wearing a bathing suit because I know he wants to see me in one. In my least sexy, most boyish outfit, I lace up my boots and take the subway to Grand Central Station, worried I won't be able to find Paul, Claire, Graham, Keith, or Cole at the information booth. Embarrassingly, I actually can't find the booth until I follow a group of tourists, but no one has arrived yet when I get there. I pick a spot and wait, but then I'm nervous that they're on the other side of the booth. I walk around it in circles and then ask the lady behind the counter if this is the information booth. She says yes, but maybe she's wrong.

Just as I get nervous that they've all left without me, I hear a whoop and see brown curls flying. Paul is skipping toward me.

"We forgot to buy tickets," he calls halfway across the atrium.

"Oh shit!" All the blood in my body drops to my feet. "I forgot my money."

He reaches me. "I got yours."

"Thank you! I'll pay you back."

"Nah, I'll tell Gwen and she'll give me the money. I get her to buy me stuff all the time," he says.

"For real?"

"Yeah. They live for that shit. They're like people who want to be parents but have no kids, so we let them take care of us."

"Oh," I say. "I had no idea."

"Stick with me, Stern. I'll show you the ropes," he says. I am caught up in a fantasy where he holds my hand as we race together to the train, but instead he says, "You can grab seats if you want. I have to wait for Claire."

Claire. Why is the worst person on earth dating the best?

"No, I'll wait with you," I say. When Claire finally arrives, the train is about to leave without us so we have to sprint. By the time I slide into my window seat, we're all breathless. Out the window is just tunnel-wall blackness, and the car is freezing from an overcompensating air conditioner, and that bus-before-camp feeling suddenly slides into my body and stays. I'd been so glad to be with Paul I'd forgotten about my nerves. The doors shut and I can barely breathe: I don't know where I'm going, how long I'll be away, or how I'm getting home. My lips grow dry, and, abruptly nauseated by panic, I shut my eyes and pretend to sleep.

I feel a kick against my shin. "Already?" Paul teases.

"Didn't sleep last night," I lie. I refuse to open my eyes.

"Oooohhhh, Amanda had a big night!" Cole yells. "Did you have sexy time?"

I force a mysterious, dismissive smile and manage to get them to leave me alone. I need to keep my eyes closed, so that I can't see anyone and I can pretend that no one can see me. Eventually, the rest fall asleep, too. By the time we arrive, I'm doing a better job of seeming to be easygoing. Taylor's waiting at the station, and we load into the car and watch the landscape roll past. Everyone sighs and coos at the beauty of the countryside, but to me, any new, unfamiliar smell just reminds me of leaving home. I wish I could enjoy these things like everyone else, but I don't know if I'll ever separate the smell of fall leaves, burning wood, or anything that means "away," from my long-ingrained feelings of terror and sorrow.

Taylor and Gwen's place is enormous. There are two houses on the property. One for the family and the other to change for the pool. The other acting kids, who arrived on an earlier train, are already swimming and splashing around. We drop our stuff and follow Gwen to the pool house, where we can change. It's cold and smells like cheap coconut sunscreen, mildew, and oversoaked skin. As we're taking off our clothes, I catch Claire staring at me in the full-length mirror. I'm immediately nervous.

"What?" I'm hoping she's horrified by my bathing suit, which means Taylor will be, too.

"Nothing," she says, crossing her arms over her high-set boobs.

"My bathing suit's really ugly, isn't it?" I ask, trying to sound like that wasn't the whole point.

"Not really. I kind of like it," she says. "How did you get—" She stops herself.

"Get what? The bathing suit?"

"No, your body," she mutters. "It's just, I never saw you like that before, without baggy clothes and . . . you have a really nice body."

I put my T-shirt back on. "Same as yours," I say and nudge her out the door.

"No, my boobs are too high and my waist is really short. You have no fat on you. Like, not anywhere."

I don't want to hear an assessment of my body. My body is defective, and I hate it. All it does is fill with dread and static and noise, holding me back from being independent from my mom and home, and it won't let me be like everyone else. Yet, somehow, it also alerts men that they can comment on it or, worse—touch it without my permission. After all that waiting, my puberty came in so slowly, I barely saw it change, but now that I finally have boobs and hips, I don't want them pointed out to me. My body is girlish, and it is trying to betray who I am trying to be. Anytime anyone says anything nice about my body, I black out a little.

Other girls would be flattered, but I'm broken, and I don't want this kind of attention. I don't want to look at it, and I don't want anyone else to look at it. I hurry to the pool. Everyone's telling me to take my shirt off and come in the water, and it's so hot out that I finally tear it off at the last second before jumping in, staying there until I'm freezing. But it doesn't work: When I finally get out of the pool, Taylor is waiting there with a towel.

"Damn. I knew you'd look good in a bathing suit, but this I did not expect," he says into my ear.

I try to laugh it off as I pull away from him, keeping my body toweled up. I sit on one of the chaise lounges and watch everyone, feeling Taylor's eyes on me. I don't like this. I'd always counted on the fact that my preteen body made me invisible, but now that I have a teen body, I feel molested when people look at me. Why can't adults just take care of me without their needs getting in the way? I go into the pool house and put my baggy clothes back on. I had planned to brag to Taylor about my suspension, but I no longer feel the urge.

When I return, Taylor is at the barbecue. The sky isn't dark yet, not even close, but I feel desperately alone and sad and want to go home before the sun sets and triggers that homesick kid inside me.

"What train are we taking?" I ask Paul.

"I thought you were sleeping over," Paul says.

I feel my face drop. "I ... I'm not sleeping over."

"Oh. I am. Taylor can drive you back to the station if you want. You can figure it out with him."

"Okay," I say. "Okay."

But I don't want to figure anything out with Taylor. He's been watching me all day, and I've been avoiding him. The Taylor I like is the one who wants to be my savior, not the one who can't wait to fuck me. Gwen is counting out marshmallows and I go over to her.

"Hey, you think you could drive me to the train?"

"Taylor's gonna drive Claire, so why don't you just go with them?" she says.

"Okay." Oh joy.

"Do you need any money?"

"No, I'm good."

The air is hamburger-flavored and dinner tastes of summer. Claire flirts with Taylor, and despite the fact that I don't want that type of attention from him, I'm envious that he's paying her any at all. When he puts his hand on her arm, I feel pained by it. When he gives her his one-armed hug, I'm shot through with butterflies.

He catches me watching and I look away, but he knows, and he's heading over. "Hey, I'm driving you and Claire to the station. Can you be ready in ten minutes?" he asks me.

"I'm ready now," I say.

He smiles. "Man, I can't wait until you're eighteen," he says, knocking me with his hip.

1984

Dr. Parker Prentice

Amanda needs individualized attention, and the opportunity to engage in dialogue with her teachers. Monitor her progress carefully.

When I Turn Eighteen

THERE IS NOTHING ANYONE can do about it, not even me: I am Taylor's favorite. In the plays we write, he always sees to it that I play his sidekick. When class is over, he and Gwen and I walk away together and take a cab downtown, where we all have dinner, watch movies, and go to parties; and when Gwen's not around, Taylor and I do coke. When she is around, we just smoke pot, which is fine now that I've come up with a creative work-around. Whenever it's my turn, I take the joint and stand, go to the kitchen to get a beer or open a window, never actually taking more than a baby hit. Sometimes I don't smoke any at all. My mom knows I spend time at their house, but she has no idea what we're doing, and she never asks. I don't know why they don't have a child, but Gwen acts proud of me at random moments, the way mothers are proud of their children. When I cut Taylor's hair, she remarks on my talent, and when I sit and work on a play for hours at their desk, she crows about my focus.

I have the keys to their apartment now, and when they're going out of town they tell their doorman I'm allowed to stay there. Madison and Tatum have both left for boarding school and Amelia transferred to Trinity. My group of in-school friends has dwindled down to one: Libby, who lives downtown and, like me, is a Village kid with the freedom of an adult. Although I've admitted to nothing, she doesn't think she's smart either. We spend our time aimlessly walking around the Village, flirting and picking up boys. Sometimes we go to the Palladium, the World, or Area to dance.

Since I'm perpetually terrified of being abandoned again, not just by my school friends but by Taylor, I feel constantly forced into doing things I don't want for approval. If I knew how to get myself out of situations that scared me, maybe I'd be less afraid, but I still haven't learned how to rely on myself for my own safety. Sleepovers still frighten me, but I've bragged about having access to an apartment, and Libby wants to use it. Taylor told me I could bring boys back to his place. "Just think, you have your own apartment to have sex in," he says. Libby and I eat their food, drink their alcohol, and do whatever drugs we can find in Taylor's sock drawer. We are grossed out when we find condoms, and I'm shot through, again, with the fear of turning eighteen. Sleeping away from home, it turns out, isn't so scary when you're too drunk to remember falling asleep, and once it's done and over, and I didn't die or disappear, I might even be able to do it again.

Everything I do is done as though Taylor is watching me. Even when I'm at home, I imagine he can see me, watching me on some secret closed-circuit TV. Whenever my body starts to float away, or thrum with dread and darkness, I do a line and it supplants my despair and fear with levity and courage. I carry the drug with me all the time. Soon, I am afraid of nothing.

I'm failing out of all my classes. Even though I keep it in my backpack, I've worn my uniform only once or twice during ninth grade, and I'm told I won't be invited back if my grades and attitude don't improve and I continue to show up in my combat boots and half-punk wardrobe. Predictably, my mom responds the way she always does, with a (metaphorical) magic pill: I can leave if I'm unhappy and go somewhere else. But I know better this time: You have to test into the public schools I like, and I won't pass that test.

Although my dad provided my mom with child support, Jimmy paid my phone bill, and bought me clothes and presents and chipped in for doctors and school, when he didn't have to. Late one night in the kitchen, while he's eating a contraband steak secretly delivered by the gun club across the street, I thank him for giving me so much, and he winks and tells me to take out the garbage. A Wall Street "You're welcome."

Knowing I can't stay where I am, I start looking at schools: Calhoun on the Upper West Side is too noisy; there are no walls, and I can't hear anything the teacher says because I'm distracted by everything the other teacher is saying in the adjacent classroom. Dwight is fun because I get to hang out with Paul, but I don't want to be lumped in with the other dumb white idiots getting high together. Finally, I visit Friends Seminary in the East Village, and it's there, when I'm walking up the stairs, following behind my guide, that a cute boy with a curly mop of hair races past me singing David Bowie. "There's a Starman, waiting in the sky . . ." This is the school for me.

I don't know how I get in, because they surprise all applicants with a test, but I do. By the time I start my new school, I'll be the only kid left in this house, and I feel homesick for the chaos. It's been hard without Kara here, but she lets me call her with my problems. With Eddie leaving, though, now I'll have to go to my dad's house by myself, and I know I won't be able to handle that.

One night Eddie and I are watching TV in my bedroom and my mom comes in.

"Can you turn off the TV for a minute? I need to talk to you two," she says.

"Can you wait for a commercial?" Eddie asks.

"No, I can't," she says.

We're annoyed and turn the volume down, but we don't turn it off. "What?" I ask.

"Well . . . I'm pregnant," she says.

I stand. "Are you serious?"

"Very."

"Well, you're not going to keep it, are you?" I ask.

"Of course I'm going to keep it."

"But you're so old," Eddie tells her.

"I'm forty-two!"

"Exactly," I say. "Old. Does Kara know?"

"Not yet," she says.

I leap across the room to the phone and call her. "Guess what?"

"What?"

"Mom's having a baby," I tell her.

"Amanda, I'm studying for exams. I don't have time for jokes," she says.

"It's not a joke."

"I'm hanging up. College is really hard and I have a lot of work to do."

"Hang on," I say, and I hand the phone to Mom, who tells her the news. I'm mortified. Forty-two is too old to have a baby. Having a baby is a young person's job. Everything about this news feels gross and embarrassing. A person my mom's age shouldn't be having babies. Plus, she's not even around. What does she do all day, anyway? *I'm* supposed to be her youngest!

"Wait!" I call out while she's on the phone. "When are you due?"

"October," she answers.

Oh Jesus. I'll be at my new school already. What will people think of me when they find out my ancient mom is pregnant? I might as well just walk into my new school and say to everyone I meet: "Hi, my name is Amanda. My mom had sex, and now we all know about it."

But then, as the days and weeks pass, I realize that I'm getting what I want: another kid in the house with me. I start warming up to the idea. Maybe a baby will bring the family closer and give my siblings a reason to come home more often.

School starts and I'm one of three new tenth graders, which makes it easier and harder at the same time. I like my classmates, but most of my friends end up being in the grade above me, the one I should have been in all along. We hang out at one another's houses, or in Washington Square Park, or I invite them to the garden. I am out of uniform every day and never get in trouble for it. The kids are free-spirited, more my type of people, and we call our teachers by their first names. I quickly develop a crush on my math teacher, who's a young, cool guy named Paolo. He's the reason I'm excited to go to school every morning, hurrying out the door in case I can catch a glimpse of his beat-up blue truck on the way. He knows I exist because I'm in his class, but that's about it. Still, Taylor doesn't like hearing about Paolo, even though he keeps asking what he looks like and whether we had sex, which is such a dumb question—he's a teacher, jeez—I don't even bother answering.

One of the first weeks of school, I tear down the front steps and Taylor's there, waiting for me. "I was just walking by," he explains. "Thought I'd pick you up. See the new school, meet your friends..." He looks around.

He wants me to take him inside, though I'm not sure this is a good idea. Everyone I introduce him to looks at us strangely: Why am I walking around with a thirty-year-old man who's not my brother or my father? I have no idea how to even begin to explain who he is to me, but I feel pride that he's mine. I show him the art room, and my locker, and when I'm all showed out, I tell him we're done, and let's go.

"Where's, uh...what's his name?" Taylor asks. I pretend not to know who he's talking about. "You know. Cute teacher. Marco?"

"Paolo. Dunno." I walk into a classroom and look out the window and see Paolo loading his guitar into the back of his truck. "There," I say, pointing.

Taylor stands next to me at the window. "The dude with blond tips? He's gay."

"He's not gay," I say, defensive.

"Let's go downstairs," he says, rushing out. I follow behind him and we make it outside before Paolo's gone. He's surrounded by students, adored by boys and girls alike, and when he sees Taylor, and then me, I can tell he is perplexed, maybe even a little worried. They stare at each other for a minute. Taylor's pissed. He puts his arm around me like I'm his. "Let's get out of here."

"Where are we going?" I ask.

"I have a surprise for you," he says, steering me with his proprietary hand toward his apartment.

Gwen's in Connecticut for the weekend, and Taylor and I watch *Platoon* and power through a third of the eight ball he just picked up from his dealer, Misty. God, I love this drug. There's literally no other drug I ever need to try. Any trace of fear I felt before, any fear I may feel ever again in the future, is entirely gone. Erased. I'm in control. Off the drug, I have to pretend and lie so I don't expose whatever is wrong with me, but I feel guilty every time. On the drug, I believe my lies, even if I never remember them. I am a different version of me. No, I'm a different person entirely. I'm better, stronger, smarter, funnier, cooler, a leader. It also makes me realize things about myself I didn't before; like right now, after about ten lines of coke, I finally understand that I'm not the problem—it's intelligence itself that is misunderstood. People think intelligence is knowing the answers to test questions, memorizing information and facts, but I know intelligence is about a type of understanding and knowing that can't be tested or measured. It is about depth, a depth that involves not just your brain, but your entire body. And I have that kind of intelligence, but because others don't value it, it doesn't count, which means that everything I say and do will be wrong because the entire world is predicated upon measuring a type of intelligence I don't have. As I start to crash, I realize maybe I'm wrong and it's not the world that's defective, it's me, and I'll never amount to anything, so the best I can do is more coke.

Taylor puts his head on my lap and I'm not sure what to do with my hands. I fold them across my chest. We talk all through the movie. We gossip about the other kids in the acting school. He knows how in love with Paul I am, but although Taylor seems jealous of Paolo, he's not jealous of my crush on Paul. Maybe he just doesn't want to be replaced, and he knows Paolo could replace him. Paul's just a teenager. Taylor tells me that when he met Gwen the first thing he said was, "I want to make mad passionate love to you."

"Gross," I say. I don't want to think about him and Gwen having sex. I don't want to think of Taylor in any way that's sexual.

He laughs. The credits are rolling, and he sits up. "Hey, so it occurred to me the other day. Do you know how to give a hand job?"

"Yes!" I say, defensive. I've never given a hand job.

"What about a blow job?" he asks.

"Yes!" I say. "Stop asking me these things."

"It's just that if you don't know how, I'll show you. I can teach you," he says, his hands going toward his crotch.

"I know how!" I say and stand. "Jesus. I know how to do everything. I know how to do things that would appall you," I say. The whole point of pretending I know more than I do is to keep him from asking me things like this, to get him to stop saying these things to me and making clear that he's looking forward to having sex with me in a few years. I have no idea how to stop these conversations without losing him.

I head to the bathroom and sit on the side of the tub. The winter air has a smell that seems to grow stronger whenever I'm in over my head. Sometimes my body feels like it's growing too big for the world, which makes me feel exposed; other times it feels like it's shrinking and I'm invisible and being left behind. Now, it's growing. I try to focus on the smells: Taylor's Irish Spring; Gwen's Suave shampoo. It helps.

"I gotta go," I say, walking past him as he sits on the couch.

"I'll see you tomorrow?" he asks. Then, "I'm serious. If you need to know how to do 'biblical' things, just ask me."

"Yeah, I've fucked enough dudes to feel pretty solid on that front, but you know, thanks anyway," I say and try not to seem like I'm fleeing.

*   *   *

Taylor returns to school the next day to pick me up, but this time he's in his car.

"Where are we going?" I ask.

"You'll see," he says. At the first red light, he hands me a vial. "Help yourself."

I haven't mastered how to do coke this way, but I manage to get a little. It's not enough to stop the fear that begins surging through my body as it becomes clear we're leaving the city.

"Where are we going?" My mouth is very dry. My stomach is souring, and my body starts closing in on itself. You cannot vomit in Taylor's car. You cannot vomit in front of Taylor. If you vomit in front of Taylor, you will have given everything about yourself away.

"You have no patience."

Desperate, I figure out a way to get more of the coke into my system by rubbing it on my teeth, which numbs them. In a few minutes, my nausea subsides and my fear is supplanted by a rare excitement—we're in the country, going on an adventure, and not knowing where we're go-ing is miraculously fun. I shut my eyes and feel the September sun on my face, and the smell and sensation don't trigger a free fall. I feel the way I did when I returned home from camp: normal. How do I get this feeling to become my regular life? Will I have to do coke until I'm old? When I open my eyes, I recognize Gwen's country house.

"What are we doing here?" I ask.

"Thought it'd be fun," he says. "Maybe you want to go swimming."

"I don't want to go swimming," I say. "Besides, I don't have a bathing suit."

"Who said anything about a suit?" Taylor asks, winking.

"I don't want to go swimming," I say again, suddenly afraid. The coke high drains from my veins. Is he going to try to have sex with me? Taylor is handsome; all the acting kids think so—even the boys—and I know I'm lucky to get all his attention, but I want him to remain in his lane. I don't want to have sex with a man—I haven't even figured out yet how to have sex with a boy—but I don't know how to tell an adult, even Taylor, to back off. My whole life, every time I've ever tried to tell an adult what I need, I've been ignored.

I decide that if I get more drugs into my system, I won't be afraid to tell him to fuck off. Several lines later, we're lying on the couch, taking a breather, and he leans over.

"You sure you know how to give a blow job?"

"Oh my God, stop. Yes. I do. I'm like the blow-job queen," I say, hoping that's a real expression.

"Okay, okay. Man, I can't wait to see what you got. When do you turn eighteen?"

"Oh my God. Stop!" I say again, but I'm laughing from nerves, which he takes to be a type of flirting. I can tell from his smile.

"Maybe you want to take a shower?" he asks.

"A shower? Why would I want to take a shower?"

He shrugs. "Just asking."

"I don't want to take a shower," I say. I don't know how to steer him away. Why can't he just be like a big brother or a dad to me?

And yet I don't want to stop hanging out with him. I can't. No one else pays this much attention to me. Plus, all the drugs are free.

1984

Dr. Parker Prentice

She has a little difficulty with reality and she doesn't take to concepts. Her conceptual/perceptivity is not as strong as her sensitivity to art, people, music, etc. She needs a better understanding of herself.

Instead, she is pretending to know things she doesn't. She is in over her head, and she knows it.

What If I Give Birth to Myself?

THE WORLD IS PASSING by without me. My grandmother Puggy died. My mother has been complaining that the MacDougal Street house is too big for her; my little sister, Rebecca, is getting married; my little brother is about to get engaged; and I am just standing on the sidelines watching the world roll past me.

Wanting a baby broke up Javi and me, and the gates are nearly closed on having a biological child. So that's why, without telling anyone—not my therapist, not even Kara—I go to a fertility doctor to see about freezing my eggs. I'm forty-one years old, and while I want a baby, I'm certain I don't want to raise one alone. When my hands are filled with grocery bags, I ask myself, Could I manage this with a baby? When I have a cold, when I'm depressed, when I'm taking a shower, when I'm grumpy and overwhelmed, I stop and imagine a baby in the mix.

I'm afraid if I tell my friends, I'll allow myself to be talked into doing something I'll regret. I just want to freeze my eggs so that I can take more time. Maybe one day I'll feel ready to raise a child on my own, but I know that time is not right now.

What I want is for the fertility people to tell me I have plenty of time, not to worry, and to return in nine years, when I'm fifty. I fill out the requisite paperwork, all nine thousand pages of intake about my pathetic loser life without a partner or children, not even a dog, pretending not to notice I'm the only woman here alone.

I'm led down the hall and into a back office so cold I wonder if they're freezing the eggs inside us right now. I put my gloves back on. The fertility doctor has no identifying facial features, as if his face has been seen by too many people and just wore off. He hasn't even sat down at his desk and he's already midway through a monologue, reciting statistics about age and options, and his eyes look programmed: fervent and disconnected from reality.

"You're forty-one. You've got no time to waste. I understand you want to freeze your eggs, but it's too late, you don't have time for that. If it's a child you want, there is no point in freezing your eggs. You're much too old. IVF must start now! The statistics don't lie."

A pressure I didn't expect begins to close around my throat. I do want a child, I think, but I also want a career, and a partner. If I freeze my eggs, I can have a baby when I'm ready, which isn't now. I have no money to even freeze my eggs, so what would I raise my baby on, the barter system? His urgency sets off a cascade of doubt in me. This is not matching my fantasy scenario where he tells me to return in nine years.

He pulls out a chart and starts pointing to the downward curving lines, citing statistics and averages. I cannot concentrate on the words coming out of his mouth, although I know I'm supposed to be absorbing everything and that statistically speaking, 95 percent of women between the ages of thirty-four and thirty-nine who come here panicked about their fertility wind up doing 100 percent of what he says. My fingers are numb, and my toes are cold. We wound down so many hallways to get here that if I race out of his office like I want to, I'll never find my way out. I'll probably end up in the IVF room, where he'll restrain me and force-feed me his sperm. Or however IVF works.

"I don't think I want kids right away," I say. "I really just want to freeze my eggs."

He stands. "I look forward to adding your baby's photo to my wall of fertility successes," he says, looking over my shoulder as if he hasn't heard a word I've said. I turn and see hundreds of photos of infants, families, even a few teenagers, along with Christmas cards and birthday cards. The cards are insidious reminders of my failure. Here are some pictures where something is missing. Everywhere I go, I can point to the spaces where I am missing.

"No time to wait!" he says and ushers me down the hall to a different office. "Carol will set you up with a California Cryobank account and make your follow-up appointment."

At the door of an empty office, he shakes my hand, tells me to wait for Carol, and gives me a stack of papers to bring to billing when I'm done. I should take a few days to think and call when I'm ready to start the IVF process.

"All right." I know I will never see him again.

"We don't want you to regret not having children."

Instead of waiting for Carol, I bolt down the hall, lost in the maze, but anonymous since no one's chasing me. When I finally get home, I shut my bedroom door, climb into bed, and pull the covers over my head so no one can find me: not the creepy doctor, not Carol. Not billing.

When will I ever feel like I have a place in the world, like I'm not some defective game piece that people never use?

I'm forty-one years old, but my roots are still in my childhood home on MacDougal Street. Even when members of my family move, the house stays the same. It's never left me. I pull myself out of bed and head to MacDougal Street. My mom's not there, but I eat the leftover pasta in the refrigerator, watch some TV, and call Kara.

I tell her what I did, and what happened, and she suggests that I do try to have a baby. Maybe even with a friend. Even though I specifically avoided telling her, worrying she was going to say something just like this, when she says it, it seems less terrifying. She suggests a few books on single motherhood and I order them. I think of male friends to have babies with and rule each one out, wishing I could order them online also.

Who needs Carol? I sign up for California Cryobank, which my single-mother friends all used, and then scan the hundreds of thousands of sperm donors with the ease of the seasoned OkCupid user I am. You can't see what the men look like, but the filters let you add donors to your cart based on critically important factors, like which movie star would play your sperm in a movie. I add Mark Ruffalo to the cart. Ryan Gosling. John Cusack. I try to find Dominic West. No luck. Still, my cart runneth over with impersonator sperm.

The books on single motherhood arrive and as I read them, old memories jar loose of conversations with my new mom friends who bemoan the mind-numbing boredom of newborns. I think about how many doctor appointments I make for myself, and how annoying it is when I have to interrupt my writing day to go tend to my own body. What would it mean to add in another person's doctor appointments until there's no writing time left? I don't see how I could possibly do both. My worries are pushing their way up like acid reflux. What if I give birth to myself and screw myself up even more?

Maybe I'll find a different place that will let me freeze my eggs. Then I can have a baby whenever I want, because what's the urgency? I know plenty of forty-two-year-old single moms. Forty-two is the new Thursday. Right now, my brain wants me to have a baby, but all my friends who chose to do this on their own wanted a baby with their bodies. They were driven by a profound need to make it happen, and I don't feel that need. I felt that need for a dog, and I got the dog, and look what happened.

Maybe I'll feel the profound need at forty-two, when I'll be more confident and self-assured. But what if my store is entirely closed at forty-two? If I have the baby now, the issue will be off the table, and I can focus on finding the right partner without putting pressure on this person to have a baby, because I'll already have the baby! But wait—how am I supposed to meet anyone if I have an infant? I'll never be able to leave my house. I also know that when I have the baby and people ask about my writing, anxiety will surf through me, because having a baby was a good decision for my heart, but bad for my career, and now it's too late to do anything about it except feel, without wanting to, resentment at how the baby hampers my life, which will make me feel trapped, and I'll spiral into a suicidal despair, unable to get out of bed, and they'll have no choice but to lift me out of my apartment by crane. No, I cannot have a baby on my own. Next year. Next year, I'll do it.

I log out of California Cryobank and on to OkCupid. I spend hours looking at human faces, but I'm not quite ready to go back out there. Life would be so much more convenient, though, if they just lumped these two websites together. Then I could add baby and man to cart, click free shipping, proceed to checkout, and expect my family to be delivered in three to five business days.

Who Doesn't Want to Be in a Play?

I'M AT MY TENTH-GRADE Field Day when my mom gives birth to a baby girl she names Nina. I rush home every day to hold her and sing to her and play with her. When anyone congratulates Jimmy, he just shakes his head, confused, and says, "I don't know how it happened." I like having a newborn in my house, and I invite some classmates over to check her out. I'm desperate to get my new friends to accept me, but since I'm just transferring in, I'm joining established friendships, and no matter how many memories we make, I'll never catch up.

People at my new school think it's cool that I have an entirely separate life and that I'm writing and acting in plays. We're writing one right now, and we stay up late working on it. Afterward Paul, his brother Jonathan, and I trail behind Taylor to the after-parties; those nights I sleep at Gwen and Taylor's on their couch. I call my mom when Gwen goes to bed to tell her it's too late for me to walk home. Then Taylor keeps me up late doing coke. My mom is occupied with baby Nina and she doesn't ask any questions.

I get a crush on a kid named Aram. He's a year older and not my type, though I hardly know what that would be. He's the smartest kid in school, loves sports, is frighteningly sexy, kind of a loner, never had a serious girlfriend, and already looks like a man. Friends Seminary is different from Whittaker. Our classes are mixed ages, so instead of having a small group of friends in just my grade, I have pockets of friends in several grades. And now that I smoke, I have my smoking alley friends, but I don't have a confidante. Instead, I seem to have become the one people confide in, as well as the dispenser of advice. People admit things to me that, if they were my secrets, I'd never confess to anyone. I've certainly never told my friends how I have these terrifying attacks inside my body that make me feel like I'm dying. To tell anyone would mean revealing I'm defective or crazy. I keep everything to myself, which means people get closer to me, but I don't get closer to them. The more time passes where I don't reveal myself, the more convinced I become that I shouldn't do it.

Maybe if I had a boyfriend, I'd have the closeness I crave. I'm desperate to get Aram to notice me, and since I've cowritten several plays already with my acting school, and my English teacher secretly submitted a play I wrote to a playwriting contest, I propose my idea of writing, directing, and producing a play at school to that same teacher, who loves the idea and volunteers to get permission. No other student has ever written, directed, and produced their own play independent from the theater department, and it's a big deal when I get the go-ahead. I am both thrilled and nervous. I'll ask Aram to be in it. Who doesn't want to be in a play? I also ask my friends Miranda and Wren and, even though he's a teacher, Paolo.

Our first rehearsal is just a conversation about the play and how I imagine it looking; having their attention on me, treating me like I'm a real producer, gives me a surge of confidence. Since Aram's the star, his rehearsals go longer. We spend our rehearsals talking about the play, which is about suicide, and how hard it is being a teenager, and soon we're talking about our parents and siblings, gender, sexuality, and race. I love the way he listens to me as though I actually have things to say that are valid.

I don't think he knows I have a crush on him. I had thought I was making progress with him, bonding over these big questions, but then he starts asking if he and Miranda can have a kiss in the play, one that they'd have to rehearse. Fuck no: The only kiss that will occur takes place between his stage-parents, played by Wren and Paolo, and if I have my way, the only person Aram will be kissing is me.

At school people are talking about my play, with the opening night now just a few days away. I feel lucky that in the one place I do not excel—an academic environment—I am being given an opportunity to be noticed for my strengths. That belief in me is palpable, and I wonder if maybe being creative is a type of intelligence and people just don't know it. I do everything myself: I design the lighting scheme and the sound track; I make the playbills and the tickets. The play is about a father's suicide, and the teenage son who attempts suicide but survives. It takes place in a therapist's office. The actors sit on chairs about six feet apart, with the light focused on one person at a time. Each character begins a sentence about his or her own experience, a line that is then completed by the next person, with the account changing drastically between perspectives.

Everyone thinks the sentence completion aspect is innovative, but what I don't tell anyone is that my much smarter friend Naomi wrote a story that introduced me to the idea of this kind of shared, shifting monologue. She goes to a different school, so I'm not that worried. Aram is so smart, and now he thinks I'm smart, but I'm not. I'm hiding behind a pretense. Everywhere I go, there are always two of me. There is the me getting tested and the me who doesn't know why. There is the me who suffers from countdowns and the me who pretends she's unafraid. There is the me who pretends she knows things and the me who knows I know nothing.

On opening night I look down from the balcony into the Quaker meetinghouse, at the gray pews where we spend our mornings sitting in silence. Taylor and Gwen are there, along with Paul and his brother Jonathan, plus more than half of the school. The principal of the school introduces the show, the lights go out, and the performance is better than any rehearsal we've ever had. No one forgets their lines and the lighting is perfect and it all goes by too fast because suddenly the final scene is up and Wren and Paolo kiss as the lights fade to black. I take a deep breath.

When the houselights come up, though, there are audible gasps, because Paolo and Wren are still kissing. They leap apart, but it's too late; everyone saw it, even the principal. Even Wren's boyfriend, Carlos, saw it. I don't have time to wonder whether a scandal will be good for publicity or not, because I'm called onto the stage and I bow and the applause grows and I can't quite believe how incredible this moment feels. I am being seen and recognized for something I wrote. For something I wrote about feelings and emotions. Instead of being seen for what I'm doing wrong, people are clapping because I've done something no one else has done in this school before. I've always wondered what it would be like to have people look at me the way I look at everyone else—like they know how to do things I don't—and now, right in these very moments, they are. I don't want it to end.

Afterward, Taylor and Gwen congratulate me, and I'm floating in a way that's not terrifying. Except for the two of them, all the adults in my life seem out of touch; other people are concerned about the subject matter, asking if I am all right, and do I need to talk about anything? I'm annoyed that I had to do something so big to receive a question so small. It feels like too little too late. Yes, I did need to talk about something, years and years ago, but now I'm too far in to be extracted. I vow never to be an adult so unaware of the interior life of kids.

The attention and excitement of the night feel like a drug. For the entire two-night run, I am buoyant, but when it ends I crash hard on the other side. The despair is paralyzing, exhausting, and confusing. When by Monday it still hasn't passed, I stay home. Midday, I get a weirdly frantic phone call from Aram, wondering where I am. I can hear the sounds of the schoolyard in the background. When I tell him I just needed a day of rest and will be back tomorrow, he doesn't seem to believe me.

"You're . . . uh, you're not with Paolo, are you?" he asks.

"Paolo? No. He's not at school?"

"Nope," he says. "And it's weird, because of . . . you know, the kiss."

The kiss! I'd completely forgotten about it.

"I wouldn't worry about it. I'm sure he's fine and will be back tomorrow," I say, ignoring a wave of nerves.

As I'm about to hang up, Aram says, "We're still friends, right? Like will we still hang out and stuff, even though the play is done?"

Holy shit. "Yes, of course," I say, trying to sound casual. "I mean, I feel like the play made us closer, don't you think?" I am expecting him to confess his love right there.

"Yeah, totally. Okay, I gotta get to class. Get rest!" he says and hangs up before I can say anything else.

When the phone rings again, I'm still smiling and I think it's him again because I hear school sounds before the speaker says anything.

"Yeeeuuusss?" I say, singsongy.

"Hi there. May I please speak to Mrs. Stern?" a woman asks. "This is Eileen Duva." The guidance counselor. I tell her my mother is out.

"I'd like to have a conversation with her about your college plans, and with you also. Will you be in tomorrow?"

"Yeah," I say. "What do you want to talk about?"

"Well, your grades are terrible, your PSAT scores are abysmal, your standardized testing scores are suboptimal, and while your achievements outside school are impressive, I'm afraid it's your in-school performance colleges look for, and, quite frankly, you don't have it."

"I don't want to go to college," I retort, offended but also hurt. "I want to keep doing what I'm doing. Maybe work in film, or write. What's the point of college?" Until I say it out loud, I haven't even known that's how I feel, but it's true. I don't want to go to college. If I already know what I want to do, why not just start doing it? Besides, I'm not smart enough for college.

"Do your parents know you feel this way?"

"No," I say.

She agrees to have this conversation with my mother tomorrow. My mom didn't go to college, so this probably won't be a big deal. Eddie didn't go to college either. He just went straight out into the real world and got himself an apartment and a job making T-shirts. When I think of jumping into the real world, it doesn't scare me as much as college does. I can hide how academically out of my depth I am in the real world, but

I can't in college. I wonder where Aram will go to college. If I'm not in college, I'll be able to visit him whenever I want.

I'm shocked out of my reverie by another phone call. This time it's Paolo.

"I'm in so much trouble," he says with no preamble. "I told them that was in the script, okay? That it was part of the play, so if they ask you, tell them that, all right?" he asks.

"Yeah, okay. Don't worry." I do my best to reassure him.

"Thanks . . . hopefully my one-day suspension will be all I have to deal with."

"You got suspended?"

"Yep. All for you, kid. But don't worry. It was fun and worth it," he says. This reversal is odd—instead of being his student, I feel like his teacher, and if I'm his teacher, then I have a crush on a student, whom I'm on the phone with, at home, talking about a kiss that shouldn't have happened, and annoyed by my layer of envy and resentment. Why are all these male teachers trying to fuck their students? Can't they get any-one their own age? Hearing Paolo's glee that he kissed a student, and the fact that he hasn't even mentioned Wren, or how she might feel, makes me feel contempt for him. I hope she and Carlos don't break up because of the kiss. Then it will be my fault.

Aram is waiting on the front steps for me the next day. I feel like a rock star at school; everyone congratulates me on the play, but because the topic of the play was suicide, they also seem a little wary of me, which I love. Even though I'm now dressing more like a painter than a punk, the more afraid people are of me, the more they'll believe their own stories about me, and I'll feel safe and hidden. I recognize the quandary I've got-ten myself into here, but I don't know how to get out. I wanted someone to figure out what was wrong with me, and in order to do that, I went in the direction they sent me, but that sent up a decoy that took on a life of its own and now the decoy is all they see. It's too late to reveal my truth to anyone. I'm an idiot who can't get anything right, and I'm not even try-ing to get someone to see what's wrong with me.

Eileen Duva catches me in the hall. "I spoke with your mother this morning," she says. "I think I woke her up."

"Probably. Did you tell her I don't want to go to college?"

"You're going to college," she says.

"But I don't want to!" I protest. I am not ready for my lack of intelligence to be revealed. I won't get in anywhere.

"My dear, according to your mother, you have no choice."

1984

Dr. Parker Prentice

   My conclusion is that Amanda has convinced herself she is not smart. Her efforts are spent avoiding situations where she might be challenged and exposed for who she believes herself to be. While there is no question she struggles with some specific tasks, the monumental struggle appears to be low self-esteem and insecurity resulting from an emotionally based issue. Perhaps it is time for her to be examined by a child psychologist.

One Right Way to Be a Person

WREN AND HER BOYFRIEND, Carlos, don't break up, thank God. The kiss brought them even closer together, and they come uptown to see a play I'm in with the acting school, and they meet Taylor, who does cocaine with us. They can't believe my luck that he gives me as much as I want, whenever I want. So long as I never tell Gwen, the drugs will keep coming.

One weekend when Taylor is out of town, we run out of coke. Desperate, I decide to do what needs to be done.

"I know where we can buy some," I tell Carlos and Wren. "But one of you has to come with me."

"I'll come," Carlos says.

"Yeah, he'll go," Wren says and looks out my bedroom window. "I'll wait here."

Carlos and I walk across Houston Street. I don't tell him where we're headed, but my confidence never flags until we near Avenue A. The streets smell of smoke: garbage can fires, cigarettes, pot, and, based on all the discarded vials we pass, crack. We pass open fire hydrants, parking meters covered in graffiti, streetlamps with sneakers hanging off the top of them. Last time I was here, updated posters of Etan Patz were glued to the lampposts. A computer had him age-progressed, morphing him into a teenager, a person who doesn't exist, erasing him all over again. I worried that if I looked at it for too long, the image of him I have in my head might get wiped away by the new one.

There's an audible crunch underneath our feet of used hypodermic needles and crack vials. People with Mohawks and face tattoos are sitting in doorways and nodding off on fire escapes. The scene is the same as last time, only this time we're lacking an adult.

"You sure this is safe?" Carlos asks.

"Sure," I tell him. "Don't worry about it."

I scour the lampposts for Etan's face, but already the posters have been plastered over. Two homeless teenagers with Mohawks, a guy and a girl, sit on the sidewalk with a skinny, mangy dog asleep in front of them.

"Got money? Give us money, man. Got money?" they yell at us as we walk by.

"Oh my God," Carlos says and presses in closer to me. "That guy had Africa-sized holes in his ears. With no jewelry."

"Shhh . . . be cool," I say, sounding utterly uncool.

"I'm cool," he says, insulted.

He follows me across St. Mark's and when he realizes I'm leading him toward B, he stops. "How badly do we need this?" he asks.

"Badly," I say.

"Enough to die for it?"

"We're not going to die, Carlos," I hiss, not entirely believing this.

He looks around us. "Yeah, actually, we might."

My entire body is numb, and yet my brain is focused, will not stop pushing until it gets what it needs—more drugs. I'm a pit bull who won't unclench until my teeth touch, and yet I am also the flesh being bitten. The coke already in my system has made me fearless enough to get this far, but now it's starting to wear off, and we're too far to turn back. I have no choice but to keep pretending I'm tough.

I cross the street. He runs after me and grabs my arm. "I can't just let you go by yourself," he says.

"You can, but you shouldn't," I say, tasting my own false bravado.

"I really don't want to, Amanda. I don't think it's safe."

I don't know where else to get coke, and I've come to rely on it like the medicine in my mom's bathroom cabinet. It takes away all my fear so completely that now, allowing any inkling of fear inside me is unbearable. There is only one way to escape my mental anguish and that's to numb it out, and this is the only thing that works. I am willing to face death in order to buy the thing that saves me from ever having to fear death.

"I'm going whether or not you come with me, but if you stay behind and make me do all the work, I'm not sharing with you."

He throws his head back and groans his frustration. "Fine. Fine. I'll come, but I swear to God if we die, I'll never forgive you."

"I can live with that," I say. I don't know where my words are coming from, since I am not inside my body at all; I'm not even in the same time zone as Carlos.

We're on Ninth Street now, nearing a car on fire, nearing C, the street where you go if you're suicidal and survival isn't your bag. Even Eddie doesn't go to C. This is the most dangerous place I've ever been.

"How many times have you done this before?" he asks.

"Tons," I lie. Just once, and even then, I faked my calm.

As we cross C and walk toward D, we're completely silent, powered only by our clipped steps. I can't take a proper inhale and Carlos is practically hyperventilating. I'm really hoping that instead of looking like two nervous kids from the rich side of the Village, we look more like hypertense cokeheads who need to buy more drugs.

We get to the boarded-up, crumbling town house on Avenue D. I take some change out of my pocket, and following the procedure I remember from last time, hurl it toward the window. A few minutes pass, and nothing happens. I throw a few more, muttering under my breath, "Come on, come on." A window cracks open, then widens. A metal pail is slowly lowered down by a rope. The familiar sight momentarily soothes me. I snag a key from the pail, unlock the front door, and Carlos follows me inside. We squeeze past oily, oozing garbage, not even in bags, just piles of vile old food cans and used diapers. It sounds like people are trapped inside the walls, scratching and thumping to get out. I hope we don't end up buried alive alongside them in the shallow drywall. Babies cry and shriek, and a couple scream at each other in Spanish, or maybe it's TV. Things are thrown and break. We walk up the steps, avoiding the cavernous holes where rats and roaches scurry. Spanish music, Spanish radio, and rap, all playing at full volume. It smells like burned plastic or turpentine. Streaks on the walls look like smeared diarrhea. We go all the way to the top; I knock on the dented door.

The same man from last time opens it, keeping his face hidden. I walk inside and Carlos follows. Misty is sitting on a mattress in her underwear and a wife beater. It's freezing, but she doesn't seem to care. She's folding pieces of aluminum foil. When she looks up at us I see scratches down her face and open sores. I didn't get such a close look last time. Now I can't stop staring; she has four visible teeth and no body fat.

When she speaks to us, I'm captivated by her bulging eyes. What little hair she has is greasy.

"What do you want?" she asks.

"Eight ball," I say.

"Come here, sweetie," she says to Carlos, tapping out a line on a mirror. "Try it." Carlos goes to the woman and tries it, then nods.

"You look like his namesake," she says to Carlos. "Ricardo, look, it's your namesake—Ricky Ricardo."

Ricardo turns around and looks at me. "She don't look like Ricky Ricardo," he says. I glance at Carlos, whose face is completely white.

I pay and we strip the wind as we tear out of the apartment and fly down the stairs. Once we've safely crossed over Avenue A, we're giddy with joy and new toughness. Our survival was a triumph all its own. I am almost hyperkinetic with relief. Twice now, I've gone past my comfort zone, and now A no longer scares me. My fear has grown muscles.

We do coke the rest of the night, and when Carlos and Wren start to make out, I discreetly tear off one aluminum edge, pinch a pebble, and fill the foil like a burrito, swishing it under my bed for later. I lick the mirrors we use. I like the numbness on my teeth best. I have a drawer filled with Taylor's paraphernalia: a grinder, an engraved mirror with its own velvet sleeve that I don't use, because I don't want it to accidentally wick away or absorb any overlooked residue and deprive me of precious granules.

As time goes by, I need more coke to get the same effects, to feel the same freedom from myself, to be enveloped inside a cocoon of magical intelligence. Am I becoming immune to it? When Carlos isn't around, Wren confides that she cheats on him all the time, which now makes me mad at her, and I coke-lecture her about the different ways we need to find affection because we didn't get it from our fathers. I tell her the attention from the other men is the reward she's seeking, but that it'll lead to despair when it fails to fulfill the gaping hole inside her. How do I know all this? she asks me.

"I've been around," I tell her. I'm making it up as I go along.

"Have you had sex?" she asks.

"Oh yeah. I lost my virginity when I was like fourteen," I tell her.

"To who?"

"Man, I don't even remember. I think his name was Marco. He was in college."

I'm blurring every edge of one truth to create a different truth so that I don't feel like a liar. Is something a lie when you know what a thing signifies without ever having experienced it? I continue to explain her psychological makeup to her in ways that not only sound, but feel, right.

Soon Wren is telling other people how much I know, and before I understand what's happening, I'm holding court in a booth at Joe Junior's during lunch while some new kid slides in to ask for my advice or for me to explain things to him, which I do. I'm so remarkably good at it, I convince myself of my own authority. Even Paolo asks for my advice, and he's a teacher.

There's not much I feel accomplished at, and not much I understand, but since I was a baby one thing I've never failed to recognize are feelings. Yes, I know I'm broken and defective, but underneath that conviction lies a question—what if my value lies somewhere else? What the

tests have taught me is that there exists one right answer to every question, and I am not the right answer to any question—and yet I know,
based on the way people respond to me, that I am the answer to something. I just don't know what the question is.

There can't be just one right way to be a person. Eddie isn't one right
way. Mr. Indresano and Basi weren't one right way. The adults around
me think there is just one way to be, and I am beginning to think they
are wrong.

1986

Dr. Wallace

A petite, attractive girl with long, very curly hair, Amanda came to both afternoon testing sessions rather tired. She had been up late the first night at a rock concert and hadn't slept the second night because of the heat and her inability to work the air-conditioning. I found her to be kind and patient, but skeptical of me and the process, referring to it a few times as "the system."

Homeless

IN MY FORTY YEARS of life, my mom has never before called a family meeting. Not even when Nina was born. But by now, we all know what it's about. For months our mom has been talking about turning the top two floors of the MacDougal Street house into an apartment, but the cost of construction is too high. She's been dropping hints about wanting to downsize, maybe rent the house for a while, and I'm terrified this is the first step toward selling it. The last thing I want is to sit in my childhood home being told that after all her promises, our future is being sold. That's why I'm late. I'm stuffing my bag full of things I don't need when there's a knock on my door; someone whisper-calls my name. Through the peephole I see my downstairs neighbor Haruko, her face blotched with dirty tears.

"Amanda. Amanda. Amanda. Amanda. Amanda."

I open the door and before I can register what's happening, she steps into my arms and presses her face into my neck. "I need a hug. Please give me a hug," she says, hugging me. I reach forward awkwardly and reluctantly place my arms around her. She feels smaller than she looks; her neck smells like beer and attempted suicide. Tiny beads of hostility string themselves on my lip. I resent this forced intimacy.

"What's going on?"

"I need a hug," she says.

"We're hugging," I tell her, trying not to sound impatient. "Are you okay?"

When she lets go, she starts sobbing and walks into my living room. How do I politely tell her that I need to be somewhere?

"I've done something terrible." She lies facedown on my living room rug. Probably she's killed her boyfriend. "What did you do?"

"I did something to Connery." Fuck, I was right. "Is Connery alive?"

"Yes," she says.

"Thank God. Listen, Haruko, I'm really late for something. I have to go. Can we talk about this later?"

"I have nowhere to go!" she says. "Can I stay here?"

"Why can't you stay in your apartment?"

"Connery had me committed last night. I got drunk and we got into a terrible fight, and I ended up telling him he should kill himself, just like his sister. I think I even said that his sister killed herself because of him. Then I threw a bottle at his face, so he called the police. I got out this morning, but Connery won't let me back into my apartment, so I have nowhere to stay. I'm totally homeless. Please, Amanda, please, let me just stay here."

"Fine, stay here, but I have to go. I really do. I'm sorry. Just stay put and we'll talk about this later, okay?"

She nods. "Thank you."

Eddie and Nina are already at the house when I get there, sitting in the living room with Kara on speakerphone. I sit next to Nina. I don't take off my coat. Daniel, David, and Holly are not there, and I assume my mom will call them with whatever terrible news she's going to tell us.

"Because of the housing crisis, the mortgage on the house has gone up astronomically, and because of that, I'm unable to refinance the house in order to pay the mortgage, so I need to rent the house for a little while."

"You're going to sell it!" I yell out, unable to stop myself.

"I'm not."

"You are!"

"The housing crisis is not Mom's fault," Eddie says. It's so annoying when he's reasonable. I lean back on the couch next to Nina and start to cry.

"Where will you live?" Kara asks through the speakerphone.

"I'm going to rent a place in Sag Harbor and live out there," she tells us.

"You're moving out of the city?" I toss Nina a "Can you believe this shit?" look. Nina's crying now, too. On top of the sickening homesickness I already have for the house, now I have to miss Mom, too?

"I think it's going to be good for Mom," Kara says.

"I agree," Eddie says.

Now I'm sobbing. Where's their house loyalty, their sense of justice and outrage? They know as well as I do that renting is the gateway drug to selling.

"You're overreacting," Eddie says to me.

"I'm not!" Now I'm practically hyperventilating. "You don't understand anything."

"What don't I understand?" he asks, getting mad.

"You and Kara, you have families. Nina and I don't. This house is our family; it's all we have, and now it's being taken away from us."

"It's not ours," Eddie says. "So it can't be taken away from us."

I glare at him, but I don't say what I want, which is "But it was supposed to be."

"Things change," Kara says through the phone.

Together, my mother and the house contain my roots, the proof of my existence, and without them, I'm extinct. This house was supposed to be ours! How can they pretend not to remember that? All our lives we were told that we didn't need to worry about being homeless because we'd always have a home, and the security I've attached to that knowledge is now being shattered. My mother is taking the house from us, giving it to someone else, only to disappear into some uncultivated ecosystem of tangled vegetation where I'll never be able to find her. Everyone is spinning away from me.

"I'll rent the house for a year or two and then I'll move back in."

I need this house to remain ours, always. My past, present, and future selves are all rooted here. I'm desperately sad and also furious. Not only do Kara and Eddie have their own families, they have their own homes;

and even if Eddie doesn't own his, he can afford to buy the things he needs, whereas I still come to my mom's house to eat leftover party food and steal toilet paper. I come to watch cable, take naps, ask for money, hang out in the garden, "borrow" queen-sized bedsheets, fancy towels, and, sometimes, just to make phone calls. Occasionally, I even come to see my mom, but the house itself has its own identity, a personality all its own, and I feel safe in its arms.

This house is where everything bad and good happened; it is our whole lives. But we all react in our own predictable ways, and, of course, I'm the most emotional and everyone is annoyed at how many feelings I possess.

"We have three weeks to pack up thirty-eight years of stuff. I'll need each of you to go through all your things in the basement and take what you want and throw out the rest," my mom says.

Once you pack up and move out, you don't move back in. Kara hangs up, Eddie leaves, and Mom and Nina go down to the basement. Crying, I make my way upstairs to my old room, lie on my bed, and stare out the window through the peeling rainbow decal. If I ever have children, they'll never see this house, play in the garden, know the life I once had. Outside the window, I can hear the people at the Dante and the baseball game on the Houston Street playground. I sit up and lean forward, but the lady on the corner isn't there. All my fears are the same as they were when I was a child, and sitting here now, looking for the lady on the corner, my worries about being homeless are coming true.

I've been afraid, ever since I was little, that I'd never amount to anything. I don't have anything steady or stable in my life. I am still waiting for something, it seems, but I'm not sure what. I've become the lady on the corner. Then it hits me that even the lady on the corner had something I don't have: a routine, sameness. She was there every single day, but I can't even do that; sameness is deadness to me. I can't bear it.

At least I have Calvin, I think as I head back home. He feels more like family than a roommate, but the good kind of family who doesn't take your home away from you. There's a note from Haruko on the counter.

I'd forgotten all about her. "Thanks, love! I'm back home now—Haruko." Calvin's doing the dishes.

"My mom is selling MacDougal Street! Can you believe this shit? My childhood home, gone!" I say as I walk into the kitchen. In the four and a half years we've lived together, I've never seen the expression on his face. I don't like it.

"What? What's that face?"

"We have to have a conversation," he says.

"I don't like this," I say. "Whatever it is, I already don't like it."

"So, remember a while back when I said it might be time for me to live on my own, but then I stayed?" I nod mutely. "I wasn't looking for a new place at all, but I accidentally found something that I love and that I can afford, and I'm going to take it."

I sit down. "What are you talking about?"

"I'm too old to have a roommate. I'm forty-four. It's weird, don't you think?"

"Well, yes, but it's New York City, so it's less weird. If we lived in Minnesota or something, yeah, but New York, not so much. Plus, I'm not much younger!"

"I'm sorry. I really love living with you, but I need my own space. I need to have a home that's just for me," he says, which makes me realize that I don't. I want someone around, even if they're down the hall with their door shut. Just to know someone's nearby.

I shake my head. I can't believe all of this is happening on the same day.

"Fine," I say, mainly to stop myself from bursting into tears. "When are you moving?"

"In three weeks. I'll help you find a replacement."

"Fine."

"You want to talk about this now or later?" he asks.

"Later," I say. My lips tremble; my voice is clogged and damp. I leave the kitchen and go lie on my bed to cry. I'm losing everything; I'm losing everyone. I am a failure at life.

I Am a Pinball Machine

I'M SEVENTEEN NOW, and soon I'll be eighteen. The year Taylor says he'll be legal to fuck me. I don't want Taylor to fuck me and I don't want to fuck Taylor, but how am I going to stop it from happening? Gwen is pregnant now, and I'm hoping fatherhood will distract Taylor from me, maybe even snap him back into being the father figure I was hoping for. I decide not to tell him when my birthday comes. I'm so mortified to be turning eighteen at the end of junior year instead of senior year that I don't tell many people at all.

Aram, on the other hand, is so smart he wins a National Endowment for the Humanities grant in civil rights. He's a senior now, applying to Harvard, Yale, Princeton, and Stanford, schools whose sweatshirts I don't even feel qualified to wear. I keep trying to get him to fall in love with me, but while our friendship deepens and we see each other all the time, he never tries to kiss me. My fear of rejection is too profound for me to lean in first. We spend a lot of time at my house, playing with Nina, getting her to say our names, teaching her random obscene sentences. I take long walks with Nina strapped around my chest in the BabyBjörn. Adults glare at me, and once, as I pass an older woman on the street, she snipes her disgust at me: "Babies having babies!" I stop and turn, watching her walk away, my mouth drawn open like a Victorian bridge. I will never, ever grow up to shame kids, no matter what bad choices they make. I promise this to myself, and to Nina. I put her to bed, I change her, I sing to her, I read to her. At night, she cries when

I leave the room and makes me lie down on the floor next to her crib and stay there while she tries to fall asleep. When I try to duck out, she stands and cries out, "Danda, come!"

I have turned into my mom's couch, and it's a lot more boring than I realized. I do love being Nina's point person at night because I understand exactly what she needs, but damn, she takes a long time to fall asleep.

When I'm not uptown at Taylor and Gwen's writing the next play with the theater kids, Aram and I are spending all our time together. We see plays, talk about books, see live music, go to galleries, and watch movies. One night, he invites me over to watch *Raising Arizona*, and he does something he's never done before—he pulls out a joint. My body puckers. I'm still afraid of pot, terrified at what it does to me. In his tiny room, I can't use my usual tricks—I'm going to have to actually smoke. I take small, baby puffs and try to focus on the movie. It's working, until Aram says something to me and I need to respond, which means I'll need to move my attention off my body, and that's when I feel my heart start to skid. A pinball is careening inside me, lighting up whatever it touches. I feel myself losing control.

"Don't you think?" Aram asks.

"Yep." I am going to throw up. "Bathroom," I say, standing up.

"Want me to pause it?" he asks.

"No!" I nearly shout on my way to the bathroom. If he pauses it, it means he'll hear me. "Turn it up!"

He does not turn it up. He pauses it and I throw up as quietly as I can, which is not quietly. I am crying, dizzy, mortified. I will transfer to another school. I will move to Denver. I will get surgery and become a totally different person that Aram will never recognize.

He knocks. Oh my God, why is he knocking? "You okay?"

"Yeah, I'm okay," I say, flushing the toilet. I stand, trembling and light-headed. I throw cold water on my face and run his toothpaste over my teeth and tongue. When I come out, he's standing right by the bathroom door. He listened! I can't look at him. I go for my shoes.

"What are you doing?"

"I gotta go." How is this not obvious?

"Well, let me walk you out. Was it something you ate?" he asks.

"I think so," I say, still not looking at him.

"Can I do anything?"

I shake my head, grab my jacket, and rush out. He's behind me. I take the stairs, not the elevator, and he's still behind me.

"Wait up," he says. I don't wait up.

Outside is better. Outside is wide and expansive. I am not trapped when I am outside. I see a cab and dash for it.

"WAIT!" he calls. I stand by the cab door until he catches up, feeling rude. "I hope you feel better," he says.

"Thanks," I say.

Aram lifts my chin so I'm looking at him and then he kisses me, half on the mouth, half off. I get in the cab. What was that? Did Aram just kiss me? Did Aram just kiss my vomit mouth? I am in love.

*   *   *

Aram and I have started spending time with Paul's brother Jonathan. He's gay and arty and beautiful, and when I'm not at the acting school or with Aram, I'm with Jonathan doing coke. We keep our extracurricular activities from Aram, who despite smoking pot is too straight-edge and would disapprove, just as Taylor and I keep ours from Gwen. Jonathan is determined to get Aram to officially ask me out. One weekend, the three of us go to Rockaway Beach, and when Jonathan sees me in my bathing suit, he starts making comments, trying to get Aram to check me out.

"Damn, sister," Jonathan says.

"Shut up," I say.

"Why do you wear oversized clothes? You think this body will last forever? You're gonna wake up one day with a tire around your belly pissed you didn't flaunt your wares when you had them." He seems genuinely concerned, which makes me laugh.

"I'll take my chances," I say. Maybe he's right. But if normal and appropriate people, like Aram, wanted me, I probably wouldn't be so afraid of my body.

Aram turns to look at me, and then he does a double take and smiles. As he starts walking over to us, I want him to be attracted to me, but I am also bracing myself for what's coming, nervous that he'll turn out to be just like Taylor, after all, and will say or do something crude.

"Did anyone bring Kadima?" he asks.

As he heads off in search of a place for us to play, I feel like a bad person for questioning his motives. For questioning anything about him. Out of all the men and boys I know, Aram is the safest. What he says and what he does match the things he says he believes. I trust him, I realize, and I want to be more like him.

Jonathan sits across from us on the way back to the city. "Have you two ever thought about going out? You're a cute couple."

I sputter a bit—Jonathan is very good at this game—but Aram looks over at me. At the train station, after Jonathan leaves, Aram kisses me good-bye, landing even closer to my lips than the last time. At home a little while later, I can't sit still: I have to tell Aram how I feel. Time is running out. In two months he's going to Stanford, where he'll find a fellow valedictorian who, unlike me, probably never vomits. If I don't tell him now, I never will. He'll leave and I'll have missed my window. I have to get this right.

Without giving myself time to think, I call him and invite myself over. I listen to Cat Stevens's "Wild World" over and over again on my Walkman on the train uptown. I'm sweating hard; I can't take one smooth, gliding breath, just choppy little ones. I will not let my body vomit. When I get to his place, he's in a T-shirt and sweatpants. His parents and sister are watching an Ingmar Bergman movie.

"Wanna go for a walk?" I ask, knowing if I go into his apartment, I'll end up throwing up in the bathroom. Soon we're walking and talking and it's all normal until I stop and I take a deep breath. "I think I'm in love with you."

He puts his hand to his forehead. "Oh God," he says, turning his back to me. That's it; I am going to throw up. Everything is turning black and rushing in to crush me. I take a few steps backward, but just as I'm about to run away and never see him again, he turns back and looks at me.

"I think I'm in love with you, too."

I am overcome by happiness and relief, and stunned that finally I'm getting something I wanted. He is kissing me and I'm happy—and then a deep pocket of grief scoops me up. He's going to Stanford. He's going three thousand miles away. We're going to be separated. The thing I want, the thing I've always wanted and finally have, is about to be taken away from me. He's going to leave me, and I'm in Deep Countdown.

"I can't believe I'm going to Stanford," he says, as if he can read my mind. "Why did I pick someplace so far away?"

"Don't go," I say.

"I have to, but we have the entire summer," he says.

For the first time ever, an entire summer feels too short. Why can't it feel interminable the way it did the summer I was sent to camp?

We kiss some more, and I try to shake off the countdown and enjoy what's happening. I have to go back downtown to meet Libby for dinner, and as we say good-bye I'm in such a swirl of emotions, leaping onto the train as it pulls in, celebrating the timing as a lucky omen, that I don't notice I'm going the wrong direction until I'm at 207th Street. I have to get out and switch trains, but it's an elevated stop, in a particularly terrifying place, and I know now that all my good luck is about to end. No one can achieve such happiness without having to pay for it, and as I clatter down the metal stairs to cross the street to the other side, I know I'm going to get killed at this train station and I'll never have the chance to be with Aram, to marry him and have kids and the whole big life that is finally within my reach. I bolt up the stairs on the other side and wait to get knifed in the night on the platform, but then the train comes, and miracle of all, I am not dead. No one killed me as revenge for being so fucking happy. This is because my happiness was coated in worry. The worry is still keeping me safe.

The System Is the Problem

MY LOVE FOR ARAM is so all-encompassing, so painfully full, and it's about all I can focus on. I know that grades are important to Aram, that studying and learning are a huge part of what turns him on. We have long talks about intelligence and I confide in him that I think I'm stupid, but I don't mention the learning disability or the tests. That labeling is too mortifying, and besides, I still don't know which part of my learning is disabled. His assurances that I'm not dumb bounce right off me, like compliments. I confide how hard it is for me to take tests at school, how even when I know the material I never seem to be able to answer the test questions in the moment.

"Tests are just about retained information. Information isn't intelligence. You know that," he says.

"Well, yeah, but . . ."

"You know who tests are good for?" he asks. "People who are good at taking tests. Those people have an unfair advantage, but if everyone were asked to write a play, you'd excel and they wouldn't."

"Yeah . . . okay. Maybe," I say.

"School learning isn't where you excel—"

"Because I'm dumb."

"No, because you learn through experience, and that's not the way we're taught. The organizing principle behind our educational system is predicated upon one-dimensional thinking. Our system is based on teaching to the average person, not the individual. You're an individual. I'm average."

"You are not average," I tell him.

"You know what I mean." And, actually, I do.

For the first time, here at the start of my senior year, I feel ready to really pay attention and try to be the person I've never been, the person I've been afraid I could never be, even with effort—the average person. But now, Eileen the Guidance Counselor is suddenly telling me, it's too late. I'm always the last to figure things out. While I've been mooning over Paul and then Aram and hanging out with Taylor and doing free drugs and thinking I was cooler than everyone else by writing and performing plays, everyone else has been diligently studying, strategizing how their extracurricular choices might best represent them to the schools they desire. They go on college visits and weigh the pros and cons, talk things through with their parents, parents who probably help them with homework and essays, and know when they have tests coming up, unlike mine, who know nothing about my life in or outside of school. In my grade, I'm the one who makes a show of how school learning isn't life learning and that if I already have the most important part covered, why bother with the other stuff? And now, when it's too late, I finally start to understand why I should have bothered.

The big plan that Eileen and my mom have made for me, to get around my terrible grades and test scores, is for me to take the SATs untimed. And, once again, I have to go get an IQ test to prove that I have a learning disability, because my mom is making me write my college essay about living with one. I don't want to do this. Not the testing, and not the essay.

I'm suddenly enraged. Out of nowhere, I start yelling that I don't want to do this anymore. I don't want to get tested and I don't want to write my essay on her dumb idea. Why do I have to constantly define myself according to these other ideas? I can barely get the words out; I am sobbing and hyperventilating, but my mother thinks I'm being difficult and bratty. I just want to be freed from this cage of identity other people made for me. I go to the roof and smoke cigarettes, sitting on the edge, dangling my legs over the side. I look down on the Houston Street playground and the lady on the corner. She looks so much more fragile from up here. I can see Sixth Avenue and Bleecker Street. What did that cop do when he came up here to look for Etan Patz? What was he expecting to find, six-year-old Etan smoking his cares away? I wonder if Etan would have wanted to go to college. I wonder where he is now.

I start chain-smoking. The more I think about it, the stupider and more insulting my mother's plan feels. It suggests the only way I'll get accepted into college is if the admissions office feels sorry for me. If they see that I have some hardship, they'll take me in, like I'm some wounded, helpless bird, but I don't want people to accept me for my weaknesses. That didn't work when I tried it with Tatum, and I know it won't work now. I want people to accept me because they are impressed with my abilities. If she thinks it's fine to sell me as a victim to gain access, that means she really thinks I am a victim. Her way of dealing with hardship is not my way, but the problem is, I don't have a way. Hers is all I know.

Every time something hard happens, she swoops in to solve it, with phone calls, doctors, pills, but that is not helping me. In fact, I think it's made me worse. Now I don't know how to do anything, and I'm terrified of all the things I should know how to do by now, because she's done them for me, or hired people to do them for me, my whole life. Any burden I've come up against, she's tried to erase before I can feel its weight, which means I don't know what to do when it comes. I don't know the results of my own tests, or the name of whatever learning disability I have. Maybe I don't even have a learning disability! Maybe I'm just crazy. Whatever the case, what I know is that who I am is being withheld from me. I know she probably did it out of love, but I no longer want someone to fix me. What I need is help naming, and facing, whatever is wrong with me.

But despite my fury, my mother wins. Here I am again in the waiting room, waiting to be tested for the ten thousandth time, so I can be labeled worthy of a college's pity. And really, what does "learning disabled" mean, anyway? Does learning differently automatically make me disabled? And if people can't teach me in a way that's easier for me to learn, then why aren't they "teaching disabled"? Why is it all on me? Aram is right: It doesn't actually make sense that schools expect the one way they teach to be the right way for all students. It's like having only one option at a buffet table and telling those who are allergic to the option they have an eating disorder. Why can't I be accepted as I am? Am I violating some code of humanity? I hate this waiting room, and I hate these tests, and the longer I wait, the more resentful I become.

An uppity mother keeps looking nervously toward the door and jumps when it opens. A girl about my age walks out, past her mother, and leaves the office. I recognize her fury. The mother doesn't follow her.

"Did that go okay?" the mother asks the doctor.

"Yes, Layla is lovely."

"Do you think she'll get into college?"

"Why don't we talk about all this once we've completed testing."

"Of course, it's just, she absolutely needs to get into college, and with her grades . . . you understand."

"Why don't you phone me, and we'll discuss this further," Dr. Wallace says, looking over at me. "Amanda, I'll be with you in one minute."

The mother grabs her things off her chair, pushing the door repeatedly before realizing she needs to pull. I hear her with her daughter in the hallway.

"So, how was it? What did she ask you?"

"I don't remember. A lot of questions."

"What do you mean, you don't remember? You were in there for an hour and a half. These tests are important."

"Not to me."

"Well, maybe that's the problem," the mother says.

The elevator dings. "I'm not the problem," the girl grumbles. "The system is the problem!"

I can't make out the rest, as the elevator slides them away. The system *is* the problem. That's what Aram was talking about. Maybe I've been taking all the blame for a problem that's not only mine to bear.

Dr. Wallace retrieves me. I'm tired. Aram and I were out late at a concert and then stayed up talking and messing around. I've been awake for three hours. I slept for two, and obviously even the girl who just left is smarter than I am because she knows enough to talk about the system when I can't even define "matchless" to Dr. Wallace, who is asking me vocabulary words.

"Now I am going to ask you a series of questions, and I'd like you to answer as best you can."

"All right," I say.

"When is Washington's birthday?"

A cool breeze from inside my body. A surprise splash of heat across my face. "Washington?"

"Yes."

"His birthday?" I'm supposed to know this? "March twentieth," I offer. It's my own birthday.

"Who wrote *Hamlet*?"

"Shakespeare."

"How does yeast cause dough to rise?"

"Yeast? I . . . I don't know. I don't cook. It swells?"

"What is the population of the United States?"

"I don't know. Is it like a billion?"

"Name three kinds of blood vessels."

This is just information. Information isn't intelligence, so not knowing this information can't mean a lack of intelligence.

"Um . . . veins—"

Why aren't these tests questioned? If the tests stay the same, so will I, and the cycle will never end. Is this what the girl meant by the system?

"Arteries?"

"And the third?"

"Aorta?"

"How many senators are there in the United States Senate?"

My entire life I've been trying to fit myself in. I know these tests are measuring me, trying to see how far from average I fall, but I don't understand why it's always on me to conform to some imagined ideal, some invisible normal. Why doesn't the world ever try to conform itself to match me?

"One hundred? I don't know. Can you tell me?" I ask.

No one ever tells me. They just ask and ask and ask, knowing all my answers are wrong without ever helping me to be right.

*   *   *

Aram and I have created a new level of love, and with it, a new level of grief. No one has ever felt this before. The least amount of happiness I feel with him is ecstasy. He is the organ I need most to survive.

When we're together, I feel sorry for everyone else, knowing their joy pales in comparison to ours. When he leaves for Stanford, all I can think is how lucky everyone else is, to be able to smile and laugh when I never will again, not when Aram is three thousand miles away. When I'm not sobbing, I'm catatonic. Everywhere I look I see his reflection, I feel his absence. My boyfriend is the ideal man, the man all men should be made from.

We talk on the phone for hours and send each other packages and mixtapes. I tear his letters open hungrily, and tears spill on the words in the letters I write in return. I spend less time with Taylor, which Taylor doesn't like, especially because all I do when we're together is talk about Aram.

"When will I meet this kid?" Taylor keeps asking me.

"He was in my play at school. You met him," I say.

"I didn't. I just saw him."

"Dunno. When he's home for Christmas, I guess."

"We'll have a party," Taylor says. "Me and Gwen. You can invite him."

I can't wait for Aram to meet Taylor and Gwen, who will impress on him how cool I am. So cool I have grown-ups for friends, grown-ups who are attractive and do drugs and buy us things.

Meanwhile, at school, while I've been mooning about Aram, my friends have started getting accepted to colleges. I do not. I knew no admissions office was going to take a person whose main selling point is that she has a learning disability, and who uses it as an excuse for why she has done badly in school. The rejections pour in. The only school I care about is Hampshire, though, and of course that's the one whose letter just doesn't seem to arrive.

Aram comes home for the holiday. At Taylor and Gwen's party, I'm excited to show everyone off to one another. When we arrive, it's smoky and crowded with acting kids but no other adults, the inverse of their normal parties. Gwen and Taylor are on the couch, their new baby, Hannah, sitting on Gwen's lap while Taylor rolls a joint. I'm only her sister, but still, I'd never smoke anything with baby Nina nearby.

"Aram, finally!" Taylor calls. "Hang on, pal, let me just get this thing off the ground."

I smile at Aram, who shoots me a confused look. I pull him over to the couch as Taylor lights the joint, stands, and shakes Aram's hand.

"Been looking forward to meeting you, man," he says, handing him the joint. Aram accepts it without speaking, and he takes a tiny hit before handing it back to Taylor.

"Where are your manners, kid? Give some to your girl." Aram hands the joint to me. He seems to be on automatic. "So, Stanford, huh? You're smart."

"Depends on your definition of 'smart,'" Aram says.

"Whoa, deep!" he says, elbowing Aram. Taylor and Aram are both acting strange.

"Where are your friends?" Aram asks.

My mouth drops.

"Right here." Taylor motions all around.

"But these are kids," Aram says.

Taylor puts his arm around me. "She's no kid. She's my best friend."

Hearing him call me his best friend is disturbing, and I cringe. I'm embarrassed for him just then, in a way I never have been before. When

I'm in my thirties, some high schooler is the last person I'd hope would be my best friend. Something is off about Taylor, and I've never been able to see it until right this second.

"How old are you, man? Thirty? Thirty-five?"

"Whoa. Easy, pal. If you have a problem with me, you're not obligated to stay."

"Hadn't planned on it," Aram says and looks at me. "You ready?"

"You want to leave?" I ask, incredulous.

"Yeah, I want to leave," he says. "You coming with me?"

I look at Taylor, whose look tells me I'd better stay, and then back at Aram, whose look tells me my choice will have permanent consequences.

"See you, Taylor. Thanks for the party." I follow Aram out before Taylor can respond. On the street, he walks away quickly, his steps angry. I call to him. He doesn't answer, but he's heading toward my house. By the time we get there, he still hasn't said a word to me, and he heads up to my bedroom, lies on my bed, and puts an arm over his eyes.

"What's going on? What's the matter?" I ask.

"*Those* are the people you hang out with?"

"Well, yeah. What's wrong with that?"

"That guy was rolling a joint next to his infant." I look at him, not knowing what to say. "He was smoking pot with you," Aram says.

If Aram thinks smoking pot with me is bad, there's no way I'm ever telling him what else we do. "Is that terrible?"

"Yeah, it's pretty fucking terrible. He's your teacher. He's supposed to be your role model, the ambassador of adulthood, and he thinks he's your fucking best friend?"

I don't say anything, because I don't know what to say. Everything that comes into my head sounds trite or hollow. I've been in over my head with Taylor for so long now, I can't tell what's wrong or right. Is Aram just too straight? Taylor's cool. Paul is cool. Jonathan's cool. The acting school kids are all cool. I'm cool. Aram is not cool, but he's smart and wise, and I trust and love him, and now I don't know what to say.

"Is that how you spend your time when I'm not here?" he asks. "Is that who you spend all your time with?"

"Well, sort of," I say.

Aram looks at me with disgust, the kind of expression I've lived in fear of seeing. One that says I'm worthless and shouldn't exist.

"So you smoke pot with him?" he asks.

"Kind of, yeah."

"What else do you do?"

"Nothing!" I say.

"You do nothing? You sit there in silence?"

"Well, no . . ."

"Do you do drugs with him?" Aram asks.

"Sort of?"

"Sort of? What kind of an answer is 'sort of'? What sort of drugs have you done with him?" He sits up now, angry. I don't know why I didn't see this coming. He doesn't think I'm cool for the reasons I think I'm cool. I'm embarrassed now by everything I've bragged about. When I don't have an answer he stands up.

"Did you have sex with him?" he asks.

"NO! Of course not!" I yell. "Why are you standing up?"

"I need to stand," he says.

"Are you leaving?"

"I don't know yet," he says. Now I can't breathe very well. I fold myself over and put my head in my knees until my face goes sweaty. "Has he made a pass at you?" he asks.

"I'm not sure," I say. "I mean, he's said things to me, like, about my body and about doing things to it."

"Doing *what* to it?" Aram asks. He glances out the window, in the direction of Taylor's house, as though he's going to go back there and beat him up.

"Like how he can't wait until I'm eighteen so he'll be legal to fuck me," I squeak out, and then bend over again and put my head back between my knees.

"You ARE eighteen!" Aram shouts.

"I know," I say. "I haven't told him."

"It's wrong what he wants to do to you. You know that, right?"

I nod my head yes.

"And he hasn't tried to do anything?"

"Not yet," I say. "I mean, he's asked if I want him to show me how to give blow jobs. I say no every time."

"Do you want to fuck him?" Aram asks.

"No! Aram, no! Not at all. I just..."

"You just what?" Aram's enraged. He grabs his jacket.

"Where are you going?"

"To fucking kill him." I burst into tears. Aram sits down next to me and hugs me.

"NO!" I say. "I'm ashamed."

"Of what?"

"Of myself! I got myself into this situation. I did this." He doesn't say anything. "I was so young. I didn't know what else to do but pretend all the things I didn't like about my friendship with Taylor weren't happening. And now I'm a different person. If I met him now, none of this would have happened."

"You have to decide what you want," Aram says.

"What do you mean?"

"Maybe it's not right of me to say this, but I don't want that guy in my life, and if he's in your life, then he's in mine, so I guess you need to decide which of us is more important."

I don't know what to say. "I have to see him all the time. I have the play."

Aram is quiet for a bit. "Well, if you decide you want to be with me, then in three months, when the play is done, you need to end things with him, entirely. No seeing him, calling him, nothing. It's got to be over. The guy is bad news. He doesn't want the best for you; he wants what's best for him. I think you know that. I am not saying 'you can't.' You can. You can do whatever you want, but I get to choose who I want in my life. I want you, and I don't want him."

I feel, quite suddenly, relieved. Aram is giving me an out with Taylor. I realize I've wanted out for a long time. "I want you," I say.

"You can think about it," he says.

"I don't need to think about it."

I got myself into this, and I want to get myself out. I want to be the one saving myself.

*   *   *

The next day I get rejected from Hampshire. I can't even get into what is other people's safety school. Aram tries to convince me I'm not an idiot, but I decide to take matters into my own hands. I write Hampshire a letter, appealing their decision. I tell them about all my accomplishments and how I excel at theater and playwriting and aren't my ambition and my drive amazing? Apparently not, because they reject me again.

I write a monologue about the exchange and include it in the script of our play, which Gwen has been sending out to producers. Out of nowhere, an actual producer picks it up and decides to produce it off-Broadway, at a theater on Forty-Second Street.

Holy crap. A play that I cowrote, and am starring in, is going off-Broadway. None of us can believe it. We've been working on this play-in-monologues for months, and we're proud of ourselves. Ha! Screw you, Hampshire. Now that I'm going to be a famous actress, I don't care about Hampshire, or any college. All I care about now is my career. I should get back in touch with Tatum and invite her to the opening, so she can see how famous I am. People who have seen our rehearsals start to talk about the play, and my piece about getting rejected twice from the same college is getting the most attention. It's strange to be rewarded so fully for suffering a now-public humiliation.

During a school assembly, the principal makes an announcement about the play, but as friends and teachers congratulate me, I can no longer access my earlier glee. I have never been in an off-Broadway play. Every smile or mention is yet one more mounting expectation that feels insurmountable. My only expectation is that I'll fail. At first I count the days, but then I realize the days are forcing themselves onto me and I can't slow them down. Countdowns don't take over my body as much anymore since Aram and I got together, but now they're back and I think they're worse. A twitch settles under my right eye and stays there for days. My breath comes in small batched doses, metallic and misty like Kara's new asthma inhaler. I am not just in the world, I am inside it, embedded inside the scorched core of reality, where feelings roast themselves in bright orange, and the temperature hovers at 5,700 degrees.

The previews are only two weeks away. The zipper that holds the world in place has been opened, and I feel myself being pulled toward it. I don't know what's on the other side. I might fly through at any time. All our plays have been at the acting school, but this is a real theater with plush seats and a raised stage and actual lighting. People have to buy tickets! I don't think I'm good enough to be a professional actress, a professional anything. I feel like I've trapped myself again, about to expose my entire interior self to the world, including my parents, my classmates, my siblings, and strangers. And when it's all over, I will have to break up with Taylor, and I don't know how.

It's a week before the show. It's two days before the show and I can't go to school, I'm too paralyzed by fear and dread. I feel mortified now that I wrote about Hampshire and everyone will know I got rejected twice because I'm so dumb. What have I done?

Eddie offers to teach me how to breathe, because he sees that I can't. His Mohawk is long gone, and instead of firing up Bauhaus, he burns incense. In the past year, he's gotten into chanting and meditation and something called macrobiotics, which means he eats food that smells like unshowered feet. He's been studying yoga in India, and that's where he learned to breathe. I lie on his bedroom floor, but as he tries to talk me through the stages, I can't even hear his voice. My brain is too loud and my body can't focus, and my temperature has been too high for days. I'm pretending to do whatever he says to do, but it's useless. His instructions aren't strong enough to counteract my body's instructions. Even my skin is afraid; I can feel it trying to crawl off me. My clothes are rubbing against me all wrong and nothing seems to fit me, not even my own body. My body has shrunk, but my clothes don't feel bigger; they feel like burlap against my skin.

The day rounds the corner to 2 p.m., then 3 p.m., and then the dark starts painting over the sky and I can feel it trying to reach me, to brush me into the night like one of its stray hairs. Tomorrow is the first preview. I can't go through with it. This is the actual real world, a world I am ill-prepared to join. Everyone will see that I'm not good enough.

Then, despite my mental clawing to keep the night from passing, it's suddenly time to go to the theater. I haven't eaten in days, but my stomach is full. Under the marquee I hurry past the rest of the acting kids, who are cheering and posing for pictures. I don't want any reminders of what is going to happen in three hours. My mouth is dry and my lips are vibrating and I know I will forget my lines and fuck up, and everything I've ever tried to hide will spill out of my body in front of everyone I know. And paying strangers, too.

In the dressing room I try to do Eddie's breathing, but I can't remember a thing. My mother offers me a beta-blocker, but I don't want to take it because I don't know what it will do. I can't stop throwing up. The lights dim in the house. I stand in the wings, and when the music goes on I'm afraid my heart is going to eject itself from my chest. Then my cue comes and I send my body down the aisle and onto the stage and start my monologue and I can hear my mouth being dry, but on the line that's supposed to be funny, people laugh, and suddenly my mouth moistens up, and I feel like my body and I are reconnecting. The audience is on my side. I relax.

The preview goes perfectly. Onstage, opening night, I bow twice, once as an actor and then again with Graham, as writers. Like meeting Aram, it's this applause I feel like I've been waiting for my entire life. All this time I thought I wanted to be an actress, but it's the writing that matters most to me, not the performing. The run of the play is amazing and awful and I can't wait for it to end.

When it does end, I know I need to cut Taylor out of my life. Aram talks me through how to do it. Instead of confronting Taylor directly, when the show closes, I just stop showing up at the town house, and when school lets out I leave through the smoking exit, out back. When Taylor calls me, I don't answer. When he throws pennies at my window at night and yells my name, I lie on my bed and shake, terrified he can see me, that he'll climb up the side of my house and look at me through the window and my face will give away my truth that I'm afraid of him, that I'm in over my head and have been for years, that I'm not the girl I've pretended to be, and that he's not the hero I wanted. I miss him and I don't. I feel free and trapped. I realize that while I still want to do coke all the time, I need to stop.

And so, when I finish the last of what I have, I do stop, not understanding about withdrawal, not realizing that my skin will take on the agitation of my internal self, or that my cravings for the drug will feel unendurable, sending me into spasms that swing between rage and despair. I stay in my bedroom, alternating between a fatigue so deep my bones won't lift and a feral lather, biting my sheets and throwing wild tantrums on my bed, shocked at the thoughts I have that involve stealing and selling my mother's jewelry for more drugs. I do not want to be that person. I tell my mom I have the flu and she sends up soup and medicine as I use all my willpower to remain in my bedroom until the cravings subside. It takes about a week, and no one pays enough attention to recognize the specific strain of my "flu."

The Dread, the Relief

MY MOM HAS RENTED our house to a famous film director and his family. I feel conflicted now about seeing his movies. I'm on my way uptown to meet my mom when I run into Haruko again. Last thing I remember, she was set to break up with Connery, and I assume that's what she did.

"I have the best news!" she announces near the mailboxes.

"What's that?" I ask.

She puts her hand on her stomach. "I'm pregnant."

"Oh my God. Whoa. Wow."

"Yeah, I know. Connery and I are getting married."

"Oh. Wow. Okay. Um...are you happy with that decision?"

"Oh yes! Babies change everything. Marriage too. I'm on cloud nine."

"Good for you," I say, even though I mean "poor baby."

Since Frankie was in my life, however briefly, the idea of having a newborn baby has become less appealing. What I really want is a Frankie, which means finding an already existent kid who needs a mother figure. But then my grandmother Puggy died and left a little money to each grandchild. Kara pointed out that it was enough for one round of IVF. I made the mistake of mentioning the idea to my mom, who has heard me wonder aloud many times whether or not I should have a baby on my own. She suggests I make another appointment at the fertility clinic, despite hearing about the previous visit, and despite the fact that I'm still ambivalent about having a baby on my own. I know she wants me to have a baby, but how do I know what I want until I have it? I didn't know I wanted a Frankie until I had one.

"What if I have a baby and regret it?" I ask my mom.

"You won't."

I close my eyes, preventing myself from growing visibly angry. What if Melissa dies? What if Baba dies? What if we lose this house? What if something bad happens when I leave? My whole life the answer has always been the same, but "It won't" is not an answer; it's not even true.

Before I can come up with a response, we're summoned into the doctor's office. He has the results of my blood test, and it is bad news. I can feel the heat rising, its burn in my chest. Loss. Even when I'm ambivalent, news of loss bumps me out of the world.

"With your blood results, I can tell you that you have less than a one percent chance of getting pregnant, even with IVF. It's not uncommon for women your age to come to me and think we can make miracles happen, and we can, just not the miracles you expect, or even want."

There it is: I missed it. There had always been time, and now time is gone. All my ambivalence and anxiety led me here, ensuring I would never be able to make the family I wanted. I'm the one who held me back; this is my fault. I will never have a biological child. I will never know what a child of my genetic material will look like. I won't have the experience my siblings had, my friends have, my mother had. I don't have a child because I waffled, and I don't have a partner because I waited each time when I should have left. Decisions meant loss, and so I didn't decide and now the decision has been made for me. I can't have children. I can adopt, or get an egg donor, but I cannot make my own baby.

The dread is gone, lifted; in its place is sadness, but also relief. The decision has been taken from me; now I can't choose the wrong thing because there is no longer a choice. I missed the window. Was I so afraid to make a mistake that I unconsciously did this on purpose? After all, if I really wanted a baby, wouldn't I have made it happen somehow?

When I look at my mother a grief wells inside me. I look away, so I don't find myself dissolving into a fetal ball on the office floor. I manage to wait to fall apart on the street outside, where my mother hugs me and doesn't know what to say.

When we part I walk for a while, all the way across town toward Sixth Avenue, each block a sample of upcoming seasons to walk through. The crisp first breath of winter, fire smoke followed by a shocking pocket of warmth, and then I look up, called to the sky, a lifelong reflex. It's not yet four thirty and the sun is beginning its descent, and my body responds with a tightening of dread in my chest. Dread that every evening will find me suffering from countdowns for the rest of my life. Why does this still happen to me? My body has always reacted to the sun this way; the sky and I have a private relationship that is not mine to end. What does it want from me? What is it trying to tell me? I try to do what my therapist has trained me to do, to follow the feeling to the very beginning, to when I first felt it, and identify the association. Of course: It's telling me that soon it will be bedtime and I'll have to leave my mom. That soon I'll have to go to my dad's. It's telling me that the day is dying, that things are ending and all the distractions of the day are quieting, creating more space for me to worry about all the ways I have to say good-bye.

But I am not a child anymore. Can I change my association to the sky? What if I simply decide it's the best time of day and not the worst? I look at the sunset and tell it, You are so pretty. You don't scare me. And for a moment, it doesn't—and I feel released and in control of my feelings. Until I accidentally blink the moment away.

*   *   *

A few nights later, my little sister Rebecca calls to tell me she's pregnant. I feel knocked a few feet deeper into my new reality of having "missed it," but through the pangs of jealousy I'm excited for her. We talk about names and discuss her worries and the due date, and when we hang up, I surprise myself by not bursting into tears. I'm embarrassingly proud of this.

A few days later I receive a call from my dad. Immediately I worry something else bad has happened. The last time he called me in the middle of the day, it was to report that my grandmother Puggy, his mother, had died.

"Dad, hi. What's the matter?" I ask.

"Everything is fine. I just thought I'd call and see how you were. I'm sure Rebecca's news wasn't easy for you to hear."

I'm about to protest about how happy I am for her, insist that it's no big deal, but I am so caught off-guard, so touched by this small act of attentiveness, that as I start to say, "I'm fine," I burst into tears, something I haven't done in front of him since I was small. And he sits with me there, on the phone, listening. As I realize he's not going to crack a joke at my expense, I feel a shift inside my body: I am no longer crying for the baby I won't have. Now I am crying because the person I least expected has shown up when I most needed him. The exact person I've spent my whole life afraid to need.

Waiting to Move On

THE ONLY COLLEGE THAT accepts me is in Vermont, a place I associate with death, and the first year is a disaster. Just when I've stopped doing drugs, everyone else has started. They drop acid and try to burn down dorms. They take mushrooms and crucify animals. I call Aram and Jonathan every day. Aram makes me feel better on the phone, but each time we hang up I am alone again. When I invite Jonathan to come visit he refuses, citing each horrendous incident I've described over the last three months. I agree to accompany him to the AIDS clinic for testing over Christmas break. He's worried, and I don't think he should be even after he confesses the myriad escapades around the city to which I've been ignorant. Every few weeks I write Taylor nasty, vile letters I never send, blaming him for who I almost became. I imagine the not knowing, the squirm of discomfort as he tries to make sense of what happened, why I stopped talking to him, and the reversal of power fills me with a charge, reminding me I'm nobody's bitch. I wonder if that's how he felt with me, when he used to have the upper hand.

As the end of December nears, I realize that Jonathan hasn't called me back in a few days—last we spoke, we were trying to make plans for the trip to the clinic. When I call I get his machine. I tell his machine when I'm coming home and tell him to let me know when and where to meet him. For the next week and a half, I call Jonathan and leave him messages, each one increasingly more concerned and mad.

"Why aren't you calling me back?" I ask. "Are you okay?"

"Did you die?"

"Oh my God, maybe you died and I'm yelling at your machine for not calling me back, when you can't call me back because you're dead and now whoever hears these messages is going to think I'm a terrible friend for berating a dead person for not calling me back. Call me back!"

I call Paul and ask if Jonathan's okay. He is. I ask if he knows whether Jonathan made an appointment to get tested for AIDS. He did. Paul thought I was going with him. He agrees to call Jonathan and see what's going on. Paul never calls me back. Now I'm leaving messages for both brothers to call me back, and neither does. Why are they ignoring me? I can't figure out what I did wrong.

Finally, I'm home, and soon so is Aram, and we do our tradition of going to Rockefeller Center to watch the tree lighting and go to a movie and eat chestnuts from street vendors. He doesn't know either why Jonathan isn't responding, so he leaves a message, too.

"I bet he'll call me back," Aram says, confident. I wonder if this is karma for dropping Taylor. Is this payback for unceremoniously cutting someone out of my life? I feel sorry for putting Taylor through this, but not sorry enough to reach out to him. And besides, I didn't do anything to Jonathan; I'm hardly a bad influence. But Jonathan doesn't call Aram back. He is just gone.

*   *   *

It takes me a year and a half and three colleges before I settle on a school. After the horrors of my first school, I decided to take classes at the New School and live at home, but that's no better: I fight all the time with Mom, who treats me like four-year-old Nina's full-time nanny. Finally I land at the University of Rochester, which is bland and generic, but I'm tired of transferring around and decide to stay put.

In the spring of 1991, Aram and I are in France. He has just finished his junior year abroad at Oxford, and we've decided to spend a week together in Paris before our summer jobs begin in New York. We have spent the past year dating other people. Or rather, he has spent the past year dating other people, while I waited for him, white-knuckling through the year, hoping that every phone call was not our last. Now that he's had his interactive experience with the physical landscape of British girls, and relieved me of my fears by choosing to remain monogamous, the idea of dating others has stuck in my head and I wonder, Should I do the same thing? I love Aram more than I thought a person could love, and while we have amazing conversations, and laugh more than we fight, there's an entire body of things he'd rather not talk about, things having to do with me.

While I've spent my entire life living in fear, Aram, it seems, has fears as well, and they are in contradiction to mine. Mainly, my problems are too big for him. They frighten him. He didn't want to hear about Taylor in high school, and he doesn't want to hear about Taylor now, in the aftermath. Any party I mention I've attended or person I've encountered whom he wouldn't choose as a friend threatens him, and he doesn't want to know. He's the person I've come closest to explaining my terrifying worries to, but whenever a thought or worry of mine is too dark, it triggers in him a fear that my troubles foretell something about me he doesn't want to know.

"Better left for your therapist," he tells me, which makes me feel decidedly crazy and not worth knowing. If I can't share my true self with Aram, the healthiest, safest, and most intelligent person I know, without scaring him, who in the world is left for me to tell? My therapist is nice enough, but she just wants to talk about my sex life, which I don't want to talk about, so we wind up making small talk while I chain-smoke in her office.

When we got together, when I was a senior and he was off already to school, no one could seem to believe it. Aram and me? Clean-cut, academic Aram? Who won the NEH? He's with me, the weird, artsy little freak who hangs out with that strange older man? No one could wrap their heads around it. He was so normal; I was so not. While I resented feeling that judgment from the outside world, I never felt it from Aram, but the more time passes, the more I sense that he agrees with them: He is normal and I'm fucked up. I'm tired of hiding who I am to protect others from their distress. Am I going to have this problem forever?

One of our last days in Paris, we're walking through the Place de la Concorde and we pass a mother with two little girls. One of the little girls, I realize with a start, looks just like Melissa, the way Melissa did when we were kids together. As we pass one another, I turn around to see the little girl has also looked back at me. She's staring at me with recognition, like she knows who I am. We both walk like that for a bit, staring back at the other, recognizing one another although we've never met. Is that Melissa's blue dress? Did I just see Melissa? Did she come back as herself, but in Paris? I call home that night and tell my mom about the strange encounter, and she tells me that Sharon, Melissa's mom, moved to Paris a few years ago and has two children; one of whom would be around the age Melissa was when she died.

I can't stop thinking about this. The last time I saw Melissa, she was not-Melissa. Her face was swollen from steroids. A bandanna snugged around her bald head, dethroned by chemo. I never saw her again as the girl she was, until just now. Only, who was that? And how did she know to recognize me? I don't believe in ghosts because they scare me, but now I kind of do. Was that girl Melissa? Did she not die? Did she do the thing I feared my mom would do, and pack everything up and move to Europe and not tell anyone? Because here we are now, in Europe, and there she is, not sick at all. Still eight, and healthy, like she's been given a second chance. I used to think the world should stop when people died. That we should wait until enough time has passed and we're all caught up with our mourning, but if Sharon—Melissa's own *mother*—had two new children, then she continued on; she didn't wait. She gave herself a second chance at being a mom. She gave Melissa younger siblings, and those siblings grew, which creates the illusion that Melissa grew also. Etan is kept alive by the news and by lore, by age-progression images and new developments, so maybe Sharon is keeping Melissa alive by having new children she could tell Melissa-stories to, and they can carry with them memories of their sister they never met.

When everyone else was moving forward, even Sharon, I waited. Maybe that little girl turned not because she recognized me, but because she saw in me a trapped little girl, just her age. I am twenty-one, but on the inside I am still eight. Everyone else has moved on, even, in some ways, Melissa herself, the person I've been waiting for. And here I am, still waiting to be known, to be solved. Aram doesn't want to solve me. He wants the undiscovered part of me to remain a mystery, but I'm beginning to think the unknown part of me is actually who I am. And I think I want to know her.

The Body

I'M ALMOST DONE with my junior year of college. Aram and I are still together, but I am dating other people, as he has done, when I begin hanging out with someone I shouldn't. His name is Carl, and he's everything Aram is not. Carl smokes, drinks, has secrets, a dark past, plays guitar in a band, and sings like a ragged rock star. He's a version of the quintessential bad boy, and he's a bad choice for me, but he makes me feel something Aram never could: normal.

We seem to always be smoking on the steps of the library at the same time every day. Soon we're doing it together. The more time I spend with Carl, the more I realize that with Aram, the safety I feel comes with a side of judgment. Aram and I bonded over art and ideas, but Carl and I bond over the bad stuff, the hard parts of life that Aram never wants to know. Instead of feeling like the fucked-up one, I feel accepted. As I spill my life to Carl, I realize how ironic it is that Taylor, who once so covetously sought to unearth the dark parts of my life, has become the story he was so anxious to hear. It's a challenge getting Carl to open up in return, and I savor the rewards of each effort. I don't feel inferior to Carl, but the more we share, the more I realize I do feel inferior to Aram.

Aram knows about Carl and Carl knows about Aram and neither likes the situation. Aram is secure, healthy, and wholesome. He is smart, self-reflective, has good judgment, and is intellectually engaging, but he's also so academically focused, he's become boring. Carl has, in spades, what Aram lacks: edge. It's this darkness in Carl I'm drawn to, although

I don't know why. He needs someone to take care of him. He's fragile, damaged (he claims), and needs someone to rescue him, and I recognize these feelings. I'm afraid to spend my life feeling like I'm too much for someone, like everything that makes me me is better left to a therapist. All the things about me Aram thinks are troubled are just basic, everyday, normal things to Carl. My gut tells me I shouldn't, but I accidentally fall in love with him.

I am issued ultimatums. I must choose. It's either Aram or Carl. Two entirely different people who offer two entirely different lives, one of which I feel I'm inferior to and the other to which I feel equal. When summer comes and Aram and I are together again, he seems so simple and basic. Nothing like the complicated, secretive Carl. Early on, my gut told me Carl was not my guy, but I convinced my gut to believe otherwise, and now all of me is convinced. Aram is a good boy, and Carl is not. I fall somewhere in between. After four years together, I break up with Aram, with Carl at the ready to lift me up. Going from one person to another makes breaking up seem easy.

I am not that worried about Aram. He and his family are close—too close at times. They have meetings to discuss their feelings, and nothing ever goes unresolved. I find it all so weird and uncomfortable, unnatural even. In my house, nothing is discussed: We just get in fights and apologize when someone cries, but nothing is ever resolved. That type of communication feels natural to me. Carl is my kind of unhealthy. We're made for each other.

Senior year of college I have my first ever stalker. He's Dutch, and at first he's just annoying, constantly inviting me to a play or a concert after I've said no thanks, I have a boyfriend. He's relentless and won't let up. I tell him to stop asking me. Carl tells him to stop asking me, but he won't. Before long he's barging in on conversations, inviting himself to sit down when I'm alone with friends. Then it escalates. He appears places without my knowing I'd been followed: the bank, an out-of-the-way art gallery; and then, he shows up in my classes. I file a complaint with the school, but they do nothing.

This is becoming a familiar pattern. Last year I took driver's ed; on the first lesson the teacher drove me to the highway, and once we were on it, he said to think of the gear shift as his dick: I should touch it as much as possible. It was a driver/student car with two steering wheels, and somehow, through a barrage of lewd suggestions, I drove us home, where he sat in the car, below my bedroom window, for hours. I had no choice but to tell Jimmy, who stormed outside to tell the guy off, but the second he saw Jimmy, he drove away. We called the school and told them what happened; they promised to fire him, and then a week later they sent us a bill. The guy kept working there. I want to call Jimmy now and tell him about my stalker, but I'm too far away for him to scare the guy off.

A month or so after classes have begun, the stalker walks into my art class, eating a peach. He walks over to me and eats it slowly, right in my face, the juice dripping down his chin while he smiles. I flag down the teacher, who tells the guy to set up an easel, because—as I'm horrified to discover—he's now in this class, too. I file another complaint. The school does nothing. When Carl walks in, I think it's because he knows what's happening, and he's come to drag my stalker away, but instead he tells me there's been a phone call and I need to call home. Instantly, I am back at camp, being tapped on the shoulder and walking through a dark field toward the end of my life as I know it.

"Is it my mom?" I ask Carl.

"No," he says. "It's Jimmy." The words sound so strange coming out of his mouth.

Not until that moment had I ever given thought to Jimmy dying, but now that I fear he's dead, I realize how attached I have always been to him. While he wasn't the most involved parent, often exasperatingly absent when he was physically present, I knew he loved me and he knew I loved him.

When I call, Kara's already home. Jimmy's had a heart attack. He's in the hospital now, but it sounds like maybe he's going to be fine. I don't need to come home, she says. I shouldn't worry. I'm relieved, but not enough to return to class, or to get up off the couch. I'm glad he's okay, but I'm still shaken; I'm not ready to lose Jimmy. When I was in high school, Jimmy got a fancy car, and one night while he was driving, some guys jumped in, put a gun to his head, and then pushed him into the street and took the car. He wasn't hurt, and he joked about it after, but the image of what could have happened stuck with me. I want this to be the same, and I imagine him now, being released from the hospital and regaling us over and over at dinner for the rest of our lives about that time he had a heart attack and we all overreacted and thought he was going to die.

I'm still on the couch an hour later when Kara calls back to say Jimmy had a second, more serious heart attack, and now he probably won't make it through the night. I need to come home. Mom is too upset to talk. When this second call comes, my roommate is there, but Carl is gone, and I am too confused and overwhelmed to move. My roommate gets me a ticket for the first plane out, drives me to the airport, and, somehow, although I don't remember even getting on a plane, I arrive at the hospital. It's late, near eleven, and my mom, Kara, and Nina have all gone back to MacDougal Street to get some sleep. Neon lights dance on medical machines and there is my stepfather, with tubes down his nose and throat. When I notice his eyes are taped shut, I begin to panic on his behalf. The nurse explains that it's to help keep them moist, since he can't blink.

I hear my own voice, hysterical. "Well, did anyone tell him that? Does he know why his eyes are taped shut?" The nurse shrugs, and I sit down next to Jimmy; he squeezes my hand to let me know he can hear me. I explain about his eyes and tell him he's going to be okay. The nurse motions to my Walkman and says maybe I should play him something. I ask if he'd like to hear a song and he squeezes my hand again. I slip my headphones over his head, set them on his ears, and press Play. "Riding on a Railroad" by James Taylor is what's playing, and he seems to like it. Standing there with my stepfather, the man who did the best he could being a dad to a houseful of kids that weren't his, I know I'll never hear this song the same way again.

I sit with Jimmy for a while, talking to him, not knowing whether or not I should be telling him he's in a hospital and that he's had a heart attack, but knowing I'd want to know if the situation were reversed. Being with Jimmy like this, with life's surfaces stripped away, just the two of us, in a life-or-death situation, feels like our most intimate moment. He has always been practical, no-nonsense, and deems my emotions and vulnerabilities silly, but now he is the vulnerable one. He listens as I explain what's going on, and then I tell him I'm going to get some sleep and I'll see him tomorrow. He squeezes my hand and I feel it tell me he's scared.

At home on MacDougal Street, Mom, Kara, and Nina are all upstairs, in Mom and Jimmy's room. Nina just turned six and is asleep surrounded by all her new presents. Eddie is at his apartment, and Daniel, David, and Holly are at theirs. Kara gives me the play-by-play. The nurses don't know if he'll make it through the night. I tell Kara and Mom I played him a song, and he squeezed my hand. I sleep on her couch and when we wake up, we're relieved the phone didn't ring. When we call the hospital they tell us he's still alive. Every morning we go to the hospital, and every night we fear a phone call will disrupt our sleep telling us what we don't want to hear. After several days he has surgery, and all seems okay, so I'm told to return to school.

The surgery seemed to make things worse for him. Every few days I get phone calls that things look dire and I need to return, and each time he pulls through. One night Mom is waiting on a phone call from the nurse. Kara tells me to keep the phone clear and she'll call to report. Carl is with me and we're pacing. When the phone rings I lunge for it.

"Hello?"

"I am going to rape you," the voice tells me.

I hang up fast, stare at Carl, then look at the curtainless windows, sprint to the door, double-lock it, and burst into tears. Carl doesn't know what to do. Jimmy, I know, would. He'd have someone put in an alarm system and hang blinds. He'd have dealt with the external danger, even as he'd leave the internal world to someone else.

That weekend Carl drives me to the city. Because my stalker's por-
tentous phone call struck me as particularly apocalyptic, a sign of bad
things to come, I pack not just my favorite things, but items I've imbued
with false power and luck: the gris-gris necklace Jonathan gave me to
wear on planes so they won't crash (which I still carry, though Jonathan
hasn't spoken to me in three and a half years), some earrings Aram gave
me, a shirt I love, my journal, and a worry stone. I'm hoping these things
will commingle their power and keep Jimmy alive. In the car down to
New York, I wonder what I would have done had I been given the opportunity to come home before Melissa died. Would I have been brave
enough to sit with her in the hospital, hold her hand till the end? Would
I have tried to save her, and would I be a different me if I had, knowing
that she died anyway? All weekend long, I sit with Jimmy at the hospital. Nina is there, sitting on the radiator, kicking her legs against it and
playing with an American Girl doll. My mom is chasing down doctors,
taking notes, and gathering information. Holly knits in the waiting room.
Daniel and David are walking around the neighborhood looking for roast
beef sandwiches. Eddie is in and out. Kara is at home answering the
phone and making calls. Jimmy has bedsores, and he is sedated. There
are no more hand squeezes. He's a shade of beige-green that matches
the hospital lighting. I hate it here. Although the nurses are nice, I'm
afraid of all the sickness. The smell reminds me of the nursing home
they put Baba in and the urine he left on our couch cushion. In the
waiting room, Holly won't stop knitting. She looks like a little girl, scared
and alone, and I can't stop thinking that if Jimmy dies, she, Daniel, and
David will all be orphans. Even if they're in their twenties.

The morning that Carl and I have to head back to school I want to
stop quickly and see Jimmy one last time, so we park the car outside the
hospital and hurry upstairs so I can spend one more minute with him,
in case it's my last. Carl comes up, too, and stays in the waiting room.
I duck into Jimmy's room and sit beside him, studying his motionless
face. Without Jimmy, I wouldn't have stepsiblings; there'd be no Nina.
He's the Lego piece that connects our family. Without him, will we still

be a family? Even if we fight and not everyone gets along, we're all we have. How much will we lose if we lose Jimmy?

Carl is motioning to me from the waiting room; it's time to go. I tell Jimmy I love him, give him a kiss, and say I'll see him soon. When we get downstairs, there's glass on the sidewalk. The windows on the car have been broken, and all our stuff has been stolen: Carl's guitar, my bag with all my good-luck charms, and every last one of my favorite things. I'm too in shock to know what action to take. Carl goes to buy garbage bags and tape to cover the windows, and I stand next to the car, feeling un-recognizable to myself. Those good-luck things not only kept me alive, they kept me connected to the people who gave them to me. Now I feel pulled apart from Jonathan and Aram, and from my own self, and from all the luck I ever thought I had. My charms have instilled me with the confidence of someone protected by the Secret Service, and now how can I trust the world? I know this means that Jimmy is going to die. I recognize this for the bad omen it is. Am I still connected to Jonathan and Aram without the things they gave me? We drive seven hours back to Rochester, freezing, the car empty of our possessions, windows cov-ered with garbage bags.

Thanksgiving is a few days away when Kara calls again, and I under-stand that this truly is the end. I need to get there before he goes. I want a chance to say good-bye, so he can know I appreciated him, even if I didn't always show it. But when I arrive my mom's body is flung over Jimmy's, and she's baying and howling. I missed it. I missed saying good-bye, and I feel oddly left out of an experience I'm not sure I even wanted to have. Nina doesn't have a father. She's just turned six years old, her siblings are all in their twenties, and her father's just died, which means she doesn't have a mother now either, at least until she's done grieving. His body is waxy and skinny. His face has lost its shape, melted into an expression I've never seen. Like a sculptor is trying and failing to repli-cate him.

The doctors now call him "the Body." They think because he's dead he's no longer human. The Body must be brought downstairs. The Body

must be moved. The Body is fifty-nine years old. The Body's name is
Jimmy. I don't want them to take him away just yet, although I don't
want his body to be my final memory of him. Eddie comes racing in. He
was at a concert, and he missed it, too. When he sees Jimmy he bursts
into tears, which triggers Mom to wrap herself over the Body again. I
find it ironic that it was only in death he was able to reach his goal
weight. Though I've held his hand in this bed countless times over the
past few weeks, now I don't want to touch him. Though I know better, I
still worry, the way I did as a child about Melissa, that his death is contagious somehow.

It's November 20, 1992. I'm twenty-two years old. Tomorrow the sky
will turn back on, blue or gray as ever; eventually the snow will melt, the
grass will grow, a gentle breeze on a hot day will lure me to follow it into
the future, into time that won't stop existing, that exists right now even
without Jimmy. Time is my enemy. My resistance to moving forward is
telling me something. I know I'm supposed to carry Jimmy with me, into
every future stage of my life, but I want to stay stuck in time, and it's
this fact I'm embarrassed to recognize, because I'm not exactly certain
what it means.

Soon the entire country will be celebrating Thanksgiving. Mom is
hysterical with grief, collapsing in the bathroom, and waking up four
times a night to burst into tears and cry into Nina's neck, but Nina just
goes about her business, unwilling or unable to mourn. The image of my
mother thrown over Jimmy's body, the sound of her keening howls, will
not leave my head. She's fragile. Because she believes she can't handle
the realities the world throws at her, she doesn't handle them, leaving
the reality to Kara. It's Kara who takes care of Nina, as she once took
care of me, and a small part of me feels threatened. We're keeping Mom
propped up, but no one's keeping the rest of us upright. It feels like
there's no room for anyone else to grieve.

We all take turns with Nina, but Kara is the designated caretaker. I'll
have to go back to school at some point, but I don't want to. I want to
stay home until I'm old. Nina doesn't have the same fears I had, but

she's attached to Mom, just the way I was, sleeping in bed with her. But Nina is also more like Mom than I was. Unlike me, she cares how she looks, happy to spend time smoothing ponytail bumps and festooning herself with bows and ribbons. She has temper tantrums, though, interminable ones that strike when she doesn't get what she wants. We're all grown and out of the house, so to Nina her siblings are more like parents. It will just be her and Mom in that big house together when we're gone.

I call Jonathan to tell him the news of Jimmy's death, but he doesn't call me back. I write him a letter, but it goes unanswered. I don't understand. It's been three and a half years since I saw or heard from him last, and the only sense I can make of his disappearance is that he changed his mind about having me join him when he got tested because somehow he knew he was positive and he'd feel ashamed or embarrassed in from of me. I miss him.

Back at school, where no one understands the depths of my pain, I feel out of place. People try to commiserate by telling me about a cat who died or an aunt who passed away. I spend most of my time off-campus, trying to make up the classwork I've missed so I can graduate on time. Someone keeps calling and hanging up, somehow knowing to do it always when the sun is setting, kick-starting that fading trigger that has shadowed me for years on the street side of life. I'm sad; I'm depressed. Carl keeps asking if he did something wrong, if I'm mad at him. He doesn't seem to understand that I can have feelings that have nothing to do with him. If I were with Aram, we'd have long conversations about death, about the term "passing away" versus "died." He'd give me the space I need. He'd understand about the grieving process. Carl just wants to know if I still love him. I miss Aram. I want to hear his voice.

The phone calls won't stop. Outside I always feel like someone is trailing me. Everywhere I am I feel Jimmy's absence, which makes me feel unsafe, and now, with a stalker, I really am in danger. There's no one to call: My mother is grieving, my sister is caring for Nina, and my boyfriend feels threatened by my despair. It's winter, which makes the world feel smaller, and the sun sets earlier. After all these years, no one knows what happened to Etan Patz, only that something horrible happened to him when he was walking down the street, just the way I'm doing now. I begin to skip classes that meet at night. I see friends during the day, or invite them to my house at night, but I try not to go outside.

I meet with a university administrator and tell her the situation. She says she'll speak to the boy and get back to me. While I wait, new fears invade my ability to function. When I was small, I was afraid that when I woke up my whole family would be dead. Now, though, I simply fear I won't wake up myself. What if I die in my sleep like Melissa? I stay sitting up all night, and when I do fall asleep, I jolt myself awake, relieved that I'm not dead.

Carl works a block away from my apartment. One night, I'm supposed to go meet him there, but the minute I reach the sidewalk I'm gripped by a premonition that if I take one more step I am going to be killed. I dash back and lock myself in my apartment, call Carl, and tell him I can't come, I can't go outside. He doesn't understand. What's the big deal? It's night, same as ever. But nothing's the same as it was. It's dangerous, and unhinged, like after Etan disappeared. Reality has ripped one of our players off the board, yet it expects us to continue on as though that didn't change the game. To child-me, night became less scary when Jimmy moved in, because the worry of protecting everyone myself was alleviated, but now night is my responsibility again, and Jimmy isn't here.

The paranoia gets worse and I make an appointment with a therapist. He was supposed to be a campus therapist, but it turns out his office is off-campus, and I'll have to take a bus to see him. Each time I do, I am a lost sixth grader once again, terrified I will be raped and killed. Each time, I am grateful to the driver for letting me live.

The therapist is a student, inexperienced and not entirely helpful, but he listens to me and says soothing things that make me feel understood. He's easy to talk to, and before I know it, I feel attached to him and look forward to the days I'm in his office, so I can explain my crazy feelings and he can nod and not ask me to reassure him or tell me my feelings are too dark to deal with. I keep asking him what I have, what's wrong with me. I am still searching for a name for these feelings that have been plaguing me since childhood. They left when I took drugs with Taylor and trickled in and out after that, but now they're back and worse, more feral than ever.

"If you had to diagnose me," I push again, a few weeks in, "what would you say I had?"

"Well, I'd probably say you had mixed personality disorder."

"What? Are you serious? Like Sybil?" I ask. How could I have been so duped by this guy?

"It's just a guess."

"Well, that guess sucked."

I might not have the right answer, but I do know he's wrong, and that all my teachers were wrong, and my mom was wrong. I don't think I'm learning disabled, and I don't think I have "alters." I keep seeing him, though I no longer trust him. I badly need someone to talk to. Sometimes I am tempted to wrongly diagnose him, just to show him how it feels.

Carl is useless, too. What he's always been best at is letting me care for him, but when it's my turn, he's lost, a little boy constantly asking me what I want him to do. When I'm silent because my fear won't allow me to open my mouth, he'll ask if I'm mad at him, or if he did something wrong. He'll ask if I love him. Yes, I nod. As soon as he's reassured, he falls asleep.

One morning I'm called back for a meeting with the school administrator. She's met with my stalker, she says with a smile. She was charmed. "It's a cultural thing."

"What do you mean?" I ask.

"He's Dutch. He's just showing his affection like a European. It's sweet."

"He called and told me he was going to rape me."

"He said that wasn't him."

"So you're not going to do anything?"

"I can ask him to write you a letter of apology, if that's what you really want. But I think you should give him a chance. He's charming."

I leave the office, feeling more naked than infuriated. He's standing outside the office; he's followed me here. I'm stopped in my tracks, and he comes close to my face and slowly blows on it, then walks away. I have nowhere to run, and no one to take care of me. I am crying and hyperventilating on the steps of the administration building. No one can help me. Not even my own self. I'm the last person I'd put in charge of me.

Waited My Whole Life to Be Normal

THE SCHOOL THERAPIST WRAPPED things up with me abruptly, eager, it seemed, to report to his superiors he'd completed this assignment and was ready to move on. Though I couldn't bring myself to respect him, I still was not ready to move on.

"What am I going to do now?" I asked him.

"Look in the Yellow Pages," he said.

"I'm not looking for car parts," I told him.

He shrugged. "You'll find someone."

After graduation, dread follows me back to New York and turns back into the dread of my childhood, only worse. Carl and I live together with Tatum, whom I've kept in touch with all this time, in a small railroad apartment on Thompson Street in SoHo, not far from my Mac-Dougal Street home. Around the corner is the lumber store where people claimed to see Etan Patz the day he disappeared, and a handful of blocks away is his parents' apartment, and the bus stop where he never arrived.

Buses, ironically, become my default source of transportation. Subways are impossible. The second I descend the stairs, I become convinced the entire system will crumble and I'll be buried underneath. I try cabs, but that's worse. The second I close the door, the driver sinks the locks down, my heart starts pounding, and I become convinced I'm in the process of being kidnapped. All that's left is walking, but even that fails, because everyone who walks behind me is going to cut my throat, and everyone walking toward me is obviously going to stab me. Buses, then, are how I roll.

For a while I decide this way of living is doable, and it doesn't hamper my lifestyle much. But soon it's not just transportation that sets me off, it's being around other people. It's going to parties, or bars. I can't even take cabs with other people, or get into friends' cars. Before long I'm making excuses to get myself out of everything, and Carl is annoyed. He's been playing music all around town, and I can't get through an entire set without having to leave. There are always too many people, and they are breathing in all the air, not leaving any for me.

Then a friend of ours from college comes to stay with us for the weekend. As Lori is on her way up the stairs to our apartment, I begin to panic. I prop our apartment door open so more air will get in, but it doesn't work, and overcome by nausea, I speed to our bathroom to throw up. Carl isn't helpful. When I'm upset or overwhelmed I become mute, or monosyllabic at best, and he takes this as a sign that I'm angry with him, and I wind up having to reassure him for days when I'm the one who needs calming.

Given my freak-out, instead of staying at the apartment, Carl and Lori and I walk to Scratcher, Carl's favorite bar in the East Village. I have trouble keeping up my end of the conversation, busy trying to talk myself out of whatever it is I've fallen into. I use the technique of my childhood and try to distract myself with mundane thoughts: Think about things that are dull, things that are orange, things that are clothes, things to do with my hair; but I can't shake the reality that we're walking toward a crowded, enclosed place with only one very narrow door from which to escape. What kind of twenty-four-year-old is scared of going to a bar? But I can't help it—I need to leave soon after we arrive. I leave Carl and Lori inside, pleading sickness, and the second I'm outside I feel much better.

On the walk home, alone, I'm free of social obligation, the pressure relieved. When I'm with other people, I seem unable to function, but when I'm alone, I can. It has begun to feel as if triggers are everywhere, even places they shouldn't be, like at my mom's house, where I can't stay for long without feeling sick. All the places I once relied upon to guard me have been reversed; now, being alone, hiding from everyone and everything, feels safest.

Soon I simply stop going anywhere, refusing to venture out of the apartment. I turn down a job because it's in an office, and just hearing the offer turns off my breathing valve. I think Carl is erasing me. I miss Aram. I made a mistake. I never should have left him. Why did I do that?

Before long, though, there is no more me. I don't feel anything resembling a self; the only thing I feel is despair and claustrophobia. Is this what Melissa felt when she was dying? Did she really die in her sleep and feel no pain? I want to talk to Jonathan. I don't understand where everyone went. Did I help kill Jimmy because I knew he ate steak in secret and I promised I wouldn't tell Mom? I am responsible for his death because I should have told Mom, and I am responsible for Melissa's and Baba's deaths because I left home when I should have stayed, and Etan Patz because I failed to find him. What if, in the moment I pretended to find him, I took the police away from actually finding him? Maybe he was walking by just as I was dragging the cop away? How many people are left in my life? Will I meet more people I'll come to love and then kill without meaning to? Every day I feel the world shrinking.

What is wrong with me? Things aren't good, and they're not right. I'm worried I am going crazy; maybe I've always been crazy and no one told me. That's why no one would ever give me a diagnosis—because how do you tell a kid she's nuts? But what kind of nuts am I? Right from the start of life I was scared, and I know that it's not about intelligence but psychology, and my psychology feels abnormal.

Carl suggests smoking pot as a way to calm down. I haven't smoked pot since high school, but who knows, maybe it'll work. We don't smoke much, or maybe we smoke too much, it's hard to say, but all of a sudden, I am terrified of Carl. I need to get out of our apartment. I don't want him to come near me or touch me. When I get outside, he yells down to me from the fire escape, and I start running up Sixth Avenue to my sister's house. I have to get there before I die. My entire body is closing in on me. I'm being murdered from the inside; my own body is doing it, and I don't think that's even suicide. I can't tell whether I'm out of breath from running or from dying, and I slow down and get to her building and wave to the doorman, who knows me, and it isn't until the elevator door closes on me that I realize what a massive mistake it was to get on an elevator. I breathe as slowly and evenly as I can, and seven years later it opens on Kara's floor; I stumble to her apartment and let myself in. I find her in her bedroom reading. Her husband is in the kitchen. As soon as she sees me she realizes something is wrong, but I can't hear anything she says.

"I'm dying. I can't breathe. I'm dying," I say.

She shuts her book. "You're not dying. You're freaking out, but you're not dying."

"I think I'm having a heart attack. My breath is trying to stop."

"I don't think you're having a heart attack," she says.

"How do you know? What if you're wrong and we don't go to the hospital and then I die? You'll have to live with that for the rest of your life."

"You're not having a heart attack."

"I'm crazy, aren't I?"

"What do you mean?"

"You can tell me the truth. I must be crazy and it's like some big family secret that no one will tell me, but I need to know. I know you know."

"You're not crazy," my sister says.

I'm frustrated. Kara is the only one I can trust to tell me the truth, but she's refusing.

"I swear I can handle it. There's no other reason for the way I am."

"I promise you, you're not crazy. There is no secret we're keeping. I think maybe you're a little stoned and having a freak-out," she says. "That happens to people all the time."

"It does?"

She nods. "Sure. You're not crazy. You're just having a bad reaction to pot. Let's lie down and read until you feel better." It works.

A few hours later, I can go back home. But it doesn't stay better for very long. Maybe Kara doesn't know. Maybe Mom never told her I'm crazy.

Carl starts going out without me. I am glad not to have to entertain anyone or deal with visiting friends using up my allotment of air. I used to keep the windows open when people came over, but now that no one does, I keep them closed and locked. I don't want anyone creeping in. I refuse all invitations, even dinner at my mom's house just blocks away. I can't even go to Kara's house. I wish everyone would leave me alone.

Soon even the thought of going anywhere makes me scuttle to the bathroom and vomit. I'm crying all the time, too, and can't get out of bed. I'm depressed and scared and I know that something's very wrong with me, but I also know that no one will be able to figure it out because me is the problem, and that can't be changed.

I don't know how long I've been crying. I have to cut my skin to make sure I still feel things, but I don't, so I have to cut myself a bit deeper, and now I'm afraid that I'm actually dead but stuck among the living. The whole world is in on the secret that's being kept from me: My family, my friends, every doctor, every tutor, all my past teachers, even that bad free therapist was in on it. My mom must have called him. Called them all. Told them my sickness needs to be hidden from me because I am weak. My poor mom, to have a daughter so crazy everyone has to keep it from her. I'm crying so hard now, crying for my family who's had to bear this secret about me and treat me normal at the same time. I call my mom. I don't check the time.

When she answers I greet her through snot and tears and a clogged throat.

"What's the matter?" I can hear her sitting up in bed. It must be late.

"I know," I tell her, "that I'm crazy. I know now. It's okay. You can stop pretending."

"What are you talking about?"

"It's okay," I say, emphatic. "Really. It's better for me to know. It's the right thing to do, you know, to tell me the truth about me."

"Manda, there's nothing wrong with you. You're not crazy. You have a learning disability, that's all."

"I don't have a learning disability!" I yell. "I'm crazy. I can't leave my house. I can't stop crying. I am afraid of everything. I'm going to die. If I leave the house, I feel like people are going to kill me. For months—" I can no longer speak through the sobs.

My mom convinces me to get a cab to her house, even though she's only five blocks away. I sit on the side of her bed and cry and cry and she leaves a message for her therapist and I sleep in her bed and in the morning, I see her shrink, whose job it is to tell me I'm crazy. Unless, of course, my mom got to him first and told him not to. Or unless this creepy cabdriver kills me first.

I'm sitting across from my mother's therapist. Like every other teacher, tutor, doctor, and evaluator whose office doors I've tripped in and out of, no wiser or better than before I arrived, I know how it goes now, and I'm disappointed in the outcome before the session has even begun.

"Can you tell me what brings you here today?" he asks.

"I'm crazy and no one will tell me the truth," I say, sounding completely crazy.

"And why do you think you're crazy?"

I tell him everything: how I am afraid of the world, how I can't go to sleep because I'm afraid I won't wake up, how just having friends visit makes me throw up, and throughout all of this I have to keep my worries hidden.

"Can you tell me what happens in your body when this occurs?"

I tell him what's been going on and when I finish listing the symptoms, I look him in the eye and confess again, "I'm crazy. These are all the things a crazy person does."

"And when do these things happen?"

"I don't know. There's no one thing that sets it off. I mean, one time

I was in a restaurant and they dimmed the lights and I freaked out and had to leave. I freak out in cabs and on the subway and walking down the street and well, just, always."

"And how long has this been going on?"

"God, I don't know. Since I was very young. A baby. Before I could talk."

"My goodness. And you're how old?"

"I just turned twenty-five."

"It sounds to me like you have a panic disorder."

"A panic disorder?" I say the words, never having heard them before, and they fit right inside my mouth. "Panic," I say again. "That's it. That's the word I've been trying to come up with, and that's it, yes! It's panic!" I am so pleased I can hardly believe this moment is occurring. I have the name for the thing I've suffered from my entire life, and it's only one word long.

"I don't understand how it's taken this long for someone to diagnose you," he says.

"You and me both," I say, practically punchy.

"It's rather obvious, if you ask me," he says. "Textbook, even. You have all the symptoms, but because you've gone so long without a diagnosis or treatment, your condition has grown extreme. Without treatment, panic spirals out of control and branches into other disorders, which is what's happened here. At the moment, I'd say, on top of having a panic disorder, you are also suffering from social anxiety, clinical depression, and general anxiety disorder. That's the bad news. The good news is this is all treatable. I can prescribe you medication that will help manage your emotions, but I am also prescribing therapy. You must take the medication in conjunction with therapy."

I can't believe that my mom was right all this time. Medication does solve everything! "How long do I have to be on the medication before I'm cured?" I ask.

"Well, it's not quite that simple. There is no 'cure' per se. This is a treatment. A lifetime treatment. You have a biological disorder. You don't just have panic attacks, which are situational and circumstantial, you have a disorder, which means the attacks come on without any known pattern. Anxiety is hereditary. It runs in families. Your mother is my patient, so I can't use her as an example, but people are born predisposed toward certain things—weight, let's say. This doesn't mean people are fated to struggle with their weight, but it does mean that if unhealthy eating habits are already in place when they're born, they will, most likely, wind up struggling with their weight."

"So my emotions are struggling with their weight?"

He laughs. "You could say that. But, as I said earlier, there are treatments. If one doesn't work, we try another. Although you may often feel as though you are dying, you are not. What you have isn't terminal, it just can feel that way."

I smile. I like this guy. "What kind of medication do I have to take?"

"We'll try you out on an antidepressant called Zoloft and see how that goes. It might take a little while to find the right medication, but if you have patience, we can do it. Just remember, you've spent twenty-five years unmedicated, untreated, and undiagnosed, so you can hang on a few more weeks or a month until we find the exact right thing for you. Okay?"

I feel out-of-body, but in a good way. The matter-of-factness with which he's said all these life-altering things astonishes me. I've spent my entire life battling some impossible, invisible plague no one ever seemed to see, and this guy did it with such ease, as though panic disorder is easy to establish, obvious to anyone who would take the time to ask what my symptoms were; *textbook*, even. I feel weirdly solid, like I'm a valid human being. I didn't even realize my feelings were categorizable as symptoms. Panic disorder. The air is softer, expansive, as though the world has suddenly opened and is unfolding every opportunity my panic had once ruled out. Every single thing in my life now makes perfect sense: the connections I couldn't bridge; the choices I couldn't make; the strange switches the natural world and all its sunsets turned on and off in me. He hands me a prescription.

"I'll come up with a few names for therapists you can see. Since I'm your mom's therapist, I can't see you both." Now he's pressing another paper into my hand, with the name of a psychopharmacologist he wants me to call so she can help me find the right cocktail. "You need to call her today if possible, okay? You can't just take medication and not see anyone."

I promise, and I walk out of his office into a new world. Outside, I lean against the building. The relief, like my panic, is all-encompassing and everywhere. It's in the pollen dusted on cars, the dirty pacifier lost in the gutter. Everything I see and feel and smell is folded into my liberation. I'm going to be totally normal before long, like everyone else. It suddenly feels so clear. All those years of feeling dumb, of everyone insisting I had a learning disability, are about to melt away, while my panic, my gloriously treatable panic, will be eradicated with a pill. I'm not just going to change; I'm going to be a brand-new me. For just a moment, I imagine returning to my eleven-year-old self, walking down that hall with an unwavering confidence behind Dr. Rivka, and whispering from the future, No matter what she asks you, tell her your symptoms. But then I'm back and I think, it took only twenty-five years, but you got what you've always wanted. What now?

Forever Mama

I MISS FRANKIE, I miss Javier, and I miss my home. Maybe if I had gotten Pilot now, when I feel more confident as a caretaker, I'd have been able to make it work. Now, at least I realize that I can be some-one's safe thing, the way I was for Frankie. But now that I will never be a mom, at least to a baby of my own, whose safe thing will I be? Maybe I can find Pilot somehow and get her back. When I first started thinking about having a baby, I read parenting books, but I didn't do that before I got Pilot. But maybe I should. I've discovered the more I teach myself about what I don't know, the less afraid of life I feel. So yes, I will buy books about separation anxiety in dogs, watch videos, and find a trainer, and then I will search for Pilot. If I find Pilot, I can get a do-over and show her that we can be a family. I'll tell her I'm sorry I failed her the first time around. We'll be a family and maybe even move away from here and make our own secret garden upstate.

But now, just like Javi and Frankie, Pilot already has a family. The one who took her when I gave her up. Even with dogs my timing is bad. I'm ready to give up entirely, until on Petfinder one midnight I come across a small, sweet-looking dog named Penny who was just rescued from a kill shelter in Tennessee. I apply for her. Out of twenty-three people I am the first, and I win the dog. It's raining the day I pick her up and her fur is matted, making her look half her original size; it's not love at first sight. I'm disappointed by how small she is, but she looks like she's smiling. Her ears are black and floppy, her body is white, her belly is spotted like a cow, and she has a black pirate-eye. When the foster woman hands me the leash, the dog sweetly licks my calf and then sits patiently beside me. Oh, she's lovely. I write a check, and the dog and I walk away, neither of us knowing what we're doing.

As we're walking to Petco, she licks every leg she passes, trying to see inside swinging purses and absorbing the world with an outsized, limitless curiosity. Even before I'd met her, I had a short list of names, and Busy was one of them, so that when a woman stops and says, "Such a busy little thing," Busy jumps off the list and onto my brand-new family. Busy Stern.

In the cab on the way home, I am overwhelmed by the silence. I want her to like me, so I start to feed her treats. One after the other. We're halfway to Fort Greene when Busy throws up all over me. Okay, no more treats. I scoop the vomit up using the Petco bag. Busy and I stare at each other.

"Are you okay?" I ask.

What have I done? Who is this animal? Have I made *another* mistake?

Like so many of my OkCupid dates, Busy doesn't look like her picture. Her nose is too pointy. She's too little. I feel embarrassed by her physical traits as though they were my own. I hate that I feel this way, and by this point in my life I've had enough therapy to know I'm treating her like a narcissistic extension of myself, but I don't know how to stop. In the apartment, I follow the books' instructions, keeping her on the leash while introducing her to each room, but that seems to overwhelm her. I take her leash off and she follows me to the living room. She stares at me. Then she pees on the floor. I call my friend Laurie.

"She's not too little?" I ask, standing over the dog.

"No," Laurie says, standing next to me.

"Too pointy?"

"Nope."

"Maybe I should take her back. Maybe there's another, better, bigger dog for me out there."

"No, this is a really good dog. Look how sweet and loving she is."

"Look how skinny she is," I say.

"You'll fatten her up."

"I'll give it two weeks. If I still feel this way in two weeks, I'm taking her back."

"You won't. I know dogs. I'm telling you this one is special."

"Yeah, well, that's what they said about me, too."

After Laurie leaves I decide to face the potentially unendurable task of leaving Busy alone. I have a plan of action. Ten minutes, three times a day at first, and then longer increments until she's used to it. I set up a video camera to film what she does, so I can know when she's used to it. Yet, with all these things in place, I'm still terrified she'll be Pilot, second edition. Deep breath. I wonder if I'm more afraid to leave her alone than she is of being left alone, and that's when something strikes me. With Pilot, the rescue folks told me to do everything with as little fanfare as possible, so that Pilot wouldn't absorb my panic, and I did that, but I'm realizing now, I did it only through my actions—emotionally I was still a mess. And she must have picked up on that. I was reinforcing the very thing I was afraid would happen. So now, I use all my energy to really not care. Or worry. Ten minutes, big deal.

I walk out the front door and stand on the stairs and soon I hear her crying and I can't stand it. I feel the pain that's driving her to cry, I can feel her terror inside me, not knowing where I am, where I've gone or why, or if I'll come back. I want to save her, soothe her, make things better, and my instinct is to comfort her, but I don't. My mother did this for me, thinking it would help me, but it did the reverse. One thing I know to be true is that in order to get over a fear, you must face it. To save her will reinforce her sense that she needs to be saved, that she *should* be afraid and sad and panicked without me, the way I felt without my mom, and that's a feeling I don't want to pass along as my legacy. I didn't want that for Frankie, and I don't want it for an animal. I can hear her cries all the way from the lobby, so I force myself to leave the building and walk around the block, taking in the early July heat, and when I return she is still crying. I spend the rest of the day, and the week, leaving and returning, leaving and returning, in longer and longer increments.

At first she sits by the door and cries. Then, after a few days, her cries fade to whines. Toward the end of the week she whines less but continues to wait by the front door. Eventually, she heads toward the living room when I leave and waits for me on the couch. And by the end of the next week, once she realizes I'm gone, she goes into the living room, grazes her toy basket, pulls something out, and begins flinging it from one side of the room to the other, racing after it. My sweet, vulnerable little dog is entertaining herself, and I'm proud that I have been able to train someone to be self-reliant, to trust that when I leave, I always return.

Being able to do for Busy what I needed someone to do for me fills me with a certainty and groundedness I've felt only with Frankie. There's a hole in my heart and Busy seems to fit it perfectly. Now I know what it looks like to grow free from panic. I know how to do this, I think.

Busy is patient and wildly affectionate. She's easygoing yet playful. She's not at all like Pilot, and, unlike me, she's quick to learn and easy to teach. She is my true complement. Where I am a hyperactive New Yorker, she is West Coast calm; where I am always in a rush and tossing back coffees, she is a leisurely European taking time with her espresso. But we are both eager to please, both dislike sudden lunges—by dogs or people—in our direction, and both dislike being left behind.

At the farmers' market I introduce her to everyone, and I feel a sense of family fulfillment I haven't felt since Javi and Frankie. At the dog park I imagine she's me as a kid, and I do what I wish had been done for me: I'm consistent. I stand in one place. I make sure she knows that every single time she turns back to check on me, I will be exactly where she left me. I don't want my concerns to become Busy's, and if she's to take her cues from me, my cues must be steady and calm, even if I'm faking it. When I'm hosting Happy Ending, I set the tone for the entire night. From the second I step onstage, my energy and presence matter, because they tell the audience how to feel, just the way a parent's energy and presence tell their child how to feel. If I'm strong and assured, the audience won't worry about me, or the show, or themselves; they'll be able to focus and be present. But when I'm nervous, they're nervous and the show suffers; and over the course of the night I watch in horror as it grows into an insecure teen, awkward and constantly angling for reassurance.

Over my life I've worried so much and feared so many things, and though many of those things actually happened, here I am, still alive, having survived what I thought I couldn't. I didn't turn out the way I thought I would: I didn't get married and I didn't have kids, and the not-having didn't kill me either.

As I'm watching Busy learn to enjoy independence, I think back to a dinner I had with my mom right after I had to give Pilot away. I was proud of myself for doing a difficult thing, and I wanted to be recognized for it.

"After everything she endured, I finally realized I had to do what was best for—"

"You," she said, pleased to be able to finish my sentence.

"No," I said, confused. "For Pilot."

This exchange nagged at me and I am only now understanding why. Years ago, she was me and I was the dog.

I wish I had realized then that giving Pilot away to guarantee her happiness at the expense of my own represented exactly what a good parent does. A good parent puts their child first, before themselves and all others, and that's what my instincts had suggested without having to be told. I chose her, and when I saw she needed more than just me, I chose for her, giving her what she needed. I chose her future happiness. I was a good parent at the exact moment I thought I wasn't.

I think back to another parenting revelation I had nearly two decades ago—which I promptly forgot—when Kara invited me to sleep over with her and May, my six-month-old and first-ever niece. I was besotted by the baby, and while Kara's role in life had expanded to include that of a mother, her role in my life hadn't changed in the ways I feared. In the morning, Kara let her snuggle with me and she crawled my body awake. May's existence offered my narrow frame of feelings another layer I hadn't felt since Nina was born—hopefulness. It was a tough transition, and while Kara was a natural, being a new mom was hard. She and her new mom friends were overwhelmed and depressed. I wanted to be as good a sister to her as she is to me, but I didn't know how. I noticed that the babies absorbed the emotions of their caretakers. Their moods altered to mirror their moms' or nannies' nerves. I wondered then if that's what happened to me when I was a baby during my parents' divorce. Maybe I picked up all the bad energy and stored it like a sponge, but could there be a solid, calm Amanda, free of other people's troubles, still buried underneath? I learned a lot just by watching May take in the world, surrounded by adults who loved her but who were all struggling on their own terms. I wondered then if emotions were transferred in utero, if my mother's emotions seeped into me. All the inexplicable feelings I have possessed, it occurred to me, may not even have been mine.

I don't have a baby, but I do have a dog, and I understand my job even more clearly now.

Back at home, after the park, Busy puts one sweet little paw on my leg, and as my love swells, the dread comes with it: One day, this perfect little beast will be dead. What am I going to do without her? So many people I've loved have died or fallen away. Now I'm afraid that all the time I have with this dog will be spent anticipating the day I no longer have her.

Since I was small I've had one foot in the future, never fully present with the time and space inside which I'm standing. Growing up, my mom always focused on what I didn't have or couldn't do; she was always in the future somehow, too, trying to get me help, trying to fix me. My dad also was focused on the externals: how we looked, acted, and how we did in school. The focus on what I lacked took precedence over what I had, and without realizing it, I adopted that way of thinking—my lack became my focus, too. Without meaning to, I co-opted a precept I didn't and don't actually believe.

I want to raise a dog the way I would a child—to be self-reliant without the need for enmeshment. I will be present and attentive. I will nurture even that which I do not understand. I will try to understand. I will put myself second. I will be a good mother and pay attention. When there is no longer any Busy in my life, I will think back without regret, grateful that I was conscious and present with her for every one of her days. So I stop and look into the eyes of this dog I still think is too skinny and too little and I say, "Busy, I am your forever mama and this is your forever home and we are a forever family." Then she puts her head on my leg and falls asleep.

Maybe Javi was right and there really are two kinds of people: those who worry and those who are grateful. But we're not beholden to the "kind" of person we've been. If I worry all of Busy's life, I'll have missed it. If I'm always so afraid of death, I'll never actually live.

I try hard to stay present and attuned to the moment, but I can't help it, a few minutes later I lower my head and make sure she's still breathing.

Take Care of the Animals

I'M THIRTY-ONE AND have finished my first book. I have a literary agent, and I clean my brother's yoga school for money; I'm dating a few different people, but no one seriously. After a long period of things not being all right, a phone call with Kara has shocked me into making some choices.

I call her, crying and depressed.

"Are you taking your medicine?" she asks.

"Yes," I say.

"You know, something occurred to me the other day."

"What?" I'm standing, staring at the chair I'm too depressed to lower myself into.

"Maybe you should go away somewhere. To a farm in the country. Help with the animals. Life would be so much more manageable for you. You could go for a few months, or longer if you wanted," she says.

"A farm?"

"Yeah."

I can smell the country and picture the surroundings, the calm slowness of being in nature, and while I do feel that pace would work for me, I can't shake what she's really saying to me—that the real world is too much for me.

"I'll think about it," I tell her.

When I hang up I sit on my desk and look around my messy apartment. My bedroom floor has been turned into my closet; half-finished art projects are scattered about. I had a bowl of popcorn for dinner last night, and the bowl is in the closet where I fell asleep crying. This is not the apartment of an adult. Can I really not survive the world like everyone else? Kara has presented me with an out. Life would be so much easier on a farm taking care of animals, but is that the right choice for my life? There is so much I want to do, but life does seem harder for me than for others. Do I want to leave real life for a simpler, easier state of existence? The idea makes me feel embarrassed for myself, but it also makes me angry. I know I'm more capable than it seems, but in my family I've been the emotionally unstable one for so long, I'm not sure anyone expects much of me, and that's the standard I've been living down to.

I haven't heard from Paul, or any of the acting kids, in years, and I am surprised when he calls. He's married now, to a woman named Claudia, and he's still acting. We catch each other up on life, and since I know better than to ask after Jonathan at this point, I ask about his parents instead.

"They're doing really well," Paul says. "Considering."

"Considering what?" I ask.

Then, silence.

"Oh my God. You don't know," he said.

I want to vomit.

"We didn't really call anyone or anything; we just let the word spread, but I guess it never reached you," he says.

"When did it happen?"

"Two years ago," he says.

"What was the date?"

"February 21, 1999."

"Was there a funeral?" I ask.

"Yeah. I'm sorry, Amanda. We didn't do a good job of telling people. It was overwhelming, but I have some small things of his that I've given people over the years. You should come uptown sometime and pick something out," he says.

"Okay." I'm quiet for a moment. "Can you tell me why he stopped talking to me?"

Paul takes a big breath. "He didn't know he'd live for ten more years. He thought it would be fast, and he didn't want to put you through any of it. He didn't want you to see him get ugly, with sores. He moved to New Mexico, away from everyone. It wasn't just you he cut off, but you were the first. It was unimaginable for him to leave you with memories of him at his worst."

"Wow," I say. "That's just . . . That makes me really angry."

"I know. That's why I never told you. I knew if you knew why, you'd force your way back into his life, and he just couldn't handle you seeing him sick. He just . . . he couldn't. He could barely handle his own family seeing him that way."

"I wish you had called to tell me. I wish I had known. All this time, two entire years, he's been dead and I haven't known."

"I'm sorry. We did the best we could. We let a lot of people down."

"Send your parents my love, and you, too, okay?" I say.

"Yeah, I will."

"And Paul? I'm sorry. I'm so sorry you lost your brother."

"Thanks, Amanda. I'm so sorry you lost him, too."

When we hang up, something happens to me I can't describe. I feel enraged and reckless; I want to obliterate myself. I'm so ashamed I spent the last two years not knowing Jonathan was dead. How can I account for that time when everyone was mourning and I was drinking and fucking and laughing and going to parties, in between having panic attacks over things that meant nothing—nothing compared to this? I'm a terrible person. I didn't know, I didn't know. Why didn't I know? I never even assumed he was dead; it never crossed my mind.

I still can't believe that for someone so attuned to death, I missed the ones I should have been there for. I've had two best friends die, and I didn't get to say good-bye to either of them because their deaths were withheld from me. People have been keeping the difficulties of life from me since I was small, protecting me from my own truth. I can run away to the country and live on a farm and keep protecting myself from the world as if I really am helpless, or I can fight back against the world and face off against everything I fear, one fear at a time.

Certainty

IT'S BEEN THREE YEARS since my mom sold our house. One afternoon I'm early to meet a friend and close to MacDougal Street. I've passed the house before, but that was before the new owners moved in. I feel the urge to spy on them, see if they're treating the house right. I walk on the Dante side of the street, facing the row of houses, but it's too dark to see inside. I notice that the facade looks faded. I see dried watermarks. The house has been crying.

I want to know who took our place, to see who is standing where we stood, saying and doing and thinking where we did all those things. They don't know about us, just as we didn't know or think about those who came before us. I want to tell them about Dead Man Smith, and warn the kids that Norman Bates lives in the basement. They should know about Ciggy, Sasquatch, and the lady on the corner; and if Jimmy comes back, they should direct him our way. But maybe it doesn't matter. Even if I ring the bell and tell them everything I think they should know, I'm just a firsthand person telling stories to a secondhand person, who will inevitably tell some third-hander, and on it goes, until the people I hope will be remembered aren't people at all, but the stories of people who were once real. I guess that's who we all are. The stories of ourselves other people tell. Somewhere, though, is the story of us that never got told, some original self that never happened.

I cross the street and notice that newspapers and trash have collected on the ground outside the front door. The camera Jimmy put up is rusty and broken, dangling by its wires like a nearly severed head. The windows in front are covered by cardboard, so I can't see inside, down the hall, and into the secret garden. The paint is chipping, the window guards are rusted, and the gold letter slot on the front door has grown a green patina. As I stand and stare, passersby eye me, suspicious. I want to reassure them I'm not a Peeping Tom or, worse, a tourist. I used to live here; this was my home. But now, it seems, we sold it to a ghost. It feels too early for me to be on the other side of this house's history, but here I am, locked out, with the view blocked by cheap cardboard. No one moved in. I open the mail slot, but I can't see anything.

Someone bought it and let it sit here for years, and it's grown saggy with despair. Stale tears have eroded the paint, leaving milky streaks down its front. Now it's twice the price. Only wine and real estate are covetable with age. There it sits, the house I grew up in, where everything I feared would happen, happened; where the people and things I love no longer converge and can't be found. All the garden kids are gone. No one lives new lives on top of our old one. There are no children racing around, sliding down banisters, racing out into the garden; there is no one giving thought to the people who came before. Three years on, the house stands like a premature gravestone. If Jimmy comes back, he won't know where we went.

As a little girl, when I left for my dad's house on the weekends, I always feared the house would be gone when we returned, and in its place a black empty rectangle. But this is worse. The house is here, but its soul is gone. The garden is no longer mine, nor is the school around the corner. Everything important in my life used to orbit in relation to this house, and this house meant my mother and my mother meant home and home meant safe and those things together meant I wouldn't die. Until Etan Patz disappeared, at least.

*　　　*　　　*

When I was in sixth grade, a man was apprehended for luring two small boys into the sewer system. His name was Jose Ramos, but the newspaper dubbed him "the Drainpipe Man." A known pedophile, he was finally sent to prison in 1985, but he became a suspect in the Patz case when it was revealed that he dated the woman who occasionally cared for Etan. That woman, Sandy, had walked Etan to the school bus in the weeks leading up to his disappearance. Without a body, the Patz family could not pursue a wrongful death suit, and so, in 2001, twenty-two years after their six-year-old son disappeared, his parents declared him legally dead.

Then, on May 24, 2012, out of the seeming blue, a day before the thirty-third anniversary of his disappearance, a fifty-one-year-old man named Pedro Hernandez confessed to killing Etan Patz. I was forty-two years old and on my way to a picnic in Fort Greene Park when I received the alert on my phone, and I sat down on a nearby stoop, shaking as I read the claims. In 1979, Pedro Hernandez, then an eighteen-year-old stock clerk, was working at the deli adjacent to the school bus stop. When Etan arrived on the corner, gripping his soda money, Hernandez told him to follow him to the basement to get his drink. Hernandez claims that halfway down the stairs, something came over him, and he put his hands around Etan's little neck and strangled him. He tossed his school bag behind the refrigerator, and put Etan in a box, placed the box inside a garbage bag, and, later that day, hauled the boy down the street and discarded him in an alley.

I didn't go to the picnic. I turned around and went home, turned on the news, and read everything I could. But I could not stop shaking. How could this be? I kept thinking. How is it possible that all this time, and all these years we've been waiting and looking and hoping, he's been dead? It made no sense to me; it didn't add up, not just because the story seemed odd, but because when it comes to this case, I am still a nine-year-old, just as Etan is still six. He disappeared between 8 a.m. and 8:10 a.m., but to me, he didn't die. He's been alive all this time because I never knew that he wasn't. Despite the confession, we will never truly know what happened to him. He got swallowed by the in-between, and life stopped. For some of us life never started again.

And yet, through all that, and through all those years, not once did my loyal house abandon me. It never disappeared or cut itself out from the world. We, my family, are the abandoners, leaving no one to care for the house that cared for us. The building is my memory, the one solid object that means my past, and here it stands now, an empty legacy that won't carry any of us with it. Soon we'll be the memories, but with no children of my own, who will remember me? I never gave birth to those who would miss me most. Will anyone feel the loss of me? Like Etan's posters, will my memories simply be plastered over one sunny day?

I still have my key, and people say to let myself in. But after all the years of being afraid someone might break into the house, I can't now be the intruder. An era is over, my mother says at least twice a year, when the iconic places in the Village fall victim to inflated rents, when some-one we've known forever dies. But we're the era now, and we're ending.

The landscape is always changing. Behind every new store is an old one, behind every person is an entire lineage, and inside all of us are choices we make again and again until we decide to make better ones.

*   *   *

Now I'm late, and I rush down the street just as a cavalcade of young mothers three abreast push their carriages toward me. I step off the curb and into the gutter, the same one I sank into when my mom told me Melissa died. They pass and I watch their backs grow distant. I am not a part of that world, and I never will be. Neither will Melissa or Etan or Jonathan. We are all just moments in time, a blink in a trillion-year history, even if our existence sometimes feels endless. While I'll never know if the life I never got would have been better than the life I have now, I do know the lives Etan, Melissa, Jonathan, and Jimmy never got would have been.

To Be the Same

WHEN DID IT START? It started before I was born. It started before my mother was born. It started when friction created the world. When does anything start? It doesn't; it just grows, sometimes to unmanageable heights, and then, when you're at the very edge, it becomes clear: Something must be done.

Left untreated, anxiety disorders, like fingernails, grow with a person. The longer they go untended, the more mangled and painful they become. Often, they spiral out of control, splitting and splintering into other disorders, like depression, social anxiety, or agoraphobia. We rise and fall upon a merry-go-round of their features. Separation anxiety handicaps its captors, preventing them from leaving bad relationships, moving far from home, going on trips, to parties, applying for jobs, having children, getting married, seeing friends, or falling asleep. Some people are so crippled by their anxiety they have panic attacks in anticipation of having a panic attack.

I've had panic attacks in nearly every part of New York City, even on Staten Island. I've had them in taxis, on subways, public bathrooms, banks, street corners, in Washington Square Park, on multiple piers, the Manhattan Bridge, Chinatown, the East Village, the Upper East Side, Central Park, Lincoln Center, the dressing room at Urban Outfitters, Mamoun's Falafel, the Bobst Library, the Mid-Manhattan Library, the main library branch, the Brooklyn Library, the Fort Greene Farmers' Market, Laundromats, book kiosks, in the entrance of FAO Schwarz, at the post office, on the steps of the Met, on stoops, at the Brooklyn Flea, in bars, at friends' houses, onstage, in the shower, in queen-sized beds, double beds, twin beds, in my crib.

I've grown so expert at hiding them, most people would never even know I'm suffering an attack. How, after all, do you explain that a restaurant's decision to dim their lights swelled your throat shut, and that's why you must leave immediately—not just the restaurant, but the neighborhood? If you cannot point to something, then it is invisible. Like a cult leader, anxiety traps you and convinces you that you're the only one it sees.

The small things you once overlooked begin to accumulate: your grandmother's agitated voice messages when you don't return her phone call inside of an hour, how out-of-sorts your father gets when someone is sitting at the table he's reserved, your mother's anger when someone makes a mistake. We expect anxiety in others to look like the anxiety that exists inside us, but it often doesn't, and so we don't recognize its sundry forms, even when the distress we feel inside our bodies isn't our own but someone else's.

Life is not marked by "aha" moments. There are no narrative conveniences that give our messy stories the tidy shape of a novel or a movie, but there are occasional bouts of epiphany; and recognizing that my grandmother's agitation was anxiety led me to widen my scope, silently probing others for signals that they, too, were anxious. With practice, I began to see it in my friends, which made me feel less alone and less defective. And then, one day, as I was joking at my own expense—as I often do—and a friend said, "Why do you always do that? Make jokes out of your sadness?" the roots exposed themselves to me, and I realized my dad's jokes weren't meant to hurt my feelings; he joked because my fear of him left him feeling rejected. Recognizing in others what I thought existed only in me gave me a context for their shortcomings, and I was overwhelmed by compassion. I couldn't see what they suffered from because I suffered from it, and they couldn't see what I suffered from because they suffered from it.

Anxiety, as the doctor had said, is inherited; it runs in families. In retrospect, that seems so obvious. We can't recognize in others what we can't see in ourselves. My suffering went undiagnosed all those years not because they weren't looking, but because they couldn't recognize what they saw. For better or worse, we can teach others only what we understand. I've walked through the world like a subject in search of its story. In my family, we always looked to others to tell us who we were. We asked, What's wrong with this picture? What does not belong? Each person begins, after all, as a story other people tell. And when we fall outside the confines of our common standards, we will assume our deficits define us.

From birth to death, we are measured and weighed, plotted on a line of percentile curves and compared against an invisible normal. We are appraised on our ability to answer questions whose responses are either right or wrong, which telegraphs to us that we are either right or wrong. We are tested, examined, assessed, and evaluated, and the numerical-value results become who we are—but it's in the chasm between "you" and that invisible normal where anxiety grows, telling you there's been an error and the error is you.

This is where I spent my life, wasting my cleanest fuel on a misguided channel-crossing away from who I was and toward some interpretation of who I was supposed to be. At first I thought my feelings were the learning disability, until I realized it was my brain they were after. Beyond "learning disabled," I was told so little, not even the name for the disability they said was "mine." When I tried to get answers, my questions hung there without closure, and that incompleteness seeped through me, cementing worry into belief that what was slow and different about me was my own brain; that I was stupid. Where I thought one thing was the matter with me, now I understood there were two. The accumulated efforts to correct me left me feeling defective, and my inability to be fixed became my identity, and it's followed me all the way here.

The message to people who learn differently, who are poor test takers, or who display any physical, emotional, or intellectual variance, is that we're not who we should be, and who we are isn't right. My fear and my conviction were the same: that I was the flaw in the universe; the wrongly circled letter in our multiple-choice world. This terrible truth binds us all: fear that there's a single, unattainable, correct way to be human. We rely on measures that disregard human characteristics such as empathy and emotion to tell us who we are.

Unconsciously, we consider these results our worth, and we shrink or expand our self-image to fit inside these notions, but we are not our results, just as we are not who other people imagine us to be, and yet we are placed and displaced according to these returns. We spend our lives unwittingly applying this system of measurement ourselves, raising our children on it, and teaching them to pass it down.

I dragged my youthful beliefs into adulthood, granting myself the grand fears of my childhood by building a type of altar to my concerns and making good on old worries. When I was finally diagnosed at age twenty-five, I had to accept a different truth and learn a new way to be me.

In the end, so many of the things I feared would happen, happened. People died; they disappeared; we lost our house. It's all come true, and here I am now, living inside the very future I feared, imagining it would kill me. Yet I am okay; I am alive. While I didn't get the things I assumed I'd have, I did get the one thing I've been seeking since I was little: a name for my suffering, and something else—the will to go toward my fears, to feel my awful feelings and live with discomfort and uncertainty in a life that often feels too hard for me.

I've spent my life trying to become the story of myself someone else was telling. I have been looking outside to tell myself who I am; I've been looking everywhere for a family to call my own, but *it's me*. I'm my family. And Busy is my family. Frankie Bird, the baby I never had, she is also my family. She's the part of me that never happened, but she's still a part of me. All these years, she's always been the family whose story I never got to tell.

For the Patz family, Etan became a story that the world can't stop telling, but what we know of the boy himself are the externals: his height and weight, the outfit he was wearing, the bag he was carrying, his route, and every theory that surrounded him, but we never heard his voice or knew what his laugh sounded like. We know only our version of him, and as such, who he was could be only the boy we invented. Etan could be Etan only to his family; to the rest of us, he was a representation, a symbol of our fears for ourselves and our children.

I used to think the closest I'd ever get to having a family happened already, that perfect April when I lived with Javi and Frankie on the small island off the coast of Maine, but I've since realized that family isn't just a feeling, it's a manner of action. I've spent years gathering supporting arguments for my claim that not creating a family of my own means I'm deficient and I've failed, without ever redefining for myself what creating a family of my own actually means. I was chasing an insular, closed system when I'm not an insular and closed person. Family is what happens between people, it's the support you provide and receive, it's the connections you build, it's pushing and pulling toward maturation, and it's witnessing. Every meaningful conversation I strike with strangers, the connections I have with my friends' children, the dedication to my friendships, the dinners I have with my neighbors, the morning chats with my friends from the coffee shop, my Saturday afternoons at the farmers' market, time spent with my family of origin, and every moment I'm with Busy is me creating and expanding a family of my own. Family is connection, and all I've ever wanted in my life is to connect with others. Just like my panic disorder, I've had a family this whole time. All that's been missing was its name.

Acknowledgments

How do you write a book about intelligence when you don't think you're smart? How do you tackle a memoir about anxiety when you have a panic disorder? These are the questions I wrestled with for the near decade I spent avoiding this book. As my friends and fellow authors published one book after another, I sat at home, stunned in front of my computer, ashamed, filled with dread, and unable to move forward until I wrote this book that I could not write.

Without my family, friends, therapist, psychiatrist, antidepressants, the ghosts of loved ones, a few ex-boyfriends, and my dog, Busy, I would still be sitting in front of my laptop debilitated by fear and preemptively gutted by imaginary bad reviews. In the four years it took to write this, I was provided with support, guidance, reassurance, advice, dinners, patronage, early reads, late reads, emergency reads, tough love, and belief that my anxiety was bad enough to write about from this spectacular group of people: Nelly Reifler, Lynne Tillman, Robert Lopez, Melissa Febos, Julie Orringer, Maria Popova, Eva Karen Barbarossa, Megan Summers, Fiona Maazel, Nell Freudenberger, Lisa Edelstein, and Tenley Zinke. Space and time to write, swim, garden, eat, breathe, play archery, and participate in the occasional séance in Bearsville, New York, were made possible due to the blind generosity of Neil Gaiman and Amanda Palmer, at whose home I wrote a substantial amount of this book.

When I needed them, Sarah Manguso and Andrew Solomon came

through like warrior ninjas with brilliant presale blurbs, followed soon after by Darin Strauss, A. M. Homes, Meg Wolitzer, and Alexandra Kleeman. And all the while, my writers group saw me through and cheered me on. My secret weapons were my agent, Bill Clegg, and my editor, Millicent Bennett. Together, and separately, they lifted, reshaped, cut, rearranged, and helped me create a narrative that matched the one I'd carried, without words, inside me for decades. And what's more, they did it with the warmth and kindness of your long-practicing primary-care physician. (Please never retire.) For putting up with my anxious phone calls (one in actual tears), and for being hands-down lovely, I thank the Clegg Agency Team: Chris Clemans, David Kambhu, Simon Toop, and Marion Duvert. My gratitude to those at Grand Central for their belief, excitement, and effort, specifically: Caitlin Mulrooney-Lyski, Andrew Duncan, Joe Benincase, Liz Connor, Meriam Metoui, Ali Cutrone, Ben Sevier, Carolyn Kurek, Brian McLendon, Rachel Hairston, Karen Kosztolnyik, Karen Torres, and Michael Pietsch. I'm indebted to my brilliant cousin Sam Terris for his publicity help, and Gretchen Koss, I can't remember who introduced us, but however we met, I'm forever grateful. (JK, Kimberly Burns—you're the best.)

Toward the end, when I nearly called the whole thing off, Kara and Eddie Stern led me across an invisible bridge and never once joked about pushing me off. Throughout it all, quietly, and in the background, Judith Rustin raised me up with her wisdom, counsel, and encouragement each time I sank, and Joseph Squitieri kept me balanced. In less than two minutes, Dr. Steven Friedfeld saw in me what no one else did, and promptly saved my life.

To all of you—my love, appreciation, and gratitude.

But we're not done!

For letting me write about them, special thanks to all my Stern and Stuart siblings: Kara, Eddie, Nick, Rebecca, Nina, Jes, Jms, and M. And my aunt Maggie Stern Terris, for always believing in me, and giving me the first round of incredible notes. While she refuses to learn how to read, I still must thank my furry, hypoallergenic heart, Busy Stern, for her patience, and for understanding what "Ten more minutes!" means. And, if you will reference the dedication, my parents, Eve and Eddie.

Finally—to you, dear book, I'm so glad I wrote you, and I'm so glad to be done.

About the Author

Amanda Stern was born in New York City and raised in Greenwich Village. She is the author of *The Long Haul* and also eleven books for children written under the pseudonyms Fiona Rosenbloom and AJ Stern. In 2003, she founded the Happy Ending Music and Reading Series, a long-running and beloved event that became an essential part of the New York City literary landscape. She lives in Brooklyn with her dog, Busy.